# Transforming Unemployment Insurance for the Twenty-First Century

"Steve Wandner's *Transforming Unemployment Insurance for the Twenty-First Century* is a comprehensive clarion call for fundamental changes in our nation's primary program to assist those who have lost jobs through no fault of their own. As his latest book demonstrates, Steve has an unparalleled evidence-driven perspective on this long-standing, but flawed, U.S. social insurance program. Any serious effort to address UI's challenges needs to reflect Steve's analysis and will benefit greatly from his thoughtful recommendations. We cannot afford to wait for another recession to improve UI. Steve Wandner has provided the proactive roadmap to do so."

—*Bill Arnone, CEO, National Academy of Social Insurance*

"Steve Wandner is the nation's foremost expert on unemployment insurance, which is why I was proud to work under him at the Labor Department. His latest book is a must-read for anyone who appreciates the history and cares about the future of America's most important safety net. Rooted in lessons from the Great Depression through the COVID-19 pandemic, this book provides thoughtful, data-driven ideas to strengthen the UI program for workers, businesses, and the American economy."

—*Josh Riley, former General Counsel, U.S. Senate Judiciary Subcommittee on Law and Technology*

"This is a thoroughly researched and sweeping book by one of the eminent researchers and practitioners of the American Unemployment Insurance system. It will become required reading for anyone trying to understand the origins of the UI system, why it is broken, and what to do about it. Highly recommended!"

—*Till von Wachter, Professor of Economics, Director of the California Policy Lab, Director of the Federal Statistical Research Data Center, University of California, Los Angeles*

"The unusual stresses placed on the UI system during the pandemic brought many of its shortcomings to the forefront. Here, Stephen Wandner makes clear that the system is currently not up to the task of providing for the needs of unemployed Americans even in ordinary times. Bringing all his years of experience researching UI and working with DOL to bear, Wandner traces out how we got to this stage, before providing a roadmap to how the system can be improved. I found his recommendations for reform to be incredibly thought provoking, with suggestions ranging from those that seem clearly doable, to those that seem like perhaps a heavy lift from either an administrative or political standpoint. That said, I truly hope that state and federal policymakers will read this book and take the suggestions to heart."

—*Patricia M. Anderson, Professor of Economics at Dartmouth College and NBER Research Associate*

"One of the many reasons there hasn't been meaningful UI reform in decades is the sheer complexity of the system. In a reader-friendly way, which is not easy for unemployment, Stephen Wandner dives deep with the most comprehensive look yet at UI's long and complicated history, its tortured present state, and its uncertain future. Each recommendation for reform is analyzed considering many of the system's stakeholders, providing a roadmap for both state and federal efforts. If only I and every other policymaker had been able to read this book before assuming leadership over such an important program. I wish I shared the author's 'optimistic hope that the U.S. Unemployment Insurance program will be comprehensively reformed soon,' but I am certain that many possible successful paths lie within these pages."

—*Robert Asaro-Angelo, Commissioner, New Jersey Department of Labor and Workforce Development*

# Transforming Unemployment Insurance for the Twenty-First Century

## A Comprehensive Guide to Reform

Stephen A. Wandner

2023

W.E. Upjohn Institute for Employment Research
Kalamazoo, Michigan

**Library of Congress Cataloging-in-Publication Data**

Names: Wandner, Stephen A., author.
Title: Transforming unemployment insurance for the twenty-first century : a
   comprehensive guide to reform / Stephen A Wandner.
Description: Kalamazoo, Michigan : W.E. Upjohn Institute for Employment Research,
   [2023] | Includes bibliographical references and index. |
   Summary: "This book proposes options and recommendations for comprehensive
   reform of the unemployment insurance program that was initiated as a social
   insurance program by the Social Security Act of 1935. It documents the
   development of the program and its decline since the 1970s. Reform proposals and
   recommendations are synthesized from reforms suggested by policy analysts and
   researchers over many decades"—Provided by publisher.
Identifiers: LCCN 2023014114 (print) | LCCN 2023014115 (ebook) | ISBN
   9780880996907 (paperback) | ISBN 9780880996914 (ebook)
Subjects: LCSH: Unemployment insurance—United States. | Unemployment
   insurance—Law and legislation—United States. | Unemployed—Services
   for—United States.
Classification: LCC HD7096.U6 W16 2023 (print) | LCC HD7096.U6 (ebook) | DDC
   368.4/4/00973—dc23/eng/20230414
LC record available at https://lccn.loc.gov/2023014114
LC ebook record available at https://lccn.loc.gov/2023014115


© 2023
W.E. Upjohn Institute for Employment Research
300 S. Westnedge Avenue
Kalamazoo, Michigan 49007-4686

The facts presented in this study and the observations and viewpoints expressed are
the sole responsibility of the author. They do not necessarily represent positions of
the W.E. Upjohn Institute for Employment Research.

Cover design by Carol A.S. Derks.
Index prepared by Diane Worden.
Printed in the United States of America.
Printed on recycled paper.

For Marleigh

# Contents

**Part 3: Issues and Options for UI Reform**

**Part 4: Recommendations for UI Reform**

# Tables

# Figures

# Acknowledgments

This study was funded by the Russell Sage Foundation and the National Academy of Social Insurance (NASI) and would not have been possible without their support. Further support was provided by Wandner Associates Inc. The initial report was written between December 2020 and July 2021 but has been substantially modified and rewritten since then. This book represents my review of unemployment insurance (UI) research and policy analysis. The policy conclusions drawn from that research and analysis are mine alone and do not reflect the views of NASI, the Russell Sage Foundation, or the publisher, W.E. Upjohn Institute for Employment Research.

I am grateful for the support and assistance of NASI. The key NASI contributors were Bill Arnone, president, and his staff, and the NASI UI Task Force.

While I have studied the UI program for the past five decades, I have learned a great deal from working with members of the NASI UI Task Force, both its individual members and from the chairs of the UI Task Force subcommittees.

I especially appreciate the review of earlier drafts of this book by David Balducchi and Ralph E. Smith.

Several task force members provided direct input to the report. They are David Balducchi, Rob Pavosevich, and James Van Erden. Their input has been invaluable.

This draft was greatly improved by comments and input from two reviewers, Christopher O'Leary, and an anonymous reviewer, as well as from Kevin Hollenbeck, who has overseen the production of the manuscript and provided invaluable comments and recommendations.

Special thanks to my wife for her patience and support.

Nonetheless, I am solely responsible for this book, and any errors that are in the material below are mine alone.

–Stephen A. Wandner

# Preface

This book is based on the optimistic hope that the U.S. Unemployment Insurance (UI) program will be comprehensively reformed soon. It endeavors to be a guide for such reform by providing a comprehensive review of the UI program, including its benefits and weaknesses. In doing so, it includes both new analysis of the UI program, as well as a review of prior research and analysis. The book examines the problems and challenges facing the current UI program. It considers a variety of options for program improvement and analyzes the strengths and weaknesses of each. Finally, the book makes recommendations regarding a comprehensive approach to UI reform. While it would be preferable to have comprehensive reform enacted by the Congress as described in this book, in the absence of such federal legislation, states should consider enacting similar legislation and adopting similar administrative approaches to improve their own state UI programs.

Given its ambition and scope, this book can be heavy reading. If you are interested in UI but you want to lighten your load, there are three ways to access this book without reading the whole volume:

1) The easiest way is to go to Chapter 14 in Part 5 and read the conclusion, which contains a series of general program reform recommendations. Then, if you are interested in exploring more about any particular issue, you can locate further discussion in Part 4.

2) If you want to get directly into the discussion of the individual issues, options, and recommendations, you can turn first to Part 4.

3) If you want to get some more background regarding the context of the options and recommendations, you can sample Parts 2 and 3 as well as read Part 4.

Work on this book began in December 2020, when the nonpartisan National Academy of Social Insurance (NASI) announced that it had initiated a Task Force on Unemployment Insurance to provide state and federal policymakers with information and analysis regarding potential approaches to improving key aspects of the UI program. The Task Force's work was financed, in part, by the Russell Sage Foundation.

As the principal investigator for the UI Task Force, I produced an earlier, unpublished report in July 2021 to help "identify, assess, evaluate, and document a range of options to address weaknesses in the UI system" (NASI 2020). That report reflected the work of a group of 19 Task Force members who were assembled to study various aspects of UI reform, including 1) eligibility, benefits, and reemployment services; 2) financing; and 3) administration, equity, statistics and research. The earlier report reflected the discussion and input of the members of the Task Force in areas of their expertise and interest.

This book is a revision and expansion of the earlier report. It now reflects my views and opinions, rather than those of NASI or the Task Force members. It relies heavily on a large body of UI research as well as my own work over a period of five decades as a policy analyst and researcher on unemployment and UI program issues.

The UI program is one of several social insurance programs—a publicly sponsored program that provides benefits funded by compulsory tax payments by employers (and often employees) to insure against risks of a public concern, including the need for income during periods of unemployment, post-retirement, and ill health. In the case of the UI program, it pays partial, temporary wage replacement to covered wage and salary workers who become unemployed through no fault of their own. While it covers nearly all wage and salary workers, it does not cover the self-employed or contract employees. Normally, the UI program does not pay benefits to workers who quit their jobs or were fired for cause. It also does not pay benefits to new entrants to the labor force, and it does not pay reentrants unless they have worked during a recent period before leaving the labor force. UI benefits are financed through state and federal taxes on employers (and sometimes employees) that are intended to suffice for the UI program to be self-financing.

Throughout most of the history of the UI program, however, the national and state UI agencies have done more than simply oversee and pay benefits and collect taxes for the UI social insurance program. These agencies also have administered a wide variety of unemployment assistance programs which have been funded out of federal general revenue but are not themselves social insurance programs. These programs have included extending benefits beyond periods considered to be insurable UI durations, generally considered to be 26 weeks. They also have included payments to address public policy concerns (e.g., the temporary shutdown of airlines after 9/11) and to workers adversely affected by natural disasters and international trade.

This book also considers most permanent UI programs existing under current federal and state law, as well as proposals to create new ones. In addition, it discusses proposals for new social welfare programs, such as a Jobseeker's Allowance, funded from federal general revenue to new entrants and reentrants to the labor force as well as to other uninsured workers.

In general, this book does not address the 2020 pandemic recession and the period after it. Although the UI program was designed to deal with unemployment in good economic times and bad, the bad times are normally business cycle recessions. The extremity of the pandemic and the necessity to shut down much of the U.S. economy resulted in an unusually severe strain on the regular

UI program. The negative effects of the pandemic on the regular UI program reveal many of the challenges to and weaknesses of the regular UI program and the urgency for reform. Accordingly, this book also suggests options for improving the UI program and preparing for a future economic downturn as severe as the recent pandemic experience.

# Part 1

# Introduction and Overview
# of the UI Program

# 1
# The Basics of the UI Program

## FEDERAL AND STATE RESPONSIBILITIES

The Unemployment Insurance (UI) program was established in 1935 under Titles III and IX of the Social Security Act.[1] Employers began paying taxes into state accounts in the Unemployment Trust Fund in 1936, but to allow the Fund to accumulate reserves, payment of UI benefits did not begin until 1938.

Administratively, the UI system was established as a federal-state program. The Social Security Act sets conformity requirements for the states' participation in the program, but the federal government frequently has had difficulty enforcing these requirements with the mechanisms available to it. The federal government thus sets the broad legislative and administrative framework for the 50 states plus the District of Columbia, Puerto Rico, and the Virgin Islands. States administer their own programs under conforming state laws that set the parameters of the state UI programs, including initial claims and continued eligibility criteria, benefit amounts and durations, tax levels and taxable wage bases, and the level and type of reemployment services provided to UI claimants. Like Social Security and Medicare, UI insures against a contingency. In the case of UI, the contingency is the beneficiary becoming unemployed. In the case of Social Security, it is living to 62 or 67, while for Medicare, it is becoming ill and needing health care.

Responsibility for the UI program is divided between Congress, the U.S. Department of Labor (USDOL), and the states:

- Congress establishes the federal statutory framework.

- USDOL determines whether individual state UI programs are in conformity and are complying with federal law and regulations. It also provides programmatic guidance and direction to state UI agencies.

- Within the federal framework, state UI laws and procedures establish most of the specifics of the program—e.g., benefit eligibility, levels and duration of benefits, as well as state tax rates and the state taxable wage base. As a result, programs vary widely across the country.

## THE BASIC UI PROGRAM

The UI program is generally defined as a social insurance program that provides temporary, partial wage replacement to experienced, covered workers who are unemployed through no fault of their own and are actively searching for work. It is a social insurance program because it insures covered workers against the insurable risk of short-term unemployment by having a premium paid against that risk while they are employed. The following are definitions of the various components of the UI program:

- **Temporary benefits.** Under federal law, benefits for the basic ("regular") UI program generally are paid for up to 26 weeks, as determined by the states. While most states pay up to 26 weeks of benefits, in the years following the 2007–2009 recession, 10 states reduced benefit durations below 26 weeks, and in many states there has been other tightening of eligibility requirements and benefit payment provisions.

- **Partial wage replacement.** Benefit amounts are generally set once a year by the states at half (or slightly more than half) of an unemployed worker's prior wage up to a maximum amount.

- **Experienced workers.** To be eligible for UI benefits, unemployed workers must have had recent attachment to the labor force, measured by a certain minimum amount of earnings in a recent four-quarter period, called the UI base period.

- **Covered employment.** Although coverage was far from universal when the program was established in 1935, federal law has since expanded coverage, especially in the areas of agricultural, state and local government, nonprofit, and domestic household workers. While today nearly all wage and salary employees are covered by the UI program, there is a growing segment of workers in the freelance and contract economy that remain without coverage.

- **No-fault unemployment.** Qualifying workers must have been laid off through no fault of their own, such as lack of work. They cannot have quit their jobs or been fired for cause. They also cannot be new entrants into the labor force, and they cannot be reentrants into the labor force unless they were out of the labor force for only a short period of time and have sufficient recent earnings during their base period to qualify.

- **Actively searching for work.** The UI program has a work-search requirement (the "work test"). UI recipients must demonstrate that they are able, available, and actively searching for work while receiving benefits, a requirement that is necessary if UI is to be considered a social insurance program that works to minimize the moral hazard of providing UI benefits by ensuring that recipients are able, available, and actively searching for work. The work test is generally administered in local workforce offices by the states' Employment Services agencies.

There are two kinds of eligibility requirements necessary to qualify for UI benefits:

1) **Monetary eligibility.** Workers must have earned sufficient wages in a recent 12-month base period to be eligible for benefits.

2) **Nonmonetary eligibility.** Workers must have been separated from work involuntarily—such as through layoff—are searching for work, and may not refuse suitable work. Depending on state laws, other separations (e.g., voluntary quit or discharge for cause) may result in a total or partial loss of benefits.

The number of individuals receiving UI benefits and the overall amount of benefits paid vary greatly over the business cycle. The total amount of benefits paid out is highly responsive to the business cycle, increasing rapidly at the beginning of a recession and declining rapidly as it ends. Thus, the UI program is highly cyclical and responsive to variations in the business cycle, making the UI program an "automatic stabilizer" when it pumps purchasing power into state and local economies during business downturns. While layoffs occur throughout the business cycle, many more workers become unemployed during recessions. As a result, the number of unemployed workers tends to surge at the beginning of a recession, then decline rapidly as the recession ends. Also, during recessions, UI recipients are much more likely to exhaust their entitlement to all their regular UI benefits than at other times.

**Extended Benefits**

Since UI recipients are much more likely to exhaust their entitlement to regular benefits during recessionary periods, many of these workers will remain in difficult economic straits when they exhaust their regular benefits and may need more financial assistance before they find work. The UI program usually provides two types of benefit extensions during recessionary periods:

1) **Permanent Extended Benefits program.** Enacted in 1970, the Extended Benefits (EB) program operates in states based on "triggers" which turn the program on and off using state unemployment-rate measures. It pays up to between 13 and 20 additional weeks of benefits when a state's unemployment rate increases sharply, with states and the federal government equally sharing the cost of these benefits. From the start, however, the EB benefits triggering mechanism was revealed to be poorly designed and did not work well; it frequently hasn't paid benefits, even when unemployment levels were high, and the program design has not been improved in the past five decades. Although by federal statute the program is jointly funded by the states and the federal government, in recent recessions Congress has federalized the EB program, acknowledging that the program would not otherwise be effective. States also have been resistant to establishing more generous triggers permitted under federal statute because they have resisted the 50-50 cost sharing with the federal government. As a result, EB has not been effective at providing additional benefits, even during periods of high unemployment. Some states, however, have adopted an optional triggering mechanism that is more responsive.

2) **Temporary Emergency Benefits program.** Temporary emergency programs have been enacted by Congress in every recession since 1958. Congress generally responds to constituent complaints about the inadequacy of regular UI benefits, and this inadequacy is magnified when the permanent EB program is ineffective in high unemployment states. The temporary emergency programs have had many names, but in recent recessions they have been called emergency unemployment compensation. Temporary emergency programs also have frequently made temporary changes to the permanent EB program so that EB also adds weeks to benefit durations for the long-term unemployed. Temporary emergency programs provide additional weeks of benefits beyond the regular UI and permanent EB programs, extending benefits during the 2007–2009 recession in some states to as many as 60 additional weeks.

It should be noted, however, that unemployed workers only qualify for EB and temporary emergency programs if they were initially found eligible for UI benefits and are not disqualified during their receipt of regular benefits. As shown below, however, many states restrict access to regular UI benefits, and ineligible workers, thus, do not receive any benefits—regular, extended, or emergency.

## THE UI PROGRAM PAYS BENEFITS IN GOOD ECONOMIC TIMES AND BAD

The UI system provides partial wage replacement to covered unemployed workers in good economic times and bad. Table 1.1 shows how the UI system works over the business cycle: in this case before, during, and after the 2007–2009 recession, which officially started in December 2007 and ended in June 2009. Looking at selected years from 2006 to 2019, the data show the extent of the UI program before the 2007–2009 recession in 2006, during the recession years of 2008 and 2009, during the "jobless recovery" that extended through 2012, and in the strong recovery after 2012.

**Table 1.1  UI First Payments, Exhaustions, and Expenditures, Selected Fiscal Years**

|  | 2006 | 2008 | 2009 | 2010 | 2011 | 2012 | 2015 | 2019 |
|---|---|---|---|---|---|---|---|---|
| Unemployment rate (%) | 4.8 | 5.3 | 8.6 | 9.8 | 9.2 | 8.2 | 5.4 | 3.7 |
| Program participants (millions) | | | | | | | | |
| First payments | 7.4 | 8.8 | 14.4 | 11.3 | 9.7 | 8.7 | 6.6 | 5.1 |
| Regular exhaustions[a] | 2.7 | 3.1 | 6.4 | 7.0 | 5.1 | 4.4 | 2.6 | 1.8 |
| Payments ($ billions) | | | | | | | | |
| Regular benefits | 30.2 | 38.1 | 75.3 | 63.0 | 48.5 | 44.3 | 31.7 | 25.5 |
| Extended benefits | 0.0 | 0.0 | 4.1 | 8.0 | 11.9 | 4.9 | 0.0 | 0.0 |
| Emergency benefits[b] | 0.0 | 3.5 | 39.1 | 83.8 | 54.6 | 39.6 | 0.0 | 0.0 |
| All program payments ($ billions)[c] | 31.5 | 43.1 | 119.7 | 156.4 | 116.8 | 90.4 | 32.6 | 27.3 |
| State tax collections ($ billions) | 35.9 | 32.2 | 31.1 | 38.3 | 49.3 | 59.4 | 42.2 | 33.6 |

[a]Exhaustees of the regular 26-week UI benefits.
[b]Includes temporary federal additional benefits.
[c]Includes benefits under the Unemployment Compensation for Federal Employees and Ex-servicemember programs, and Trade Adjustment Assistance.
SOURCE: USDOL (2021); Wandner (2013).

During the 2007–2009 recession, the number of UI recipients and the amount of UI benefits paid out were greater than they had ever been during the previous history of the UI program. The number of unemployed workers receiving UI benefits nearly doubled, and those workers remained unemployed for much longer periods of time than ever before. As a result, the payment of regular benefits, together with permanent EB and emergency benefits, increased dramatically such that total benefit payments increased from $32 billion in fiscal year 2006 to $156 billion in fiscal year 2010.

As Table 1.1 shows, the UI program pays benefits to unemployed workers in both good economic times and bad, but it pays a relatively smaller amount of benefits to relatively fewer unemployed workers during good times. By contrast, in a severe recession, the number of program participants can increase sharply, and the total amount of benefits paid increases dramatically, since more workers are unemployed for much longer periods of time because of the lack of job openings. For example, in 2010, with a 9.8 percent unemployment rate, first payments were far above those of 2006, with regular program exhaustions more than twice the number in 2006. Also in 2010, regular benefits had doubled to $63 billion, but it was extended and emergency benefits enacted by the Congress that brought total payments to over $156 billion, while total state tax collection were only $38 billion.

The table also shows the fundamental problem with state UI financing. Although the main state responsibility is to pay for regular UI benefits, state tax collections do not keep up with the increase in regular UI program costs during recessions. As a result, states need to either accumulate funds to pay future benefits from their UI trust fund account before recessions, or they need to increase state UI taxes after the recession. Unfortunately, many states do neither. They either borrow heavily from the U.S. Treasury or they cut benefits.

## UI PROGRAM GOALS, PROGRAM DESIGN, AND REFORM IMPLICATIONS

As a form of social insurance, the UI program is designed to protect workers from income loss during periods of temporary unemployment. To carry out this mission, the UI program has three broad goals:

1) **Individual worker protection.** UI is paid to unemployed covered workers to provide them with partial wage replacement during periods of unemployment. As such, these payments are intended to sustain individuals and families until workers become reemployed. This goal is referred to as the program's "micro" goal.

2) **Societal/economic protection.** The UI program pays out limited amounts of benefits during good economic times, but it pays out a great deal more during recessionary periods when many more workers are unemployed and tend to be unemployed for much longer periods of time. Thus, during recessions, UI payments sustain not just the individual worker/family, but the larger aggregate payments made during recessions help to maintain consumption throughout the local, state, and national economies, thereby reducing the severity of the economic impact of the recession. This is the "macro" or counter-cyclical effect of the UI program on the economy.

3) **Reemployment.** While the UI program pays temporary benefits to qualified workers, its ultimate concern is the return of workers to productive employment. It does so both by expecting workers to demonstrate that they are able, available, and actively searching for work (the "UI work test") and by referring permanently separated workers to the Employment Service. The Employment Service provides unemployed workers with job matching, job referral, and job search assistance to help speed their return to work.

What should the UI program look like going forward given both its goals and federal law? In the next section, we consider the benefit side of the program with respect to partial income replacement, the adequacy of the benefits to workers unemployed through no fault of their own, and their being able, available, and actively seeking work. We also examine the program's financing. The following discussion makes use of the lessons learned from an extensive body of recent literature on the UI program resulting in evidence-based conclusions regarding the optimal basic design of the UI program (Bivens et al. 2021; Dube 2021; O'Leary and Wandner 2018; von Wachter 2020; West et al. 2016).

## Access

It is important that there be broad access to the UI program for experienced unemployed workers who are unemployed through no fault of their own. This includes the following criteria:

- Information on how to apply for benefits is widely available.
- The application for benefits is clear and easy to complete.
- Eligibility conditions should be reasonable for all unemployed workers regarding both initial eligibility when first applying for benefits and continued eligibility when filing weekly or biweekly claims for continuing benefits.

State UI administrative processes thus should include

- widely available information on how to apply for benefits
- clear and easy to complete applications for benefits
- reasonable eligibility criteria for initial benefit application and for filing weekly or biweekly claims for continuing benefits

**Adequate Benefits**

An adequate UI benefit program is measured by benefit amounts and durations, such that the UI program should do the following:

- Make the weekly benefit amount adequate to maintain a reasonable standard of living during short periods of unemployment.
- Set the maximum benefit amount at a level that provides adequate benefits for both low-wage and middle-income workers.
- Set the maximum potential duration of benefits so that it is sufficient to carry workers through their period of work search during good economic times.
- Provide additional benefits during recessionary times, whether through permanent programs triggered on when unemployment is high or by temporary emergency benefit programs.

**Sufficient Revenue**

Financing should ensure sufficient revenue over time to pay adequate benefits, with taxes reflecting employer past layoff experience and with taxation anticipating the need for greater funding during future recessions:

- The federal and state taxable wage bases should be sufficient in conjunction with tax rates to fund the UI program. The taxable wage base also should be a high percentage of total wages so that the tax is reasonably progressive.
- Under state experience rating provisions, employer taxes should reflect the prior layoff experience of individual employers.
- The financing of the UI program should be forward-funded such that states accumulate enough funds in their state accounts in the Unemployment Trust Fund in the U.S. Treasury to pay benefits during a typical recession without going into debt.

**Reemployment Services**

Most UI recipients are not temporarily laid off but become permanently unemployed and need reemployment services to speed their return to work. The following guidelines are recommended:

- To maintain the integrity of the UI program as a social insurance program, the UI Work Test should be administered by the Employment Service in accordance with the mandate in the Wagner-Peyser Act.

- To help UI recipients who are not subject to recall return to work, recipients should be given staff-assisted reemployment services from the Employment Service.

- Under federal UI law aimed at helping dislocated workers, UI recipients should receive intervention reemployment services and eligibility reviews early in their spells of unemployment.

## Making Unemployment Payments

Since the state UI programs often are called on to make benefit payments other than UI social insurance benefits, the UI program must be able to pay various forms of unemployment assistance mandated by Congress:

- Quickly add weeks of benefits during a recession based on any future reforms of the Extended Benefits program.

- Pay additional and sufficient weeks of temporary emergency benefits, similar to that which has been enacted by the Congress in every recession since 1958.

- Develop UI administrative infrastructure that creates the capacity to increase replacement rates for workers during future severe recessions like that during the COVID-19 pandemic.

- Make payments for new unemployment assistance programs. Congress has mandated that the UI program pay for an array of programs addressing special issues including adverse employment impacts on trade impacted workers, workers in federally declared disaster areas, airline workers after 9/11, workers involved in logging in the Redwood Forest, and, most recently, payments for uncovered and other workers during the COVID-19 pandemic through the Pandemic Unemployment Assistance program.

As will be discussed in the rest of this book, many problems exist in achieving the program goals listed above. These problems relate to a wide variety of issues, including the methods of administration of the state and federal programs, inadequate current legislation, and the lack of necessary UI federal and state fundamental statutory reform over many decades. For the UI program to always be able to fulfill its mission of providing adequate, temporary income support to individuals who become unemployed through no fault of their own, and to act as a countercyclical force during recessions in states and across the country, the program must maintain its strength over time. Throughout this book, however, we see that rather than remaining strong, the UI program has been weakening over many decades.

## Note

1. For a more extensive discussion of the UI program, see Wandner (2018) and O'Leary and Wandner (1997).

# Part 2

# UI Program Issues and Weaknesses

# 2
# A Historical Timeline

The weaknesses of the current UI program stem from many causes. From a federal statutory perspective, weaknesses were engrained by decisions that were made in the initial design of the UI program that was enacted in 1935, as well as from subsequent federal legislative decisions and/or inaction that progressively weakened the UI program. While the UI and other Social Security programs were created by the same legislation, the divergence in their paths over time illustrates the lost opportunities to build a stronger UI system. More generally, many of the problems that have emerged in the UI program since the mid-1970s had their origins in the 1935 federal legislation and the failure to address those problems over the next several decades.

## ENACTING UI AS PART OF THE SOCIAL SECURITY ACT OF 1935: LAUNCHING THE COMMITTEE ON ECONOMIC SECURITY'S "EXPERIMENT"

"The plan of unemployment compensation, we suggest, is frankly experimental. We anticipate that it may require numerous changes with experience." Committee on Economic Security (1935)

The United States was late in enacting a social insurance program to provide public pensions and unemployment insurance. In contrast, old-age pension and disability assistance programs were first enacted in Germany in 1889, with unemployment insurance benefits added in 1927. Other European countries enacted social security programs, including unemployment insurance before the Great Depression. The United States lagged behind other developed nations.

Because the federal government was slow to enact and implement a UI program in the United States, individual states began to consider the enactment of UI programs on their own. By 1935, when the United States finally enacted a social insurance program that included UI, several states, including Connecticut, Massachusetts, New Jersey, New York, Ohio, and Pennsylvania, were actively considering enacting their own UI programs, while Wisconsin had already enacted a UI program and paid its first UI check in August 1936. At that time, Wisconsin was the leading state with respect to UI policy and implementation. The decision to create a federal-state program was due in part to Wisconsin's desire to retain its state program (Nelson 1969).

Although the Social Security Act of 1935 gave birth to both UI and Social Security, the paths that the two programs have taken since then have been very different. This divergence has largely been shaped by decisions made before the law was enacted but also by the vastly different public policy paths that followed enactment. In the case of the UI program, those decisions resulted in the program failing to meet its original expectations.

President Roosevelt determined that he would promote enactment of a program of economic security (ultimately renamed Social Security) that would include old-age assistance, assistance to dependent children, public health assistance, and unemployment insurance. Before the enactment of the Social Security Act, there was a debate within the Roosevelt administration about what Social Security and UI would look like. During 1934, some members of the presidentially appointed Committee on Economic Security (CES) argued that both Social Security and UI should be made national programs. President Roosevelt, mostly because of political considerations, prevailed in having Congress enact a federal-state UI program instead. As a result, Social Security became a national program, while UI became a federal-state program, under state administration, with state laws establishing eligibility criteria, benefit durations, and benefit amounts (Cohen 1985). This decision had, and continues to have, substantial repercussions, contributing to the long-term weakness and decline of the UI program.

After studying UI programs in other countries and Wisconsin—the only state in 1934 with UI legislation—the January 1935 CES report recommended a compulsory UI program that paid benefits to workers who were involuntarily unemployed. For administrative and other reasons, the CES report further proposed that employees would be covered with significant exceptions for employees in small establishments; agricultural and domestic household workers; federal, state, and local government workers; the self-employed; nonprofit, charitable, and education workers; and several other groups of workers. UI taxes would be collected to create reserves from which benefits to unemployed workers would be paid. Benefits were expected to replace 50 percent of lost wages up to a low maximum benefit of $15 per week, payable only after a four-week waiting period. If workers exhausted all their entitlement to UI benefits, the CES recommended creating a permanent system of public service employment rather than a means-tested unemployment assistance program (National Conference on Social Welfare [NCSW] 1985).

The UI proposal was considered and enacted into law during the Great Depression. The latest annual unemployment data the Committee had was an estimated national 39.2 percent unemployment rate for 1933. Given the continuing high unemployment rates and the uncertainty about the economic future, policymakers and actuaries took a very conservative approach to the proposed UI benefit payments. The CES report expected that the UI program would initially be able to pay only 12 to 15 weeks of benefits, with weekly benefit amounts of no more than $15 per week. The payment of these benefits was expected to require a payroll tax of 3 percent on total wages to fund those benefits, based on the unemployment experience of 1922–1930, not including the Great Depression years of 1931–1933. The CES thought that such a short UI potential duration of benefits might be sufficient because they also expected the UI program to be supplemented by a public service employment program, which never materialized. The CES acknowledged that "benefits can be paid only for periods which . . . will seem short. The benefits are small" (NCSW 1985, p. 33). Thus, the UI program proposal was limited in scope with respect to coverage, benefit levels, and benefit duration. At the same time, the UI taxable wage base and tax rate were expected to be high to afford even these limited benefits.

The levels of state benefits and taxes in the CES report were suggestive. States would set eligibility requirements, benefit levels, benefit durations, and other provisions. The CES cautioned states to be conservative in setting benefit durations so that their state trust fund accounts (in the U.S. Treasury) would remain solvent. While the state taxable wage base had to be at least as high as the current $7,000 federal taxable wage base, states could set their own tax rates and taxable wage bases equal to or greater than the federal rate. The CES left it to the states to decide who would pay UI taxes: employers, employees, and/or the state. There were no recommendations for having automatic upward adjustments of UI benefits or taxes to reflect the cost of living (NCSW 1985).

The Committee believed that the federal government should pay not only for the administration of the UI program, but also for the administration of the U.S. Employment Service (ES), since the ES—established by the Wagner-Peyser Act of 1933—was expected to work jointly with UI state staff in public employment offices and provide labor exchange services as well as administer the UI work test for eligibility for UI benefits, which the CES report called a "willingness-to-work test." As a result, federal funding for the ES would have to increase to fund these expanded services which would be provided to UI claimants (NCSW 1985). This meant that a federal tax rate would be set on a federal taxable wage base, with UI administrative funds allocated to the states as state grants.

Given the uncertainty regarding economic conditions and the fact that UI would be a federal-state program operating with wide state discretion, the CES encouraged state experimentation with benefit and tax provisions and program administration. It expected that with experience, the UI program would be modified and improved. It said: "The plan of unemployment compensation, we suggest, is frankly experimental. We anticipate that it may require numerous changes with experience, and, we believe, is so set up that these changes can be made through subsequent legislation as deemed necessary" (NCSW 1985, p. 43). Furthermore, the Committee explained, "Congress can at any time increase the requirements which State laws must fulfill and may, if it sees fit, at some future time, substitute a federally-administered system for the cooperative Federal-State system we recommend" (NCSW 1985, p. 36).

There were at least two problems with the CES formulation of how the UI system would evolve. First, the UI system became not one but 53 experiments in the 50 states and three other jurisdictions that established UI programs. The new experimental programs were mostly determined by the states on their own as they implemented and developed their UI programs, and each program went in its own direction. As described below, some of these experiments succeeded, but most of them failed. Second, the federal modifications and improvements to the UI system that were anticipated by the CES and were needed as the UI program evolved never materialized. Congress neglected the UI program over most of the last 85 years, making mainly small changes to the program, with only one major attempt to reform and improve the system in 1976.

The Unemployment Trust Fund, established under Title IX of the 1935 Social Security Act, was initially empty. To raise sufficient funds to pay UI benefits, taxes were levied on employers beginning in 1936 at 1 percent of total wages, increasing to 2 percent in 1937 and 3 percent in 1938. By contrast, the taxable wage base for Social Security was restricted to $3,000, although it would increase rapidly in future years. With the enactment of the 1939 Social Security Amendments, the federal UI taxable wage base was reduced to $3,000, the same as the Social Security level (NCSW 1985).[1]

## Social Security

Like the UI program, Social Security also is a social insurance program. But unlike for UI, the CES proposed that Social Security be made a national program, with benefits and taxes set and administered nationally. Nonetheless, the two programs started with the same taxable wage bases to ensure the solvency of both programs. The CES presented a general proposal relating to benefits and taxes that was made specific under the 1935 Act. Under that Act, starting in January 1942, benefits were to be paid as a percentage of total wages, as was the case for UI (NCSW 1985). Social Security taxes began to be collected in 1937 on a taxable wage base set at $3,000, the same as UI. The tax was set at 1 percent of taxable wages in 1937, and tax rates were to be increased in half-percent increments until the tax rate reached 3 percent in January 1949. The initial taxable wage base of $3,000 also did not have automatic adjustments and thus would have the same problems that UI has if Congress had not taken action to raise the Social Security taxable wage base (NCSW 1985).

To be eligible for Social Security benefits under the 1935 Act, workers had to be 65, have earned at least $2,000 in the period beginning in 1937, and had earnings in at least five different years beginning in 1937. As a result, payments of Social Security benefits would start slowly beginning in 1942 (NCSW 1985). The 1935 Act included old-age assistance that was a means-tested benefit. While the Social Security payroll tax system for old-age annuities was ramping up, old-age assistance would be a more important source of support for workers 65 years old and older than old-age annuities (Ball in NCSW 1985). Thus, Social Security evolved based on the needs of recipients in a way that UI did not.

Although Social Security also began as a modest program, it expanded over time with repeated federal legislative changes and improvements to both the benefit and tax sides of the program. In contrast to the UI program, Social Security eventually would become a balanced program such that both payments and revenues generally increased together either legislatively or through annual indexing. The lack of steady benefit and revenue improvements and reform of the UI program have made it a far weaker program than Social Security.

## DEVELOPMENT OF THE UI PROGRAM, 1935–1949: THE EXPERIMENT STARTS SLOWLY, PICKS UP SPEED, BUT BEGINS TO FALTER

The CES's expectations about the UI program were not realized. By the time UI benefits became payable in all states in 1942, the United States had entered World War II. With both men and women in the armed forces and working in defense industries, the United States experienced a period of full employment. UI taxes continued to be collected before and during the war, and, with little joblessness and scant payment of benefits, the Unemployment Trust Fund grew. The major postwar recession that some economists predicted did not occur, largely because of the pent-up demand for consumer durables (not produced during a wartime economy) in both the United States and other countries. The UI program was financially sound, and state UI programs withstood a mild recession in 1949 without the need for federal intervention. During the entire post–World War II period, however, tax rates to fund UI benefits have remained much lower than the CES expected, remaining below 1 percent of total wages for the past four decades (O'Leary and Wandner 2018).

As a result of a long period of low U.S. unemployment and low benefit payments at the start of the UI program, Congress largely ignored the program. When a major recession did occur in 1958, Congress responded, not with major UI reform but by enacting temporary emergency benefits that added weeks of benefits to the states' regular benefit programs. This has become Congress's principal response in each subsequent recession. Thus, rather than adjusting or reforming the UI system to respond to workforce and workplace shifts, Congress has let state UI programs continue largely unchanged. An exception was the modest 1976 UI amendments that increased UI coverage, increased the taxable wage base, and made other legislative changes. Recognizing the incomplete nature of the 1976 reform, Congress called for the appointment of a national UI commission, but the recommendations of both this commission and a subsequent commission again were not adopted (Advisory Commission on Unemployment Compensation [ACUC] 1996; National Commission on Unemployment Compensation [NCUC] 1980).

Through the mid-1970s, congressional neglect did not have significant adverse effects on the UI program. States found that, with low levels of unemployment, they could increase UI benefit amounts and maximum potential durations of benefits without significant tax increases. Indeed, in the 1970s all states increased their maximum potential durations to 26 or more weeks of benefits (O'Leary and Wandner 1997).

Because the CES's dire actuarial forecast did not materialize, between 1938 and the mid-1970s, most states substantially liberalized their benefit programs in other respects as well. In 1938, states imposed waiting periods of 2 to 4 weeks before they paid UI benefits. By 1985, all states had either no weeks of waiting or 1 week. Similarly, over this period, the range of the state maximum weekly benefits increased from $15–$18 to $84–$225. Maximum potential durations had standardized to 26 weeks, except for three states that provided up to 30 weeks of benefits (Price 1985). Only in the last four decades have state UI benefit and tax provisions significantly diverged, with many states sharply curtailing both benefit payments and tax collections (O'Leary and Wandner 2020).

A key UI program weakness, however, has been the lack of balance between UI taxes and benefits. This imbalance has resulted from the lack of a national process for automatically increasing (indexing) both benefits and taxes each year. Driving that imbalance has been depressed UI tax rates and taxable wage bases. Together, they have kept UI benefits below an adequate funding level in many states. First, the federal taxable wage base has only increased three times since 1935, and it has been stuck at $7,000 since 1983. In addition, many states have not raised their state UI taxable wages much above the insufficient federal taxable wage base floor. Second, states have limited the increase in UI taxes necessary to pay for the increase in UI benefits that are paid during recessions. The result has been insufficient tax revenue to fund adequate state UI benefit programs and, in many states, downward pressure on all aspects of benefit payments: program access, eligibility, benefit amounts, and benefit durations.

Because the UI program depends on the ES to conduct the UI work test and provide job matching, job search assistance, and labor market information services, and because the largest population served by the ES is UI recipients, it is important to have the two programs either administered together or work closely together. Since 1935, however, that mostly has not been the case.

The UI national office began as an agency administered by the Social Security Administration (SSA) predecessor agencies—identified as SSA below—while the ES was administered by USDOL. Although they were briefly brought together at SSA in 1939, it was only in 1949 that UI and ES were brought together and administered by USDOL.

## ADMINISTRATION OF UI AT USDOL: 1949–1975

The Bureau of Employment Security was created within SSA to operate the UI program, and when it transferred to USDOL in 1949, the Bureau administrator oversaw not only UI but ES as well. Thus, UI and ES were administered together at the federal level, facilitating the coordination of policy at the state and local levels, and that relationship continued for two decades.

The decline of the federal administration of the UI and ES programs began in 1969, when the Nixon administration placed primary emphasis on expanding job training. The USDOL training agency was the Manpower Administration—later renamed the Employment and Training Administration—and initially the Bureau of Employment Security was a part of it. However, later in 1969, the Manpower Administration was reorganized, and the Bureau was eliminated as part of the reorganization. The UI and ES programs were again separated—each headed by its own administrator within USDOL. This resulted in less coordination between UI and ES with respect to programs and policy, thereby weakening the program (Blaustein, Cohen, and Haber 1993).

Also important for the UI program was the weakening relationship with the regional office staff, who were in close contact with individual state UI programs and were charged with monitoring the states, offering guidance and providing technical assistance. This weakened relationship was due to the implementation of the Nixon administration's philosophy of the New Federalism that emphasized greater decentralization of federal programs. The greater separation between the UI national office and the state UI agencies left the state UI agencies increasingly on their own, since UI national office staff did not travel much to the state UI agencies and provided less oversight, advice, and guidance. As federal guidance and oversight declined, state programs began to increasingly diverge.

The UI program's effectiveness has always been tested during and immediately after recessions. For each recession, the key questions are whether the state UI programs are ready for the significant increase in claims and benefit payments and how they respond to the need to increase revenues after the recession is over. The weakening of federal oversight and guidance was not immediately apparent during the relatively low unemployment of the early 1970s, but the UI program was tested by the severe recession of 1973–1975. That recession resulted in high program costs, high levels of state indebtedness to the U.S. Treasury, and the need for states to make legislative decisions about setting UI benefit and tax provisions.

It became clear that it was a mistake to administratively house the national UI office in the Manpower Administration in USDOL because the Manpower Administration was primarily a training organization, with little emphasis or experience in the administration of a social insurance program that pays benefits and collects taxes. When the UI program was organizationally separated from the ES, there was far less coordination between the ES and UI programs at both the national and local level. As a result, the UI national office lost much of its control of staff in the regional offices. The states were increasingly on their own as their federal partner weakened.

## ADMINISTRATION OF UI AT USDOL: 1975 TO THE PRESENT, AS THE PROGRAM FURTHER DECLINES

The UI national office has continued to decline in the period since 1975.[2] It has been operating in an agency and a department whose top priorities have not included operating a social insurance program like UI. As a cabinet agency, USDOL changed radically over the past five decades, becoming primarily a regulatory agency, with declining emphasis on the operation of programs. In 1975, when the Manpower Administration became the Employment and Training Administration (ETA), its primary emphasis remained on training rather than on running other employment and unemployment programs. Until the pandemic, the renamed Office of Unemployment Insurance (OUI) was only of minor concern to ETA, with OUI being only 1 of 10 offices within ETA.

### USDOL Becomes a Regulatory Agency

While USDOL had some regulatory responsibilities throughout its history, it became a primarily regulatory agency beginning in the 1970s with the establishment of six new regulatory agencies under its auspices (see Table 2.1).

**Table 2.1  USDOL Regulatory Agencies, Dates Established**

| USDOL regulatory agencies and establishment dates | Date |
|---|---|
| Women's Bureau | 1920 |
| Office Labor-Management Standards | 1920 |
| Wage and Hour Division | 1938 |
| Occupational and Safety and Health Administration | 1971 |
| Pension Benefit Guaranty Corporation | 1974 |
| Employee Benefit Security Administration | 1974 |
| Mine Safety and Health Administration | 1977 |
| Office of Federal Contract Compliance Programs | 1978 |
| Office of Workers' Compensation Programs | 1981 |

SOURCE: MacLaury (n.d.).

The 1970s were a time of overall growth for USDOL. Staffing increased rapidly to accommodate the new regulatory agencies. Given the decentralization of program administration, employment and training staffing declined sharply, from 37 percent of USDOL staff to 16 percent. That decrease continued unabated in the 1980s. While the rest of USDOL lost staff due to one reduction-in-force, ETA Assistant Secretary Albert Angrisani further reduced staffing dramatically by electing to conduct a second ETA reduction-in-force. By 1989, ETA staffing had declined to 1,963, down from 3,887 in 1969, and ETA had only 11 percent of the total USDOL staff, down from 37 percent in 1969 (Table 2.2).

**Table 2.2  USDOL Full-Time Equivalent Employees by Function, Number, and Percent, Selected Fiscal Years 1959–2019**

| Function | Regulation | Employment and training | Bureau of Labor Statistics | Management, executive direction, and program development | Row total/ % of total employees |
|---|---|---|---|---|---|
| 1959 | 2,078/37.9% | 1,420/25.9% | 958/17.5% | 640/11.7% | 5,096/93.1% |
| 1969 | 3,422/32.8% | 3,887/37.2% | 1,537/14.7% | 1,423/13.6% | 10,269/98.3% |
| 1979 | 12,821/59.0% | 3,507/16.1% | 2,087/9.6% | 2,928/13.5% | 21,343/98.3% |
| 1989 | 10,467/59.5% | 1,963/11.2% | 2,097/11.9% | 2,419/13.7% | 16,946/96.3% |
| 1999 | 9,618/58.9% | 1,604/9.8% | 2,406/14.7% | 2,202/13.5% | 15,830/97.0% |
| 2016 | 10,194/64.8% | 1,426/9.1% | 2,280/14.5% | 1,837/11.7% | 15,757/95.5% |
| 2019[a] | 9,751/65.0% | 1,379/9.3% | 2,242/14.9% | 1,609/10.7% | 14,999/95.1% |

[a]Budget request level for 2019; other data are actual.

NOTE: Full-time equivalent employees are the staffing level that are authorized by the federal budget. The "on-board" staff who are actually in place is usually smaller.

SOURCE: Krueger (1999) for years 1959–1999. USDOL (2017, 2018) for 2016 and 2019 (President's Budget Request). Excludes the international labor function and "other" functions.

## The UI National Office Declines Steadily

During the 1980s, both the UI national office staff and resources shrank from small to tiny. Between 1979 and 1989, the national UI office staff declined from 325 to 113, with most of the declines occurring in the early 1980s as part of the two ETA reductions-in-force (Figure 2.1).

**Figure 2.1  USDOL Staffing from Federal Unemployment Tax Act Funds,
Fiscal Years 1979–1993**

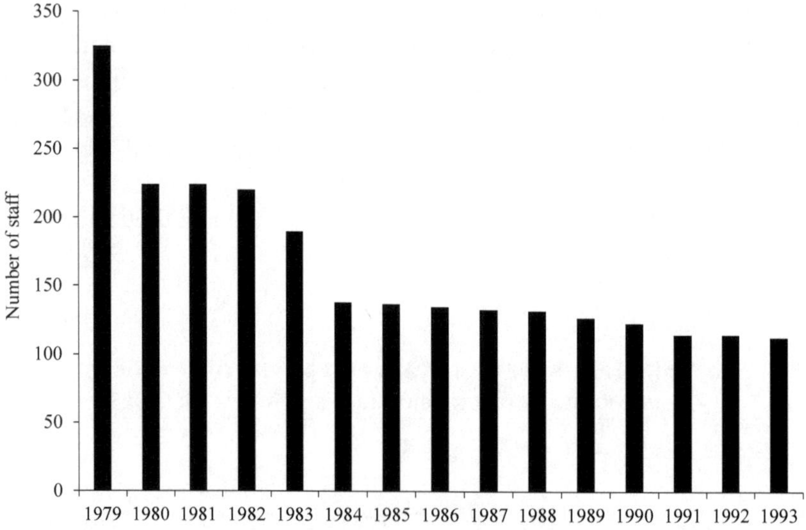

SOURCE: Ron Wilus, Chief Actuary, Office of Unemployment Insurance, from an undated and untitled UI actuarial document justifying budgetary staffing increase, developed by the UI Actuarial Division in 1993, received by the author January 1, 2019.

Thus, by 1989, national UI staffing comprised only 127 out of an ETA total of 1,963 (6 percent). This was less than 1 percent of the total USDOL staff (16,946), even though the UI budget was overwhelmingly the largest component of the total USDOL budget.[3]

The decline in national UI office staffing has continued since 1993. By 2015, staffing had dropped to only 66. Table 2.3 shows the distribution of the reduction in staffing. The declines were bigger in program operations and smaller in the functions that support the UI national office. Thus, the staffing for monitoring, guiding, and providing technical assistance to the state UI agencies' UI programs was all but eliminated.

UI national office staff continued to decline after 2015. The UI national office full-time equivalent staff was further lowered from 63 in 2016 to 62 in 2017 and 57 in 2018 (Snidar 2018).

Thus, since the mid-1970s the UI national office has been a small agency within USDOL. At the same time, USDOL has become primar-

**Table 2.3 UI National Office Full-Time Equivalent Staff on Board by Function, Selected Years and Ratio of, 1976–2015**

| Function | 1976 | 1996 | 2015 | 2015/1976 |
|---|---|---|---|---|
| Total | 145 | 94 | 66 | 0.46 |
| Front office | 9 | 4 | 8 | 0.89 |
| Actuarial, reporting, finance, and legislation | 31 | 24 | 21 | 0.68 |
| Actuarial | 11 | 10 | 5 | 0.45 |
| Reporting | 4 | 4 | 5 | 1.25 |
| Legislation, state, and federal | 16 | 10 | 11 | 0.69 |
| Research | 7 | 10 | 0 | 0.0 |
| UI program operations | 59 | 21 | 15 | 0.25 |
| State and federal benefits | 55 | 15 | 11 | 0.20 |
| Tax | 4 | 7 | 4 | No change |
| Information technology, data analysis and validation, and performance measurement | 28 | 24 | 17 | 0.61 |
| Clerical | n/a | 15 | n/a | — |

NOTE: As of early 2021, no staffing plan had been prepared since 2015. The 1996 organization chart is broken out by professional staff by function and clerical staff for the entire organization; no similar clerical/professional breakout is provided for 1976 or 2015. UI research staff were transferred to an ETA research office in the mid-1990s.
SOURCE: For 1976, estimated using the 1976 USDOL Telephone Directory. For 1996, based on organization chart (Johnson 1996). For 2015, based on Office of Unemployment Insurance 2015 staffing plan (USDOL 2015).

ily a regulatory agency, with policy priorities supporting the work of the regulatory subagencies. Within ETA, the national UI office is only 1 of 10 offices, and a small one at that. The national UI office was already a small subagency in the 1970s, and it has continued to decline over time. Today, the Office of Unemployment Insurance is so small that it cannot be an effective partner to the state UI agencies regarding program administration. Rather than having an effective national partner, the UI program has become more of a state program rather than a true federal-state partnership. The wide divergence in state UI programs, many of which seem inadequate, is likely a result of the lack of federal leadership that has allowed the development of a "race to the bottom" among the states.

## The U.S. Employment Service Is Eliminated

Two essential functions of the UI program are to ensure that UI recipients are 1) able, available, and actively searching for work (the "UI Work Test"); and 2) receiving job matching, labor market information, and job search services to facilitate their return to work. These functions are performed by ES staff in local public workforce offices. At the national level, it is critical that the UI national office and ES staff coordinate with state and local offices to provide these services and to ensure that there is communication and coordination between local UI and ES staff. That coordination became impossible as the U.S. Employment Service was eliminated and its functions were absorbed by the national office training program, the Office of Adult Services, beginning in 2006 (Table 2.4).

**Table 2.4  Organizational Placement of Employment Service Programs in the U.S. Department of Labor, 1977–2021**

| Date | Name of employment service organization |
|------|------------------------------------------|
| 1977 | United States Employment Service |
| 1991 | United States Employment Service |
| 1998 | United States Employment Service |
| 2002 | Division of U.S. Employment Services/America's Labor Market Information System (ALMIS), Office of Career Transition Assistance |
| 2003 | Office of Adult Services, Office of Workforce Investment (OWI) |
| 2004 | Division of Employment Services and ALMIS, Office of Adult Services, OWI |
| 2005 | Division of Adult, Dislocated Worker, Employment Services, and Workforce Information, OWI |
| 2006 | Office of Adult Services, OWI |
| 2007 | Division of Adult Services, OWI |
| 2008 | Division of Adult Services, OWI |
| 2021 | Division of Adult Services and Governance, OWI |

SOURCE: Annual U.S. Department of Labor Telephone Directory, selected years 1977–2008. For 2021, USDOL website (https://www.dol.gov/agencies/eta/workforce-investment).

By the early 2000s, the organization named the United States Employment Service had been reduced to a division, and by 2006, it had been eliminated completely. Currently, any coordination between the UI and ES programs occurs mostly at the state or local level since coordination has largely been eliminated at USDOL.

## Notes

1. In 1939 and now, states may enact laws requiring higher state taxable wage bases on employers. As of this writing, only three jurisdictions continue to have a fixed wage base of $7,000—Arizona, California, and Puerto Rico (Ernst and Young 2019).
2. This section makes use of material from Wandner (2019).
3. For example, for FY 2021, of all USDOL's mandatory budget authority of $28.38 billion, UI budget authority was $27.39, or 97 percent (FY 2020 Department of Labor Budget Summary Tables, https://www.dol.gov/general/budget/index-2020).

# 3

# Downward Trends and Wide Variation among States, 1980–2019

The decline in the UI program resulting from legislative and administrative changes and diminished funding and staff is revealed by the changes in program activity and outcomes over time, as well as by the increased state-by-state variation in the adequacy of benefits and the sufficiency of taxes collected to fund those benefits. This chapter discloses alarming long-term trends and wide variation in the UI program between states that have developed over many decades.[1]

The figures discussed below illustrate features of the UI program that point to the need for reform:

- Figures 3.1 and 3.2 illustrate the need for taxable wage base reform discussed in Chapter 10.

- Figure 3.3 shows the steady, long-term decline of UI benefits and taxes that have occurred in the absence of the enactment federal benefit and tax standards.

- Figure 3.4 shows wide variations by state in benefit recipiency which is the basis for the options for increased access to UI discussed in Chapter 8.

- Figure 3.5 illustrates the declining scope of the UI program as it serves less of the unemployed while the percentage of workers on layoff—the UI target population—has been increasing over time.

- Figure 3.6 illustrates the need for increased potential duration of benefits discussed in Chapter 8, while, in fact, potential durations of benefits have been declining.

- Figure 3.7 illustrates the close relationship between unionization and UI benefit recipiency with resulting large state differences in unionization and recipiency, as illustrated by the sharp contrast between New Jersey, North Carolina, and Florida discussed in Chapter 4.

- Figure 3.8 shows the significant differences in the percent of the Black population receiving UI in the states of the South and most of the rest of the country that have raised the concerns about differences in UI receipt by race discussed in Chapter 5.

- Figure 3.9 shows the sharp decline in the real budget expenditures on the Employment Service over time as the need for more reemployment services for UI recipients has increased, a topic that is discussed in Chapter 11.

## GRAPHIC ANALYSIS OF UI DECLINE THROUGH 2019

The federal UI taxable wage base that is the basis for the financing of UI program administration, the Employment Service, the federal share of Extended Benefits, and the federal loans to states when their state UI trust fund accounts become insolvent. It also sets a minimum wage base for the state tax systems. The tax base together with UI tax rates determine the capacity of the UI program to finance an adequate level of benefits and services.

Figure 3.1 shows what has happened to the federal UI taxable wage base since the program's inception. In the late 1930s, the UI and Social Security programs were administered together, and in 1939 Congress set the taxable wage base for both programs at $3,000, such that the UI taxable wage base was set at close to 100 percent of total wages. The UI and Social Security taxable wage bases remained at $3,000 until after World War II. Then, in 1949, the UI program was administratively separated from the Social Security program and came under the jurisdiction of the USDOL. After that time, the UI and Social Security programs and the way that they are financed began to diverge sharply.

The Social Security taxable wage base was increased by Congress in 1951 and was subsequently increased through the 1950s and 1960s. Starting in the 1970s, the Social Security taxable wage base became indexed and has increased steadily until it reached $160,200 in 2023 (Whitman and Shoffner 2011). By contrast, the federal UI taxable wage base only has been increased three times—in 1972, 1978, and 1983—and has remained at $7,000 for 40 years. Thus, the UI taxable wage base has declined to less than 30 percent of total wages.

**Figure 3.1  UI and Social Security Taxable Wage Bases and the Ratio of Total to UI Taxable Wages, 1940–2019**

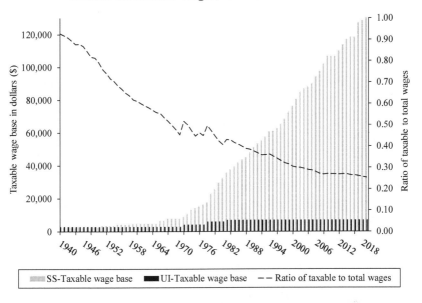

SOURCE: USDOL, Employment and Training Administration, ET Financial Data Handbook 394 (https://oui.doleta.gov/unemploy/hb394.asp) and (https://www.ssa.gov/oact/cola/cbb.html).

Although the UI and Social Security taxable wage bases started at the same level at the beginning of the programs, the Social Security wage base is now more than 20 times larger than the UI wage base—a far more sustainable and progressive approach to social insurance financing.

Among analysts of the UI program, there is agreement that, together, a substantial increase in the UI taxable wage base and tax rates must be implemented by the federal government and/or the states to fund adequate benefits. There is also agreement that, to achieve a financially sustainable UI program, the taxable wage base should be indexed, as is the Social Security taxable wage base (O'Leary and Wandner 2018; Vroman et al. 2017; West et al. 2016).

While states are free to set their own taxable wage bases at any level they choose at or above $7,000—the federal taxable wage base—the great majority of states maintain low taxable wage bases that are not much above the $7,000 minimum. In fact, Figure 3.2 shows that in 2019 only 14 states had a taxable wage base greater than $25,000, and 18 states had taxable wage bases of $10,000 or less. The result is that low-wage employers pay the UI system a much higher percentage of their wage bill than higher-wage employers.

Not only are taxable wage bases low, but most states do not raise their taxable wage base regularly, either by state legislative action or by indexing their taxable wage base to average annual earnings in the state. Only 19 states index their state taxable wage base (USDOL 2022a).

Thus, the majority of states have allowed their UI tax systems to decline as a percent of total wages, such that it is difficult for them to pay adequate benefits to UI recipients in their states.

With taxable wage bases low and states reluctant to raise taxes, it is not surprising that, since 1975, both benefits and taxes have trended

**Figure 3.2  The Taxable Wage Base from Highest to Lowest of the 50 States, the District of Columbia, Puerto Rico, and the Virgin Islands as of 2019**

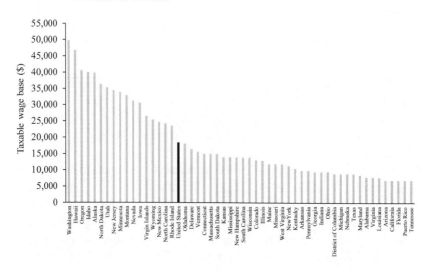

NOTE: The bold black line is the U.S. average.
SOURCE: USDOL, Employment and Training Administration, Quarterly UI Data Summary (https://oui.doleta.gov/unemploy/data_summary/DataSum.asp).

downward as a percentage of total wages (Figure 3.3). With insufficient tax revenues, benefits are constrained by available resources, and by most standard measures are inadequate.

Employers lay off workers even during good times, so the UI program pays UI benefits throughout the business cycle. Nevertheless, aggregate benefit payments are highly correlated with unemployment, that is, increasing sharply when unemployment rates increase.

By contrast, states tend to increase UI taxes only after a recession. Following such an initial tax increase, however, the states tend to decrease taxes quickly. In some states, there is a reluctance to raise UI taxes even after a recession. Indeed, after the 2007–2009 recession, a substantial number of states sharply cut UI benefits rather than increase taxes (Vroman 2018).

Because of inadequate forward funding, many states have found that their state trust fund accounts—in which the positive balance of their state UI reserves are held in the U.S. Treasury—are exhausted during recessions. State UI programs continue paying benefits because they can borrow from the U.S. Treasury–maintained Unemployment

**Figure 3.3  UI Taxes and Benefits as Percentage of Total Wages in the United States, 1975–2019**

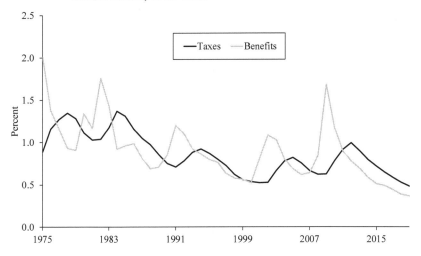

SOURCE: USDOL, Employment and Training Administration, ET Financial Data Handbook 394 (https://oui.doleta.gov/unemploy/hb394.asp).

Trust Fund. To repay loans from the U.S. Treasury, states must rebuild their UI balances in their state UI accounts. Many states opt for a heavy dose of benefit cuts rather than raising tax rates or their state taxable wage base. Examples of how states have reduced their maximum potential duration after the 2007–2009 recession are noted in Chapter 9. The result of these cuts has been inadequate and declining funding for the UI program over time.

Just as taxable wage bases vary widely by state, the UI recipiency rate also varies greatly by state (Figure 3.4). Some states make it easier

**Figure 3.4  UI Recipiency Rates by State, 2019**

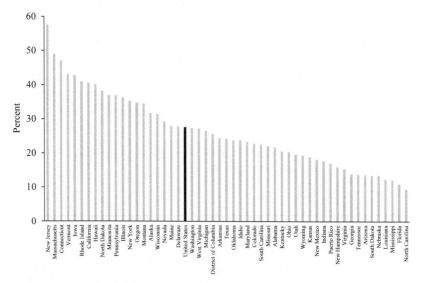

NOTE: The bold black line is the national average recipiency rate.
SOURCE: Unemployment Insurance Chart Book, Series A13, 2019 (https://oui.doleta .gov/unemploy/chartbook.asp).

to apply for and receive benefits, while others make UI receipt much more difficult. In 2019,

- only 7 states had recipiency rates of greater than 40 percent;
- 29 states had recipiency rates of less than 25 percent; and
- North Carolina's recipiency rate was the lowest in the country at only 9 percent.

UI was intended to be an earned right for unemployed workers on layoff whose jobs were covered by the UI program and who had substantial attachment to the labor force. Yet, in many states, the recipiency rate appears to be unreasonably low.

While the percentage of unemployed workers by reason for unemployment (i.e., layoff, quit, reentrant, and new entrant to the labor force) varies over the business cycle, UI administrative data (available in the online USDOL UI Database) show that over half of all unemployed workers are on involuntary layoff.[2] Since nearly all wage and salary workers work in UI-covered jobs, and the earnings threshold to demonstrate attachment to the workforce is generally not difficult to reach, the percentage of unemployed workers receiving UI benefits should be roughly 50 percent. The actual percentage is far lower in most states. For example, if the states with the lowest recipiency rates had a layoff rate of approximately 50 percent, then only approximately one in five workers on layoff would have collected UI in 2019.

Experienced wage and salary employees on layoff should generally be eligible for UI benefits. Figure 3.5 shows that the layoff rate is cyclical and tends to vary between 45 and 60 percent of those who are unemployed and that there is a small upward trend over time. The regular UI recipiency rate also varies with the business cycle, but in recent years it has declined from approximately 45 percent to less than 30 percent.

If the layoff rate is a rough measure of the need for UI benefits among unemployed workers, that need has been relatively flat, though increasing somewhat. Yet, UI benefit receipt has been declining. The reduction after the 2007–2009 recession was sharper than after previous recessions, suggesting greater difficulty for laid off workers to apply for and receive UI benefits.

Over the past five decades, as the need for UI in the U.S. labor market has increased, the availability of UI benefits has declined. While from the 1970s until 2010 nearly every state had a maximum potential duration of benefits of 26 weeks, not all UI recipients qualified for the full 26 weeks of benefits, because qualifying weeks of work depend on the amount of the wages earned during employees' qualifying base periods. Most states have variable maximum durations of benefits, and in those variable duration states, it has become increasingly difficult for lower-wage workers to qualify for 26 weeks of benefits. The result of

**Figure 3.5  Regular UI Recipients and Layoffs as a Percent of the Unemployed, 1980–2019**

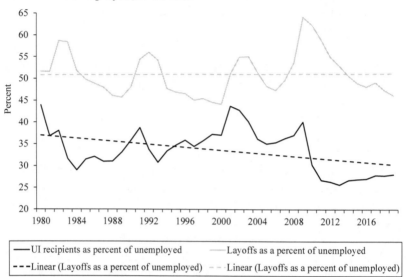

SOURCE: UI recipiency rate from UI Chart Book series A12 (https://oui.doleta.gov/unemploy/chartbook.asp). Layoff rate from Bureau of Labor Statistics, Current Population Survey, Employment Status of the Civilian Non-Institutional Population, Series ID: LNU03023622. Series title: (Unadjusted) Job Losers as a Percent of Total Unemployed.

these factors is that, on average, UI recipients have qualified for fewer and fewer weeks of UI benefits (Figure 3.6).

And over the same period, short-term temporary layoffs have declined, and the percentage of unemployed workers who are permanently separated has increased (Groshen and Potter 2003). As a result, more of both unemployed workers in general and the large subset of UI recipients have become part of the long-term unemployed—those who stay unemployed for more than 26 weeks. This can be seen by the upward trend in the percentage of the unemployed who are jobless for 27 weeks or longer.

Thus, as the need for longer durations of UI benefits has increased, the actual payment of benefits has declined. Similarly, since a much larger percentage of unemployed workers are not returning to their previous employers (BLS 2022; Groshen and Potter 2003) as automobile

**Figure 3.6 Average Potential Weeks Duration of Regular UI Receipt for Workers Fully Unemployed and the Percentage of Unemployed Who Are Jobless for 27 Weeks or Longer in the United States, 1971–2019**

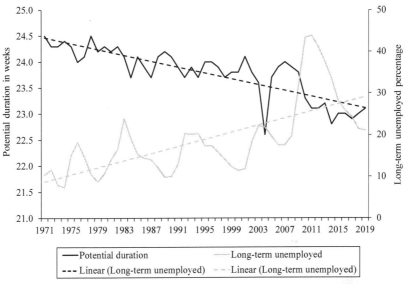

SOURCE: Potential duration of regular UI from USDOL, Employment and Training Administration, ET Financial Data Handbook 394 (https://oui.doleta.gov/unemploy/hb394.asp). Percent of unemployed workers who are long-term unemployed from USDOL, Bureau of Labor Statistics, Current Population Survey, Characteristics of the Unemployed series LNU03025703.

production model changeovers layoffs and other short layoffs mostly have disappeared, more UI recipients need reemployment assistance to get back to work. Yet, as demonstrated in Chapter 11, the availability of such services from the Employment Service has sharply declined.

Furthermore, as the potential duration of UI benefits declines, it is less likely that unemployed workers will apply for UI and receive any benefits. This is particularly true in the states that have sharply reduced the potential durations of UI benefits, such as Florida, where the maximum potential duration of benefits can be as low as 12 weeks when the state unemployment rate is low.

Union membership also appears to influence the UI recipiency rate experience by state. As shown in Figure 3.7, the percentage of union

**Figure 3.7  Union Membership as a Percentage of Employment by State, Ordered from Highest to Lowest, Regular UI Recipiency Rate for 2019**

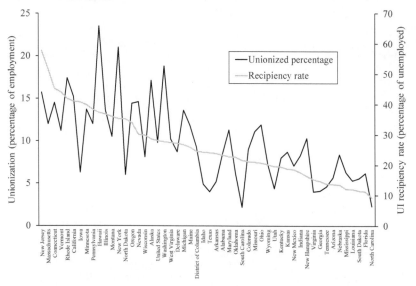

SOURCE: Unionization rate from USDOL, Bureau of Labor Statistics, Current Population Survey, "Table 5. Union affiliation of employed wage and salary workers by state" and UI recipiency rate from UI Chart Book series A13, 2019 (https://oui.doleta.gov/unemploy/chartbook.asp).

membership among employees in each state is positively correlated with state UI recipiency rates. Because employers pay nearly all UI taxes, many states' employer organizations lobby to keep UI benefits and UI taxes as low as possible. By contrast, state-organized labor groups try to maintain a high level of state UI benefits as well as state UI tax rates and tax bases sufficient to fund state UI benefits. Organized labor in the United States, however, is weak and has been on a downward trend. Nationally, approximately one-tenth of wage and salary workers are union members, and union membership varies significantly by state. One would expect that there would be a relationship between the extent of states' union membership and the states' UI recipiency rates, with more unionized states having higher recipiency rates. Figure 3.7 shows that indeed there is such a strong relationship. Since the establishment of UI benefit criteria is largely a political decision arrived at by state political officials, where unionization is high, organized labor is likely to have more power to influence state UI policy than where unionization is low.

While there are many reasons why some states pay only limited UI benefits to unemployed workers in their states, there also appears to be a close relationship between the percentage of the state population that is Black and a low recipiency rate in southern states. Figure 3.8 shows that of the 10 states with the lowest recipiency rates, 6 of them are southern states, and each of those 10 states has a high percentage of its population that is Black. Similarly, of the 13 states with the largest percentage Black population, all but 3 (Maryland, Delaware, and New York) have recipiency rates of 20 percent or less (i.e., D.C., Mississippi, Louisiana, Georgia, South Carolina, Alabama, North Carolina, Virginia, Tennessee, and Florida).

**Figure 3.8  UI Recipiency Rate and Black Share of the U.S. Population**

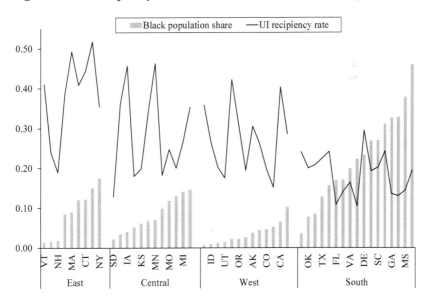

SOURCE: Percentage of Black population from United States Department of Census, State Population by Characteristics, 2010–2019, "Annual Estimates of the Resident Population by Sex, Race, and Hispanic Origin: April 1, 2010, to July 1, 2019." (https://www.census.gov/data/tables/time-series/demo/popest/2010s-state-detail .html#par_textimage_673542126) and UI recipiency rate from UI Chart Book series A13, 2019 (https://oui.doleta.gov/unemploy/chartbook.asp).

This observation is consistent with the fact that the Southern states generally have provided limited social services in other areas, expecting that their residents will provide many of these services for themselves. Goldin and Katz (2008) examine the history of educational development in the United States and find that a lack of high schools in rural areas where most Blacks lived explains why the South was the U.S. region lagging in the spread of universal secondary education. Similarly, studies indicate that the slow expansion of coverage in the Social Security system to agricultural and domestic household workers may have been based on political pressure from Southern members of Congress (Nadasen 2007; Roberts 1996).

In addition to the decline in the adequacy of benefits, over the past four decades there has been a significant decline in the funding for reemployment services for UI recipients. Figure 3.9 reveals the decline in funding for the Employment Service during a time of increasing need for reemployment services by UI recipients. Very few unemployed workers are temporarily laid off. Instead, increasingly since the 1970s, more laid-off workers are permanently laid off (Groshen and Potter 2003). Since UI recipients often cannot return to their prior jobs, many need to search for new work rather than wait for a recall to their prior jobs.

Traditionally, the Employment Service provided job matching services and job search training. These services often have been critical to successfully returning UI recipients to work in a timely fashion (Michaelides et al. 2012). However, funding for the Employment Service has been reduced since the mid-1980s in nominal terms, and the reduction has been especially stark in real terms.

What this means to UI recipients is that when they go to a public workforce One-Stop Career Center—now named American Jobs Centers—they are not likely to receive any in-person one-on-one reemployment services. Instead, they are likely to be sent to a resource room where they are expected to search for work on their own and use a computer to search for labor market information, take aptitude and other tests, search for job openings, develop a resume, and conduct other job search activities. They also are unlikely to get personal assistance in developing a resume or in learning how to successfully take a job interview.

The result is that the provision of reemployment services is quite limited. Technology-savvy, professional workers may be able to search for work on their own. Others—especially less-educated and older

**Figure 3.9  Wagner-Peyser Funding for Employment Services in Nominal and Real Dollars (1984 = 100)**

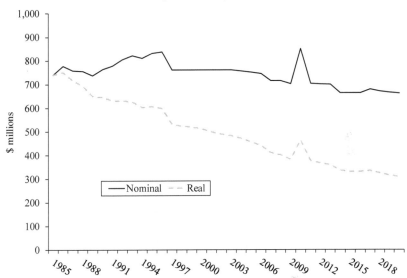

SOURCE: Wagner-Peyser Act funding from Federal Reserve Bank of St. Louis (n.d.). GDP personal consumption deflator from Bureau of Economic Analysis, U.S. Department of Commerce.

workers, as well as those who speak English as a second language or have a disability—have a much harder time searching for and finding work in the current U.S. economy.

## ISSUES REVEALED AND EXACERBATED BY THE COVID-19 PANDEMIC

Because this book generally addresses the need for long-term UI reform, for the most part it does not focus on the UI program's difficulties providing needed relief during the COVID-19 pandemic, especially since, in addition to paying out additional benefits to UI recipients, Congress tasked the UI program with administering temporary public assistance (not social insurance) programs for workers who previously had not been covered by the UI program and for whom previous methods of administration could not be used.

However, the severity of the UI experience during the COVID-19 recession revealed issues that must be addressed as part of the overall UI reform discussion. The pandemic was unprecedented because of the lockdown of the U.S economy, which caused an extremely severe and rapid increase in unemployment. It was understood that the effects of the lockdown would be severe throughout the economy, including in industries that were not previously covered by the UI program. Several of the following issues arose during the pandemic:

- **Administrative underfunding.** The UI system has been underfunded for decades. The system limped along during good times, but it had problems dealing with past severe recessions. State UI programs receive "base" administrative grants that fund a low level of benefit payments, and additional "contingency" funding when unemployment rises. Funding in early 2020 was low because of the strong economy that had been improving for many years. The UI program thus was unprepared for the sudden unprecedented surge in the volume of claims that began in March 2020. The program was understaffed and soon had problems related to claims-taking, adjudications, and appeals. Although the CARES Act provided state UI programs with $1 billion in additional funding, UI claims-takers, adjudicators, and administrative law judges are all skilled workers who could not be quickly hired and trained.[3] The additional funding helped, but it could not relieve the acute strain on the UI system.

- **Computer systems and lack of automation.** Many state computer systems are old and inflexible. At the outset of the pandemic, states had to implement three new federal programs that required developing new computer programs to administer. While states had previous experience with extending benefits in the form of temporary emergency benefits, developing new programs to pay an additional benefit—and especially to extend coverage to workers not previously covered by the UI program—was daunting and slow. The inflexibility of the state computer systems, especially the many older systems, and problems with computer programming for the new systems, slowed the implementation of the new federal programs.

- **Adjudications and appeals.** While computer systems could generally cope with the increased volume of claims and requests for benefit extensions and additions once the new computer program coding was completed, the lack of automation of parts of the claims-taking, adjudication, and appeals processes became bottlenecks. For example, many claims raised reason for separation issues that had to be resolved by adjudicators. The adjudication system is generally a manual system. Adjudicators can only resolve so many cases a day, and the limited number of adjudicators soon became overwhelmed by the caseload.

- **Inadequate communications systems.** As state UI systems fell behind in the processing of claims, claimants found it difficult to communicate with most state UI agencies either by phone or by email. Most states had inadequate telephone banks to respond to incoming calls and were unable to expand those banks that lacked call-back features. In many cases, claimants waited on the phone for hours and still did not get through.

- **Pandemic Unemployment Assistance (PUA).** The pandemic revealed that even though the UI program covers nearly all wage and salary unemployment, in a recession as severe as that in 2020, other workers also will suffer from unemployment. Congress decided to cover independent contractors and the self-employed, among others, in the PUA program, but the program had many flaws. It was difficult to determine eligibility and benefit payment amounts, and it was prey to a great deal of fraud not just by individuals but by organized crime groups because of the difficulty state UI agencies had identifying the workers, determining whether they were in fact unemployed, and the amount of their wages prior to the recession (see Chapter 13 on fraud and overpayments). The failures of PUA reveal the necessity of developing either new permanent programs to cover currently uncovered workers or a better system of administration to anticipate future temporary programs that provide employment and wage data for workers who are not part of the UI system.

- **UI as pandemic relief paymaster.** With the onset of the pandemic, Congress provided substantial relief to households and unemployed workers under the CARES Act. The Internal Revenue Service (IRS) and the Office of Unemployment Insurance were designated the paymasters for those pandemic relief payments, both to those workers who were employed and those who were not. Neither agency was prepared to assume that role, and both agencies had similar problems that included inadequate staff, weak and old IT systems, and payments that were outside the scope of their normal operations.

The description of the IRS's problems is not dissimilar to those of OUI. As Bogage (2021) explains, IRS "is morphing . . . into this dual mission of both tax administration and administering of social programs. The challenge is that IRS was not set up for that purpose and their IT is not structured for that."

While the UI system has long provided extended and emergency unemployment assistance to long-term unemployed UI recipients, what was new with the pandemic was that, in addition to paying these added weeks of benefits, the UI program was expected to pay benefits to workers with prior work experience but not previously covered by the UI program, for whom these agencies had no work history data.

- **Divergent international approaches to the pandemic.** The United States took a different path during the pandemic than did much of Europe. Many European countries kept workers on standby and paid them with short-time compensation/work sharing or wage supplements—programs discussed below. The U.S. instead chose to let its workers be laid off and receive UI or unemployment assistance. The *Economist* has contrasted the two approaches as "Preservers"—keeping workers job-attached —versus "Protectors"—having workers laid off and then receiving UI benefits (Williams 2020). U.S. policymakers may want to evaluate the outcomes of these two approaches and determine which is the better path for a future downturn as severe as engendered by the COVID pandemic.

- **Research findings.** One extraordinary result of the pandemic was the rush by researchers to understand the problems of the UI system and applicants during 2020. Many researchers understood the magnitude of the problems and wanted to help.

Researchers grabbed microdata, analyzed it, and quickly published the results.

While there is no national UI microdata set, some states have made their data available to researchers. California is one of those states. The California data have revealed much about the significant difficulties implementing the pandemic programs and their disproportionate impact on young and less-educated workers (Hedin, Schnorr, and von Wachter 2020).

## Notes

1. This section is based on Wandner and O'Leary (2021).
2. https://oui.doleta.gov/unemploy/DataDashboard.asp (accessed May 2, 2023).
3. Coronavirus Aid, Relief, and Economic Security Act (P.L. 116-138).

# 4

# Weaknesses in the U.S. UI System

## How We Got Here and What It Means

This chapter looks at how the U.S. UI system reached its current weakened state and what that means for unemployed workers both by state and for demographic subgroups. We see how the current federal-state UI system has allowed many states to engage in a "race to the bottom," with some states minimizing the benefits they pay and the taxes they collect. The result is vastly different UI programs among the states. Some states have raced to the bottom, while others have built strong programs. To understand the differences, we examine the UI program in three states with contrasting public policy: New Jersey, with one of the strongest programs, and Florida and North Carolina, with extremely weak programs.

The race to the bottom became particularly severe after the 2007–2009 recession. We consider one aspect of that decline—the decreasing number of states with maximum potential durations of 26 weeks or more.

Next, we examine the sharp differences between the United States and other western industrial nations regarding the adequacy of UI benefits and the sufficiency of financing systems to support those benefits. The statutory framework of the American UI program and states' responses to the need for increased benefits has created a far weaker UI program than that of other countries.

Finally, we examine the impact of a weak U.S. program and widely divergent state programs on subgroups of the population, including by race, gender, and age. This chapter reveals the weakness in the UI program and explains that there is little reason to expect the program to improve without comprehensive, national legislative reform.

## THE RACE TO THE BOTTOM

Some states provide sufficient funding but for woefully inadequate benefits.[1] Under the current UI system of 53 individual state programs,[2] each state is responsible for financing the regular benefits paid in that state. There exist no federal requirements as to the amount of state benefits paid or taxes collected. Policymakers have long pointed out that this structure creates an environment of interstate economic competition that leads to a "race to the bottom" as states lower state taxes to attract new firms to move to their state (Bassi and McMurrer 1997).

The race to the bottom can be observed by examining the percentage of total unemployed workers who receive UI benefits (the recipiency rate), and how much those who get benefits actually receive (the replacement rate).

Regarding the first issue, the recipiency rate has decreased over time (refer back to Figure 3.5). Much of the national decline is due to the vastly different percentages of the unemployed who receive UI benefits among the states (Figure 3.4), with the majority of states having percentages of less than 30 percent.

The second issue deals with the replacement rate: an indicator of the amount of benefits that UI recipients receive when they gain access to the UI program. It is commonly measured as the percentage of prior wages that are replaced by UI benefits. A commonly accepted standard, endorsed by numerous advisory bodies and administrations, is that UI benefits should replace at least 50 percent of a claimant's prior weekly earnings, although even a maximum weekly benefit amount of two-thirds of the state average weekly wage will result in an average wage replacement rate of less than 50 percent. Due to numerous state cuts over time, Figure 4.1 shows that by 2019, 38 states were below the recommended standard of a 50 percent replacement rate (ACUC 1996).

The prime factor leading to states' low replacement rates has been keeping the maximum weekly benefit constant from one year to the next, so that even as wages rise, a claimant's benefit cannot exceed a specified dollar level, regardless of any increase in the cost of living. In 2019, 19 states kept their maximum weekly benefit the same for over 10 years (USDOL, *Significant Provisions of State UI Laws*, various years).

**Figure 4.1  UI Replacement Rate, 2019**

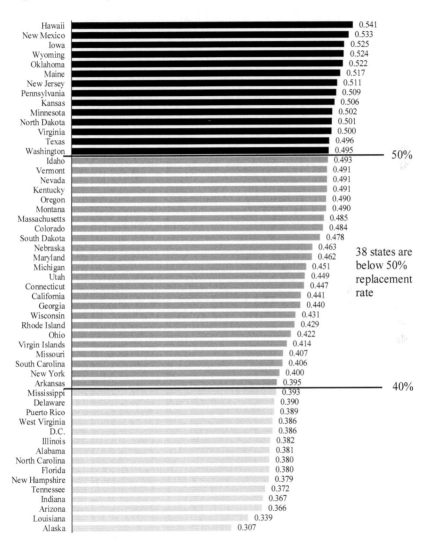

SOURCE: USDOL, BAM Data, Replacement Rate Measure No. 1 (https://oui.doleta
.gov/unemploy/ui_replacement_rates.asp).

One simple measure to bring together both issues is to compute the total UI benefits paid in a year by a state divided by the state's number of total unemployed workers for the year. This measure encompasses both the number of unemployed workers collecting UI and the amount of benefits they received (Figure 4.2). In the 1970s and 1980s, there was a relatively narrow difference between the states regarding benefit adequacy. However, the growing difference between states exploded following the recession of 2009. Several states dramatically reduced benefits and are continuing to pay a lesser amount each year. This sharp difference can be seen in the figure by comparing how the states with the five highest and five lowest benefit amounts per person diverge from the U.S. average.

**Figure 4.2  State UI Benefits per Unemployed Person**

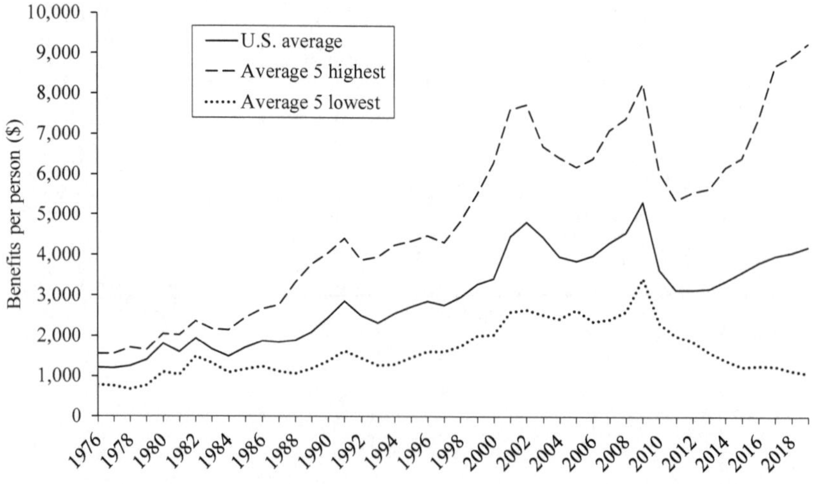

SOURCE: USDOL ETA-5159 report total benefits divided by total unemployed (CPS, Household data, Table A-11, monthly average for the year).

These data demonstrate that following the recession of 2009, this "race" has accelerated. Since 2011, 8 states reduced the maximum potential duration of UI benefit payments, and 19 states have kept the maximum weekly benefit the same for at least the last 10 years.

Finally, Figure 4.3 reveals the total amount of outstanding Title XII Federal debt—state UI trust fund account debt to the U.S. Treasury incurred by borrowing from federal UI funds—as a percentage of total wages encumbering the states as of January 1, 2021. It shows that none of the 8 states that reduced a claimant's maximum potential duration of benefits are among those states that have borrowed money to pay UI benefits.

Figure 4.3 shows the states with outstanding federal loans as of January 2021. Since the 2007–2009 recession, of the 8 states that reduced benefit levels the most (Florida, Georgia, Idaho, Kansas, Michigan, Missouri, North Carolina, and South Carolina), none have exhausted their UI trust fund balances or needed to borrow funds to pay benefits. That is true even after an extremely large 2020 drawdown in fund balances as shown by the figure.

**Figure 4.3  Amount of Outstanding Title XII Federal Loans, January 2021 (debt as percent of total wages)**

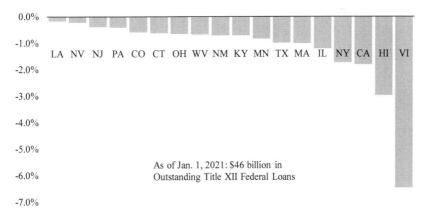

SOURCE: U.S. Department of Treasury, Title XII Advance Activities Schedule as of January 1, 2021.

The financial position of the benefit-cutting states thus appears to have significantly improved because of their cuts. Without pandemic levels of unemployment, other states have begun to imitate these benefit-cutting states (Gwyn 2022). In general, some states that have achieved reasonable solvency (e.g., reaching a high-cost multiple of 1.0 or higher) have done so because they 1) have low weekly benefit amount maximums, 2) have short average durations, and 3) use administrative means to restrict access to benefits.

We can draw two conclusions. First, states that pay low levels of benefits also make it difficult for unemployed workers to access their UI systems, as can be seen in the analysis of the North Carolina and Florida programs in the next section. Second, states that make access to the UI program difficult and pay low levels and durations of benefits tend to achieve what at first blush appears to be sound UI financing (e.g., reaching state UI trust fund high-cost multiples of 1.0 or more) by constricting benefits (e.g., having low maximum weekly benefits and low potential duration), rather than ensuring that they have sufficient revenue to pay adequate benefits (see Chapter 10). The implication for UI reform is that legislating benefit standards to address the benefit replacement rate, benefit maximum, and benefit duration is necessary but insufficient. States also may use administrative means to restrict access to UI benefits. Full interstate UI equity can only be achieved if there also is interstate equity with respect to access to UI benefits such that recipiency rates among states are similar.

## THE HIGH ROAD VERSUS THE LOW ROAD: DIVERGENT STATE PROGRAMS AND THE ACCESS TO BENEFITS

States have broad discretion on how to operate their UI programs, both with respect to program administration and the content of their state laws. The decisions that each state makes determine the extent of access to UI benefits and the generosity of those benefits. State programs vary widely because their programs are determined by the politics within each state. States that are more pro-business tend to have more constricted programs, whereas states that are more pro-labor tend to have more generous programs.

Access to benefits can be conceptually divided into three factors: 1) the ease of obtaining information and applying for benefits, 2) the efficiency of the administration of the program, and 3) the legal requirements of the UI program. There has been little research on access to the UI program in general and to these factors in particular. The analysis below is a first cut at trying to quantify the effect of these critical components on unemployed workers' access to benefits.

This section shows that if a state has components of its state UI law that provide more expansive benefits and raise adequate taxes to fund those benefits, then these factors should be associated with a higher level of benefit receipt by unemployed workers. In essence, it is expected that the cumulative effect of these state benefit and tax provisions have a direct effect on the state recipiency rate.

The components and method of measuring the presence and/or extent of each reform component has been done in consultation with other UI analysts. The components are analyzed by state and then the extent of the presence of each component is related to the state's 2019 recipiency rate. The expected result is that the number of reform components should be positively correlated to the state's recipiency.

The 25 factors listed below are based on the judgement of UI analysts. The factors are not weighted, although some factors are certainly more important than others. Table 4.1 looks at the 25 factors in New Jersey and Florida, two extreme cases, with New Jersey having the highest recipiency rate of any state in 2019 and Florida having the second lowest recipiency rate. Two thresholds are presented for the maximum benefit amount and taxable wage base because these factors vary so widely among states. The table shows that there are extreme differences between the states' UI laws.

Table 4.1 clearly shows the stark difference between Florida and New Jersey. There also are wide variations in the ability to fund a robust program, as illustrated by their taxable wages. The broad disparity in the two state programs, and North Carolina discussed below, can be seen in Chapter 3 in Figures 3.5 and 3.2. It is apparent that state UI laws matter and that there are systemic differences between the states. Below we explore some of the public policy reasons for the vast differences in recipiency rates.

We can better understand the differences between these two states if we look at them in some detail. We also briefly look at North Carolina, a state that sharply cut the UI benefit components of its UI law after the 2007–2009 recession.

**Table 4.1  Key State Statutory Components of the UI Program in New Jersey and Florida, 2019**

| Components | Analysis criteria | Florida | New Jersey |
|---|---|---|---|
| Recipiency rate (%)[a] | | 11 | 57 |
| Benefits | | | |
| Employment/wages | Most states require sufficient earnings in two quarters to affirm labor force participation | | |
| Alternative base period | Yes | | + |
| Computation of WBA | % of claimant's average weekly wage; replacement rate of 50% or more | | + |
| Minimum WBA | $100 or more | | + |
| Maximum WBA | $400 or more | | + |
| Maximum WBA | $600 or more | | + |
| Dependents' allowances | | | + |
| Earnings disregard | % of WBA | | + |
| Duration | 26 weeks or less | | + |
| Fixed (uniform) duration | Yes | | |
| Voluntary Quit WBA requalification | (10 weeks or more) × WBA | | + |
| Separation for good cause | Yes | | |
| Misconduct disqualification | 10 weeks or less | | + |
| Work search contacts | 3 or less | | + |
| Part-time work search | No base period history required | | |
| Pensions[b] | Considers employee contributions to pensions | + | + |
| Waiver of nonfraud, no fault overpayment | Equity and good conscience | | + |
| | Employer error | + | |
| | Financial hardship | | + |
| Taxes | | | |
| Maximum tax rates | More than 5.4% | | + |
| Taxable wage base | $15,000 or more | | + |
| Taxable wage base | $35,000 or more | | + |
| Employee contributions | Yes | | + |

**Table 4.1  (continued)**

| Components | Analysis criteria | Florida | New Jersey |
|---|---|---|---|
| Special programs | | | |
| Short-time compensation | Yes | + | + |
| Self-employment assistance | Yes | | + |
| Optional extended benefit triggers | Yes | | + |
| State additional benefits | Yes | | + |

[a] Percentage of all unemployed workers receiving UI benefits.
[b] Under federal pension offset provisions, states are optionally allowed to reduce benefits on less than a dollar-for-dollar basis by taking into account the contributions made by the UI applicant receiving a pension to the pension plan in question.
NOTE: WBA = weekly benefit amount.

## New Jersey: Factors That Expand Its Recipiency Rate

In addition to the statutory factors listed above—weekly benefit amount, duration of benefits, and alternate base periods—nonstatutory factors also appear to impact the states' recipiency rates. There has been limited analysis, however, of the nonstatutory factors that affect state UI recipiency rates. While the analysis of the effect of the state UI statutes above is limited and preliminary, we know even less about the other factors.

The discussion below is based on a 2021 interview with Robert Asaro-Angelo, the Commissioner of the Department of Labor and Workforce Development, and members of his senior staff.[3] The interview questions pertained to why Asaro-Angelo and his team believed that New Jersey's 2019 UI recipiency rate was the highest in the country. The factors identified by the respondents are summarized below.

New Jersey has a high-wage economy with a large percentage of workers who receive wages and salaries and therefore are eligible for UI when they become unemployed. Also, New Jersey has many seasonal workers who are familiar with the services provided by the state. These workers have high rates of UI receipt in good times and bad, but had especially high rates at the beginning of the pandemic recession.

Under their ABC method of determining the employer-employee relationship, New Jersey is strongly opposed to the misclassification of many of their workers as contractors rather than as wage and salary employees.[4] Classifying workers as contractors negatively affects workers in several ways, including by making them ineligible for UI when they become unemployed. The state strongly supports the proper classification of workers as wage and salary employees with the easier ABC test for determining which workers are in an employer-employee relationship (USDOL 2020d). New Jersey actively pursues such determinations and prohibits employers who violate its misclassification provisions from receiving state contracts. Both the state attorney general and the Department of Labor and Workforce Development's Division of Wage and Hour Compliance correct employer misclassifications. In response to state employer classification legislation enacted just before the beginning of COVID-19, the state is tasked with publishing lists of employers who, because of misclassification, are in arrears in their payment of UI taxes.

The state agency believes that several factors contribute to New Jersey's high participation rate. The state has a very liberal partial benefit formula that encourages unemployed workers to go back to work part time if they cannot find full-time work and still collect UI. New Jersey's monetary eligibility provisions for UI benefit receipt are low, and workers who do not meet the eligibility requirement using the normal benefit year may be able to qualify using the state's flexible alternative base period. New Jersey also has a considerable number of claims for Unemployment Compensation for ex-service members claims as the state has two military bases. When members of the armed forces leave the military and have not found civilian jobs, they tend to apply for benefits in New Jersey because of its high weekly benefit levels even if they return to their home states.

While some employers are opposed to paying higher UI benefits, they put little pressure on the agency and the state legislature to keep benefits low. A countervailing factor leading to higher benefits is the fact that New Jersey is a highly unionized state, and unions advocate for higher benefits. In addition, New Jersey is one of only three states that collects UI taxes from workers. Even though the tax rate is low, paying this tax makes employees feel like they are partners in the UI program and encourages them to press for both adequate benefits and sufficient taxes to support them. Employees see the UI tax removed from their pay stubs every time they are paid. As a result, they are more likely to apply for benefits when they become unemployed. The agency leadership talks about employees having "skin in the game," and they think that employees want and believe that they have a good rate of return on their investment in the UI program.

New Jersey also distributes high-quality information to employees about the UI program. The state maintains a strong system of call centers that direct individuals to an array of state services. New Jersey has a full-time NJDOL call center with staff who are fully versed in their UI system. With the onset of COVID-19 and the vast increase in UI claims, New Jersey has supplemented its permanent centers with externally contracted staff. It can maintain the quality of services provided to callers because, if the contract staff could not answer any questions, the calls were referred to NJDOL staff.

In addition, the New Jersey agency provides a great deal of information to employees about all state programs through a newly designed website. Many employees frequently use the website, in part because it covers the many social insurance programs that the state administers, including UI, temporary disability insurance, earned sick leave, and parental leave. The agency has tried to ensure that the website uses plain English and includes a chat box to answer questions.

The UI application that New Jersey uses was designed to be easy to complete. It was examined by a vendor and redesigned to increase its clarity. The application explains what the questions mean and what different answers signify, thus helping claimants to give informed answers to each question. To ensure that questions are clear, senior agency staff have asked family members to complete the application and suggest improvements. The initial claims form is interactive, pulling the claimants' quarterly wages into the application as the applicant fills out the form, ensuring that the wages used for the monetary entitlement determination are correct. New Jersey also sends a questionnaire to UI recipients asking how to improve the UI application process and makes adjustments based on those responses.

To ensure that state UI staff provide the correct information to claimants, the agency takes several actions. Training sessions are frequent. Previously, some training was in person, but since the pandemic, all training became virtual. It takes approximately six months for them to train a new claims examiner; these trainees work alongside experienced claims examiners as they learn the program.

The state UI program also sends a monthly newsletter to all UI staff to provide current and updated program information. To ensure consistency and accuracy in the information provided to claimants, staff are provided with information about what the rules are, what to say to claimants, and how to say it.

There is strong support for the New Jersey UI program, all the way from the governor to UI staff as well as the state legislature. The agency leadership reports that UI staff care about the claimants and want to be able to pay benefits if claimants are eligible. The staff work hard and understand unemployed workers' struggle to make ends meet and desire to find new jobs.

A significant bottleneck that delays workers getting approved for payment in most states is employers raising issues when contesting applications for benefits by their former employees, particularly regarding the reason for separation. Most states take a long time to make determinations regarding separation because the factual issues are discussed in a telephone call with a state agency adjudicator together with the employee and employer, and differences need to be resolved during the call. By contrast, New Jersey has made such adjudications electronic, asking for the employer's and employee's story by email. As a result, unless a follow-up is needed to resolve conflicting stories, the process is accelerated and done without telephone calls. This approach reduces the backlog in completing adjudication and speeds the timeliness of UI payments. Several other states have contacted New Jersey and are interested in adopting its approach.

As is apparent from the interview with Commissioner Asaro-Angelo and his senior staff, New Jersey has several ways in which it attempts to ensure that all unemployed workers eligible for UI benefits receive them. This includes making the benefit application process as rapid and straightforward as possible, providing accurate and consistent information and assistance to applicants and recipients, and providing generous and well-financed benefits. Employers and employees are deeply involved in and supportive of the New Jersey UI program. The New Jersey government, at all levels, supports the program. The result has been that a higher percentage of unemployed workers receive UI benefits in New Jersey than in any other state.

It also is clear from the interview summary that there is much more than an expansive state UI law that is responsible for New Jersey having the highest recipiency rate in the country. The attitude throughout the New Jersey government is that workers unemployed through no fault of their own should be able to receive UI benefits, and the Department of Labor and Workforce Development tries to ensure that these workers get the benefits to which they are entitled. The support of business, labor, and the general public is also important and appears to be much stronger than in many states. The support of business and labor for the generous payment of benefits appears to be influenced by the UI employee tax that gives workers a sense of ownership of the New Jersey UI system.

**Florida: Factors That Suppress Its Recipiency Rate**

Florida has a history of paying low benefits to relatively few unemployed workers. The maximum weekly benefit amount is currently $275 and has not been raised in 23 years. Some part-time and seasonal workers are unable to receive benefits. However, the program became much worse after Rick Scott became governor in 2010. Coming out of the 2007–2009 recession, Gov. Scott, with the support of the Florida Chamber of Commerce, Associated Industries of Florida, and the Florida Retail Federation, addressed the recessionary depletion of Florida's UI trust fund account by cutting the potential duration of UI benefits from 26 weeks to as little as 12 weeks (Garcia and Rohrer 2020).

Florida enacted highly restrictive legislation in 2011 (HB 7005) that included the following provisions (Wentworth and McKenna 2015):

- requiring that all benefit claims be filed electronically
- requiring that all applicants complete an "Initial Skills Review" test as part of their initial claim for benefits
- requiring that claimants contact five employers each week and report these contacts
- replacing the fixed maximum potential benefit duration (MPD) of 26 weeks with a sliding scale MPD that varies between 12 and 23 weeks
- expanding the definition of disqualifying misconduct

These restrictions immediately reduced the Florida UI recipiency rate to the bottom of the state rankings. As a result of a flawed computer system, the Florida UI system would not be ready to take claims during another major recession.

After the onset of the pandemic, which brought sharp increases in unemployment, it became clear how difficult it was to apply for UI benefits in Florida. The online UI application was hard to understand and complete. Answering the questions took a long time. At the end of the application, additional questions related to the individual applicants and their job search plans. The application discouraged unemployed workers from completing it. For a while during 2020, the initial claims application system, which was not designed for high levels of claims, caused the UI computer system to seize up and crash. Reports on the evening television news showed that until the system could be brought back online, applicants were required to drive to the local workforce offices, pick up a paper application, and fill it out at home. Claimants could then return to local offices and hand the completed applications to UI staff from their cars. This "filing process" made the national news and put Florida in the spotlight for poorly run UI application systems (Ghosh 2021; Mower 2020).

The Florida UI computer system, however, is not one of the antiquated systems built in the 1970s using the old COBOL language that is now known by just a few older programmers, most of whom are retired. It was built in 2013. However, it experienced serious problems from the beginning. The Florida state auditor general examined the system in 2015 and cited numerous glitches, but when auditor general staff returned three years later, those problems had not been fixed (State of Florida Auditor General 2019).

The tightening of the Florida state UI law substantially reduced Florida's recipiency rate from 16 percent in 2013 to 12 percent only 18 months later. Indeed, in 2019, former Governor (now Senator) Rick Scott bragged on camera that he had sharply reduced the number of UI recipients in Florida to 61,000 out of a population of 22 million (Oliver 2021). By 2019, Florida's state UI recipiency had fallen to 11 percent—the second lowest in the United States (Ghosh 2021; Mower 2020).

### North Carolina: Factors That Suppress Its Recipiency Rate

UI recipiency can be reshaped by major public policy decisions. The North Carolina legislature's systematic effort to reduce UI costs in North Carolina was accomplished through House Bill 4 in the 2013 General Assembly. The legislation was a direct assault on the UI system. Among the changes the law made were

- a reduction in potential duration of benefit from 26 to 12 weeks
- a reduction in the maximum weekly benefit amount from $535 to $350
- a change in the benefit calculation from earnings in the high quarter to average earnings in the last two quarters

The amendments to House Bill 4 achieved their goals. Wage replacement in North Carolina declined from 53 percent to 38 percent. The administration of the program also deteriorated (Wentworth and McKenna 2015). For example, North Carolina's UI timeliness performance measure declined to the worst in the country (Kofman 2020). That case shows that a determined public policy effort can greatly weaken the UI system. Most declines in state UI programs are slower and more indirect than was the situation in North Carolina. Often programs gradually decline over time because of factors such as the refusal to raise the minimum and maximum benefit amounts or maintaining low taxable wage bases and tax rates. By contrast, the North Carolina attack on their UI program emanating from the state legislature was immediate, strong, and direct.

From the cases of New Jersey, Florida, and North Carolina, we can see that the dramatic differences in state UI recipiency rates are related to several factors, including the intent of state policymakers and the efforts of administrators. New Jersey's high recipiency rate is the result of an expansive state UI law, but it is also based on program administration that attempts to make it easy to apply for and to continue to draw UI benefits. Florida and North Carolina, on the other hand, have low recipiency rates because of legislative and administrative action. In North Carolina, the state legislature, with a super-majority such that it could override the governor's opposition, made large cuts to the UI program. In Florida, then-Governor Rick Scott used legal and administrative means to both reduce the number of unemployed workers receiving UI benefits and keep the amount and duration of benefits as low as possible.

## REDUCING BENEFITS: INFLECTION POINTS AFTER MAJOR RECESSIONS: 1975, 2010, 2022

As discussed, the UI program was scarcely used in the United States in the period through the end of World War II. UI benefits then increased until the 1970s when they started to decline. While UI benefits have continued to gradually erode over time, there have been two inflection points that marked a change in state policy and legislation, in 1975 and again in 2010. Both of those inflection points were in response to two severe recessions, 1973–1975 and 2007–2009. In both cases, many states found their state reserves in the Unemployment Trust Fund were inadequate and responded not only by increasing taxes but also by cutting benefits.

After the 1973–1975 recession, restoring state trust fund accounts to solvency generally was accomplished by a combination of raising taxes and reducing or freezing benefits. The balance between raising taxes and reducing benefits was determined in state legislatures and, to a considerable extent, depended on the relative strength of employer and employee organizations. At that time, however, benefit reductions largely consisted of freezing increases in minimum and maximum weekly benefit amounts rather than in actual reductions in the benefit amounts or their durations.

In 2010, however, states more aggressively instituted benefit reductions. Benefit levels and potential durations were reduced. As discussed above, a North Carolina statute reduced its maximum benefit amount from $535 to $350 and its potential duration from 26 weeks to 12 weeks. Reductions below 26 weeks originally were enacted in 10 states (Alabama, Arkansas, Florida, Georgia, Idaho, Kansas, Michigan, Missouri, North Carolina, and South Carolina), although the number of states declined to 8 when Idaho and Kansas returned to 26-week maximums.

These and other changes that were made after the 2007–2009 recession reversed the historical trend of state benefit expansion. For maximum potential durations, the states gradually increased durations from 16 weeks or less in 1940 to 26 weeks or more in nearly all states from 1970 until just after the 2007–2009 recession. Given lower than expected UI costs from a program initially providing limited benefits, states were able to gradually expand benefit durations until all states were able to afford to pay up to 26 weeks of benefits. Table 4.2 shows that more states began paying more than 26 weeks of benefits in the 1950s until the new federal Extended Benefits program took over the payments of benefits beyond 26 weeks. Paying up to 26 weeks of benefits became nearly universal from 1990 until 2008. Starting in 2010, however, the consensus that states should pay up to 26 weeks began to erode, and states started to cut the potential duration of benefits—in some cases sharply, below 26 weeks—not because the states couldn't afford 26 weeks of benefits, but because they didn't want to raise taxes.

**Table 4.2  Number of States by Maximum Potential Duration of Regular UI Program Benefits (in weeks)**

| Year | 12–15 | 16 | 17–19 | 20 | 21–25 | 26 | 27–39 |
|------|-------|----|-------|----|-------|----|-------|
| 1940 | 14 | 27 | 4 | 3 | 0 | 2 | 0 |
| 1950 | 7 | 4 | 2 | 22 | 9 | 13 | 0 |
| 1960 | 0 | 0 | 0 | 2 | 7 | 33 | 9 |
| 1970 | 1 | 0 | 0 | 0 | 2 | 41 | 10 |
| 1980 | 0 | 0 | 0 | 0 | 0 | 42 | 9 |
| 1990 | 0 | 0 | 0 | 1 | 0 | 50 | 2 |
| 1995 | 0 | 0 | 0 | 1 | 0 | 51 | 2 |
| 2008 | 0 | 0 | 0 | 0 | 0 | 51 | 2 |
| 2020 | 3 | 1 | 0 | 4 | 0 | 44 | 1 |

NOTE: Table shows number of states, by year, with maximums between 12 and 39 weeks.
SOURCE: Significant Provisions of Unemployment Insurance Laws, 1940–2020.

Similar cutbacks to the UI program in response to the 2020 pandemic recession are likely to be severe and at least as widespread as in 2010. States will again want to restore their state trust fund accounts to solvency. Maintaining benefit amounts and durations are no longer viewed as sacrosanct. After the pandemic, reductions in benefit amounts and durations started to become more widespread in the absence of federal UI reform that would require the maintenance of benefit standards (Gwyn 2022). As a result, the UI program may have reached a third inflection point in 2022, and state benefit reductions may continue to be wide and deep.

## THE UI SYSTEM IN THE UNITED STATES IS WEAK COMPARED TO OTHER WESTERN INDUSTRIAL COUNTRIES

Western European governments are amazed at how weak the U.S. system is and has been for decades. In the 1980s, I attended a reception at the International Labour Organization headquarters. Representing USDOL, I was asked by UI administrators from several countries why the United States paid out such limited benefits compared to their programs. It was hard to explain.

It is worthwhile to compare the U.S. UI program to programs in other developed countries, especially since the U.S. program is such an outlier. What do the programs in other countries look like?

Overall, the Organisation for Economic Co-operation and Development (OECD) finds that the U.S. UI program is the least generous in terms of unemployment benefits of all the OECD countries (OECD 2009). The United States is similarly near the bottom of OECD countries in spending on UI as a percent of GDP (OECD, n.d.).

Compared to the 21 members of the OECD—Western European or English-speaking countries plus Japan and Korea—the United States is an outlier with respect to all three aspects of the program: UI administration, financing, and benefit payments (Vroman 2012; Vroman et al. 2017).

- **National program.** All other countries administer a national UI program with one set of laws and administrative procedures that operate throughout their countries.

- **Experience rating.** No other country applies experience ratings to individual firms to finance their UI program.

- **Low taxable wage base.** Compared to other countries that finance their programs with payroll taxes, the United States utilizes an extremely low taxable wage base. For the decade 2000–2009, the U.S. taxable wage base averaged 28 percent of total wages, whereas the 19 countries that used payroll taxes averaged between 72 and 100 percent, with 8 countries taxing total wages.

- **Employee contributions.** Employees pay UI payroll taxes in almost all OECD UI programs, and typically those taxes account for a substantial percentage of total UI program revenue. The financing arrangements in these programs are highly varied, but most rely heavily on payroll taxes. Australia and New Zealand were outliers, financing UI out of general revenue.

- **Employee-employer share of contributions.** Out of the 15 countries for which data were available, employers and employees shared the burden equally in 5 countries. In 8 other countries, the employee share ranged from 22 percent to 42 percent of the combined tax rate. The median employee share for the 15 countries in 2012 was 35 percent.

- **Recipiency rates.** Most OECD countries have higher recipiency rates than the United States (OECD, n.d).

- **Short-time compensation/work sharing.** Unlike the United States, which has a state option STC program, at least 19 of the 34 OECD countries have national short-time compensation programs (Cahuc 2019).[5] Many increase the replacement rate and duration of short-time compensation program benefits during periods of high unemployment (Wandner 2010).

In short, these programs generally are financed by payroll taxes on both employers and employees, with a substantial employee contribution. The tax rates are imposed on high taxable wage bases. Most of these countries try to avoid layoffs, if possible, by using generous short-time compensation programs during deep recessions.


## EQUITY ISSUES IN THE UI PROGRAM


The overall weak U.S. UI system has an uneven impact on subgroups of the American workforce. Whether intentional or not, there are inequities by race, gender, age, disability, and geography in the treatment of unemployed workers in the UI program. The inequities concerning the demographic groups are complex and require a number of different solutions.

The UI system was not built for the modern U.S. economy and labor force. It did not anticipate a labor force in which there are multiple wage earners in many households who need to balance work and home responsibilities. Nor did the early UI system anticipate older workers moving from one career job to another or from career jobs to "bridge" jobs—transitions that require reemployment services that the ES has not been well equipped to provide. It also did not anticipate the labor force participation of individuals with disabilities, nor did it address issues of race.

## Race/Ethnicity

Racial and ethnic inequities have been a part of the UI program since its inception and continue to the present day, particularly in the Southern states. For example, in 1935, Blacks were disproportionately excluded from coverage under the Social Security Act's old age and UI programs by the exclusion of agricultural and domestic service workers, which at that time included at least 60 percent of the nation's Black working population (DeWitt 2010, p. 51). This disparity persists in the UI program today for both Blacks and Hispanics, largely because of weak state UI programs that serve few unemployed workers, especially in the Southern states (Gould-Werth and Shafer 2012). Difficulties in completing computerized applications is also a factor. The disparity for Blacks has been growing since the recession of 2007–2009 (O'Leary, Spriggs, and Wandner 2022).

Historical racial disparities in the old age and UI programs stemmed from the limited coverage of American workers by the original Social Security Act based on concerns about the ability of the new social insurance programs to serve the entire U.S. economy. As a result, the original Social Security Act only covered workers who were regularly employed in "commerce and industry." The following groups of workers were excluded:

- agricultural workers
- domestic household workers
- self-employed individuals (including farm proprietors)
- nonprofit sector workers
- professionals, including self-employed doctors, lawyers, and ministers
- employees of charitable or educational foundations

- employees of federal, state, and local governments
- persons aged 65 or older
- casual laborers
- seamen in the merchant marine
- members of Congress

President Roosevelt's Committee on Economic Security estimated that 21.1 million workers were initially excluded from participation in the Social Security system, of which at least 15 million were white. DeWitt (2010) argues that the occupational exclusions (e.g., agricultural and domestic services) were not based on a racially exclusionary animus but were determined by administrative and technical limitations, at a time when nearly half of the U.S. labor force was excluded from coverage.

The reasons for exclusion of agricultural and domestic household workers, however, is in dispute, although there is little recent literature on the issue. Some researchers have concluded that the exclusion of agricultural and domestic household workers was racially motivated. Roberts (1996, p. 1,571) says that "[n]orthern New Dealers struck a bargain with southern Democrats that systematically denied Blacks' eligibility for social insurance benefits . . . in a deliberate effort to maintain a Black menial labor caste in the south." A similar argument is made by others including Lieberman (1995), Gordon and Patterson (1999), and Alston and Ferrie (1999).

The exclusion of agricultural and domestic household workers had the strongest adverse impact on Blacks because the employees in these occupations were overwhelmingly Black. Indeed, the effect of the exclusion of agricultural and domestic household workers from coverage was to exclude 65 percent of all Black workers from the UI program but only 27 percent of all white workers (DeWitt 2010).

The coverage of agricultural and domestic household workers came about more rapidly in the old age program of the Social Security Act than in the UI program. Amendments in 1950 and 1954 to the old age program extended coverage to both agricultural and domestic household workers in two stages (DeWitt 2010).

Agricultural and domestic household workers did not become covered under the UI program until later, also in two stages, by amendments in 1970 and 1976.[6] Nonetheless, Blacks have continued to be adversely affected by the UI program because they are a large percentage of the population in many southern states, many of which maintain weak UI programs where only a small percentage of separated workers receive UI benefits. Figure 3.8 in Chapter 3 shows that states in the South have both large Black populations and low recipiency rates, unlike in the East, Central, and West parts of the United States. Looking at the nation as a whole, there is a strong regional relationship to UI recipiency. Of the 13 states with the largest Black populations, all but 3 (Maryland, Delaware, and New York) have recipiency rates of 20 percent or less (D.C., Mississippi, Louisiana, Georgia, South Carolina, Alabama, North Carolina, Virginia, Tennessee, and Florida). Except for D.C., all the states with low participation rates are in the South.

## Gender and Age

Gender and age issues stem largely from the initial assumptions in the original 1935 Social Security Act that were based on the composition of the U.S. labor force as it existed at that time. Both federal and early state UI laws assumed that men would continue to predominate as the only family breadwinner and that they would work full time but then fully retire at age 65. Thus, it was thought that men of working age would be the only demographic group who would need UI benefits. Federal law has changed little to accommodate the changes in labor force participation by gender and age, mostly leaving it to states to make adjustments. Unfortunately, those adjustments have been uneven.

Gender and age inequities have different causes than those driving racial inequity. (This issue is discussed in detail in Chapter 8 regarding UI benefit eligibility.) Gender and age inequities stem from both state and federal governments not recognizing or adapting to the changes in the labor force in the post–World War II period. Indeed, the biggest change in the U.S. labor force following World War II has been the increased labor force participation rate of women, rising from 34 percent in 1950 to approximately 60 percent in recent years. At the same time, with the decline of defined benefit pensions and inadequate personal savings, the labor force participation rates of older workers also increased starting in the 1990s for workers 65 and older (Agbayani et al. 2016; Wandner 2018). Federal legislation limiting the receipt of UI benefits for unemployed workers receiving pensions occurred in the 1980s just as older worker labor force participation rates began steadily increasing.

These changes in the U.S. labor force have resulted in new patterns of employment (Wandner, Balducchi, and O'Leary 2015):

- Part-time work, especially by women and older workers.

- Multi-earner households.

- Workers voluntarily leaving jobs to provide care for children and other family members.

- Movement of a "trailing spouse" in households that move from one geographic labor market to another, with many states finding these workers ineligible for UI.

- Greater movement in and out of the labor force for many economic and personal reasons, particularly by women and older workers.

- Reentrants to the labor force who have been out of the labor force for reasons such as childbearing, child rearing or elder care for long enough that the reentrants do not have sufficient earnings in their UI base period to qualify for UI benefits.

- Older workers changing careers and moving from one career job to another or from career jobs to bridge jobs. Thus, they may not be searching for jobs like their prior jobs, which is what is expected by the UI and ES programs. For example, some states do not find older workers searching for part-time/bridge jobs eligible for UI, requiring full-time workers to search for new full-time jobs (USDOL 2022a).

- Older workers having lower unemployment rates than younger workers but longer periods of unemployment once they become unemployed. They also have more difficulty finding reemployment than younger workers and may need intensive services that are not available.

- Growth of independent contractors, short-term workers, freelance workers looking for temporary jobs in the so-called gig economy, where firms prefer these new work arrangements to the employment relationship. Older workers are more likely than younger workers to be self-employed and independent contractors.

None of these or other newer patterns of employment and unemployment were anticipated in 1935 when the Social Security Act was enacted. Congress has done little to adapt federal UI law to the current reality of the labor force, and states have been uneven in accommodating these changes in their state UI laws.

**Workers with Disabilities**

Unemployed workers with disabilities have been disproportionately adversely affected by the move to online claims-taking. When the UI program largely ended in-person initial and continuing claims applications in the 1990s, unemployed workers with disabilities have had greater difficulties negotiating online computer, telephone, and voice response systems that now are used to take their claims. States have varied in how well they have accommodated these unemployed workers, as well as unemployed workers with limited English proficiency, and other workers, such as many older workers, who also have difficulty negotiating these systems.

Helping these workers attain equal access to the UI program would require either improving the existing remote claims-taking systems or returning UI staff to local workforce offices so that they can assist these workers in filing UI claims and/or having their questions about the program answered.

**Geography**

Today there are vast differences between the state UI programs. Programs vary from weak to strong. The weak programs with respect to issues such as program access and state statutory eligibility criteria create equity issues for subgroups based on race, ethnicity, gender, age, disability, and other factors. This variation creates equity issues for all unemployed workers across the country. As we have seen, compared to Florida and North Carolina, unemployed workers in New Jersey are far more likely to

- have greater access to UI benefits,

- receive more benefits for a longer duration,
- have greater access to Extended Benefits in periods of unemployment, and
- be able to access reemployment services and special UI programs.

Addressing geographical disparity issues requires creating a more robust and equitable UI system across all states. Robustness should result in

- having similar recipiency rates across the country,
- accommodating the realities of the modern U.S. labor force, especially relating to eligibility and work search requirements, and
- enacting provisions that benefit low-wage workers, such as indexed minimum benefit levels, which increase annually with the increase in state average weekly work in covered employment, allowances for dependents, and monetary eligibility determinations based on hours worked rather than on earnings.

Geographical disparities could most easily be accomplished by having the UI program in the United States switch to a federal or national program with a single set of benefit and financing rules. Short of such a substantial change, under the current federal-state administrative system, greater equity would require comprehensive UI statutory and administrative reform, as well as strong enforcement of the reform elements.

## CONCLUSION

The purpose of the payment of UI benefits and the provision of other public employment programs is to bring workers into the labor force, help them stay in the labor force, and help them to find or train for new jobs. The lack of a proactive policy to help workers—including racial minorities, women, low-wage workers, older workers, and workers with disabilities—stay in the labor force has an adverse effect on the U.S. economy from both a micro and macro perspective. This chapter has addressed the need to help individual workers, but it is well to understand that the health and strength of the U.S. economy has depended and will continue to depend on keeping workers who want to work in the labor force. The UI system could play a stronger role in this effort by providing adequate income support while workers search for suitable work or prepare to return to work. A program of UI reform should keep both these goals in mind.

Part 3 discusses issues for UI reform, while Part 4 examines the options for UI reform that can accommodate the changes in the U.S. economy and labor force by modifying certain UI benefit provisions, particularly as they affect women, older workers, low-wage workers, and workers with disabilities.

## Notes

1. This section is based on an unpublished paper by Rob Pavosevich.
2. Under federal UI legislation, there are 53 programs of the 50 states plus D.C., Puerto Rico, and the Virgin Islands.
3. Robert Asaro-Angelo, commissioner of the Department of Labor and Workforce Development, and his senior staff (David Bander, Ron Marino, and Gillian Guitterez), interview by Stephen Wandner, January 29, 2021.
4. The ABC test is a three-part test to determine whether there is an employer-employee relationship. See the section on gig/contract workers in Chapter 9.
5. In addition to the United States, Cahuc (2019) identifies 19 other OECD countries that have short-time compensation programs: Austria, Belgium, the Czech Republic, Denmark, Finland, France, Germany, Greece Hungary, Italy, Japan, the Netherlands, Norway, Poland, Portugal, the Slovak Republic, Spain, Sweden, and the United Kingdom.
6. Employment Security Amendments of 1970 (P.L. 91-373), enacted August 10, 1970, covered employment in certain categories of agriculture processing. The Unemployment Compensation Amendments of 1976 (P.L. 94-566), enacted October 20, 1976, extended coverage to hired farm labor of large employers and domestic household workers of employers who paid $1,000 in wages for domestic work.

# Part 3

# Issues and Options for UI Reform

# 5

# A Brief History of UI Reform

## Past Proposals and Actual Reform

The Social Security Act of 1935 sketched out a limited, partial UI program. The Committee on Economic Security's actuaries were extremely conservative, mostly because they were dealing with an untried program in the middle of the Great Depression. Coverage of all UI programs was limited. (See the discussion of coverage in the Equity Issues section of Chapter 4.) Benefit durations were assumed not to exceed 15 weeks.

With unemployment less serious but continuing after the Great Depression, UI reform and concern for more adequate benefits have been ongoing issues for over 70 years. Among the many calls for UI reform and actual reform have been the following: 1) presidential calls for federal benefit standards, 2) the development by the UI national office of recommended model state UI legislation, 3) extended benefits legislation, 4) the Unemployment Compensation Amendments of 1976, 5) recommendations by two Congressionally established national commissions, and 6) many early and recent calls for comprehensive reform. Each is discussed briefly below.

## PRESIDENTIAL PROPOSALS FOR FEDERAL BENEFIT STANDARDS

After World War II, it became clear that the UI program would become an active social insurance program in a civilian economy that would be subject to the ups and downs of the business cycle. The Unemployment Trust Fund also had received sufficient funding by the end of the war that the UI program could be expected to expand and provide greater benefits than were anticipated before the war.

The federal executive branch unsuccessfully proposed federal benefit standards under Presidents Truman, Kennedy, and Johnson. A 1965 congressional bill proposed five standards:

1) a weekly benefit amount of at least 50 percent of average weekly earnings

2) a maximum weekly benefit amount of at least 50 percent of the state average weekly wage

3) a qualifying requirement of not more than 20 weeks of work

4) a maximum potential duration of benefits of 26 weeks for qualified workers

5) a maximum disqualification of six weeks, with a few exceptions (Haber and Murray 1966)

Thus, these presidents made clear that the UI program could afford to pay adequate benefits and that many states were not meeting what appeared to be reasonable proposed federal standards. Congress has never enacted these proposed standards.

## RICHARD A. LESTER: 1962 RECOMMENDATIONS

Richard A. Lester was director of the Industrial Relations Section at Princeton University and an early analyst of the UI program. His book *The Economics of Unemployment Compensation* (1962) made the following recommendations about how to adjust the existing UI system:

• extend coverage widely

• increase the taxable wage base

• bring eligibility requirements up to date

• create an extended benefits program

• establish a reinsurance program

• improve the experience rating system

Lester thus anticipated the creation of the Extended Benefits (EB) program in 1970, the extension of coverage enacted in 1976, and the need to modernize eligibility requirements, but he also pointed to continuing weaknesses in UI financing.

## USDOL RECOMMENDATIONS TO STATES: THE 1962 *BROWN BOOK*

During the 1950s and 1960s, the first two decades during which the UI program was administered by USDOL, the UI national office was active and provided a great deal of guidance to the states regarding recommended state UI legislative proposals. The last comprehensive set of recommendations was issued in 1962 as *Unemployment Insurance Legislative Policy: Recommendations for State Legislation,* known as the *Brown Book* among state and federal officials because of its brown cover (USDOL 1962). It was an updating of a similar book of recommendations issued by the Department in 1953. The *Brown Book* covered the full range of state UI legislative benefit provisions with recommendations but did not provide tax provision recommendations. Many of the recommendations are similar to current recommendations for UI reform, but many of these were not accepted by state UI programs at that time and still have not been adopted.

A small sample of the recommendations provided to the states during the 1950s and 1960s include the following (USDOL 1962):

- Recent base period: "The lag between the base period and the benefit year should be as short as possible." The alternate base period recommendations of today have a similar justification.

- Maximum weekly benefit amount: "The maximum benefit amount should be set at a level which will permit the great majority of workers to receive a weekly benefit amount" of 50 percent of their wage loss.

- Minimum weekly benefit amount: "The minimum benefit should be related to the wage levels in the State."

- Partial benefits: "Intended to provide a measure of income maintenance" and "give [claimants] an incentive to take less than full-time work."

Thus, many of the policy recommendations for UI reform today are not much different than the USDOL recommendations in 1962. What happened was that USDOL stopped advocating for these reforms after the 1960s, and the state UI programs began to regress from many of these recommendations in the mid-1970s.

## EXTENDING UI BENEFITS DURING RECESSIONS

In the 1950s, the United States began experiencing mild and more serious recessions. Congress spent little time focusing on the UI program during periods of low unemployment, but with the 1958 recession, Congress began enacting temporary emergency unemployment compensation programs, generally paid from federal general revenue. Such programs have been enacted during every recession since 1958.

Congress enacted a permanent EB program in 1970. This program has not worked well, even with some legislative amendments over time. As a result, Congress has continued to enact temporary emergency programs.

## UNEMPLOYMENT COMPENSATION AMENDMENTS OF 1976

Despite many small federal legislative changes, the Unemployment Compensation Amendments of 1976 were the only major reform of the UI program since its inception. The amendments responded to the strain of the 1973–1975 recession and were enacted with bipartisan support after extensive legislative hearings by the House Ways and Means Committee. Some of the components of the amendment were as follows:

- coverage: extended to agricultural, domestic household, non-profit, and state and local government workers
- federal taxable wage base: increased to from $4,200 to $6,000
- federal tax increase
- extended benefit trigger change
- eligibility and disqualification changes: preventing states from prohibiting disqualification based on pregnancy, but also disqualifying undocumented aliens and individuals receiving pensions
- established the National Commission on Unemployment Compensation (NCUC)

## NATIONAL COMMISSION ON UNEMPLOYMENT COMPENSATION

The establishment of the NCUC was a recognition of the limited scope and nature of 1976 amendments and the need to consider much more basic program changes, on which Congress was unable to agree.

In its final report (NCUC 1980), the NCUC was able to agree on many recommendations, including the following:

- Increase and index the federal taxable wage base to 65 percent of the national annual wage.
- Establish a reinsurance system to protect states against unusually heavy benefit costs.
- Establish federal benefit standards including: 1) a maximum weekly benefit of two-thirds of the state average weekly wage, 2) replacement rates of at least 50 percent, 3) no more than 39 weeks of work can be required for 26 weeks of benefits, 4) no cancelation of benefit rights except for fraud and disqualifying income, and 5) repeal the restriction of the 1976 amendments on pensions, professional athletes, and undocumented alien workers.
- States should provide up to 26 weeks of benefits to workers with strong labor force attachment.
- Improve EB triggers.
- Establish an unemployment assistance program separate from UI with income testing to provide benefits.
- Increase administrative grants to states for both UI and ES.
- Remove UI benefits from being subject to income taxation.

## ADVISORY COUNCIL ON UNEMPLOYMENT COMPENSATION

Given no legislative reform in response to the 1980 reform proposals of the NCUC, a decade later Congress established the ACUC as a provision in the Emergency Unemployment Compensation Act of

1991. The ACUC issued four reports, making relatively few recommendations, some of which were made with dissenters because of divisions among the Council members (ACUC 1996). Nonetheless the Council made some recommendations, some calling for federal legislation and others exhorting the states to act. In summary, they recommended the following:

- an increase in the federal taxable wage base to $8,500
- promoting state forward funding by paying an interest premium on state trust fund balances and preferential interest rates on loans for states working to forward fund
- EB triggers be changed to use of total rather than insured unemployment rates, and the trigger threshold be adjusted to reflect the new trigger mechanism
- that benefits replace 50 percent of prior wages and the maximum weekly benefit amount be two-thirds of the state's average weekly wage
- that workers seeking part-time employment not be barred from UI receipt
- that states eliminate seasonal work exclusions
- that state work requirements not exceed 800 times the state minimum wage
- that UI benefits be tax exempt
- that USDOL report a measure of UI recipiency

Thus, the two commissions raised many issues but few were resolved. Congress did not take up the recommendations of either commission, and many of the issues that the commissions considered still remain unresolved.

## UI MODERNIZATION

UI Modernization was the name of the UI reform program that was part of the American Recovery and Reinvestment Act of 2009. It made

$7 billion in financial incentives available to states to adopt specified reforms that consisted of

- providing alternative base periods
- paying dependents' allowances
- compensating workers voluntarily quitting for compelling family reasons
- paying unemployed workers searching for part-time work
- paying training benefit extensions

The UI Modernization provisions represented a partial approach to UI reform. Even for the reform components that were proposed, not all states took the financial incentives and enacted the laws. In addition, there was the possibility of backsliding as states could enact a provision, take the financial incentive, and then revoke the provision. Given incomplete take-up, it appears that providing financial incentives to states is not a path to comprehensive UI reform and that such reform likely would require federal benefit and tax provision requirements.

## PURSUING OPTIONS AND MAKING RECOMMENDATIONS FOR UI REFORM

This chapter shows that the need for comprehensive UI reform has been clear for many decades. In response to that need, there has been no shortage of past recommendations. In the absence of substantial UI reform, there have been numerous recent proposals for comprehensive reform, especially since the end of the 2007–2009 recession. These include recommendations discussed below, including by the Obama administration, the Century Foundation, the Hamilton Project, Georgetown University, the Center for Law and Social Policy, the National Employment Law Project group, von Wachter (2019), Dube (2021), and O'Leary and Wandner (2018). Most of the rest of this book examines approaches to and options for UI reform suggested over the history of the program. It synthesizes past reform proposals and recommends reforms based on evidence and policy analysis by the author.

# 6
# Disincentive and Incentive Effects of UI Benefits and Taxation

Discussion about UI reform can be better understood after reviewing the behavioral responses to both the UI and reemployment programs. This chapter addresses the following issues. How do individual employers and employer organizations try to limit the scope of the UI program? How do employees who receive UI benefits respond to the offer and receipt of UI benefits? And how do UI recipients respond to incentives and reemployment services that might help them return to work?

Unemployment insurance exists to partially replace lost earnings during periods of involuntary unemployment, but like other social insurance programs, UI has behavioral effects on both benefit recipients and the employers who pay the UI taxes that fund those benefits. With UI, the effects on recipients have been much more studied than the effects on the employers who pay the UI tax, but the response of employers also is well known. It is important to be mindful of the effects of these incentives to understand the current UI program, the need for UI reform, and the approaches to reform that are likely to be the most effective and have the least disincentive effects.

The UI program as conceived in the original Social Security Act of 1935 was designed primarily to mitigate cyclical unemployment. The original UI program was too modest to address the unemployment crisis presented by the Great Depression. The system did not pay benefits until the 1940s, and it was designed to address short-term temporary layoffs, such that many of the workers laid off would be recalled when the U.S. economy returned to more robust growth. That expectation was borne out until the beginning of the 1970s, after which changing domestic and international conditions led to the great majority of layoffs being permanent. Employers now have little expectation of rehiring dislocated workers, and workers must search for new work, often quite different from their previous jobs (Groshen and Potter 2003; Wandner 2010).

Worker dislocation has a negative effect on the future earnings of unemployed workers. They tend to remain unemployed longer, and when they do become reemployed, they tend to work for substantially lower wages (Jacobson, LaLonde, and Sullivan 1993). Public policy should address the longer durations of unemployment and likely wage loss when workers are finally reemployed by providing permanently displaced workers with income support while they are unemployed and help them find the best possible jobs, even if those jobs result in lower wages (Jacobson, LaLonde, and Sullivan 1993). The reemployment of permanently displaced workers—the goal of UI and public workforce policy—must be understood as it relates to the incentive structure of the UI program for both employers and their former employees.

## EMPLOYER INCENTIVES

Employers tend to try to minimize their payment of UI taxes for their former employees, since the UI tax is experience rated (Lachowska, Sorkin, and Woodbury 2022). That is, the more workers they lay off and the more UI benefits those former workers are paid, the higher their employers' tax rate will be in future years. Employers thus can pay less in UI taxes by resisting an increase in their UI experience rating based on benefit charges assessed to their UI account. They can do this by lobbying at the state and national levels to keep their UI taxes low as well as by minimizing both the number of their former employees who are paid UI benefits and the amounts that they are paid. Employers have been effective at keeping UI benefits low through political activity at both the federal and state levels (Levine 1997).

### Individual Employer Responses

Most research regarding the employer response to the UI program has addressed two issues. First, the impact that experience rating provisions have on employers, especially in reducing layoffs or avoiding being charged for separations (Lachowska, Sorkin, and Woodbury 2022). And second, the extent to which employers help state UI agencies police the integrity of the UI system by responding to whether their former employees are entitled to receive UI benefits. By providing information regarding an employee's nonmonetary eligibility (e.g., the reason for the separation such as layoff for economic reasons, fired for cause or voluntary quit) employers can supply critical information. Employers, however, have a financial incentive to help deny their former employees UI benefits to minimize their own UI costs.

Employers do not necessarily police the system by themselves. Many large employers hire third parties to monitor and challenge the claims of individual employees. To justify their existence, these firms have an incentive to attempt to have claims denied that would otherwise be charged to the employers for whom they work. The result tends to be a confrontational relationship in which some unrepresented workers who might otherwise be found eligible are denied UI benefits.

## Group Employer Response

By denying claimants access to UI benefits, employer organizations and UI cost management companies at the state and national level also work to minimize the cost of UI benefits to their members, including the national organization Strategic Services on Unemployment and Workers' Compensation (UWC).[1] They also lobby state and federal agencies, state legislatures, and Congress to minimize the amount of UI benefit payments and the UI taxes needed to pay those benefits. Employer groups have been highly successful at the federal level. Indeed, their efforts have ensured that there has not been major federal UI legislation since 1976, and the federal UI taxable wage base has not been increased since 1983.

Employer organizations and UI cost management companies also have been particularly successful at the state level, especially in states where trade unions are weak, where employer groups face little opposition when lobbying state governors and legislatures. As a political economy concept, political decisions are determined by the relative countervailing strength of the opposing parties. In the United States, those opposing parties are organized business and organized labor. However, since unions are weak in most states, political power lies mostly with organized business, except in the small number of states with high levels of unionization. As a result, there is a strong relationship between the extent of state unionization and the UI recipiency rate

(O'Leary and Wandner 2018). The UI program is robust mostly in the few states in which unionization is greatest. Business's resistance to UI reform also is evident in the opposition by business representatives to some proposed reforms contained in two UI commissions' final reports (ACUC 1996; NCUC 1980).

## EMPLOYEE DISINCENTIVES

For many years, it has been suggested that providing UI benefits to unemployed workers has a disincentive effect on workers' job search behavior and increases their duration of unemployment. This issue has been studied throughout most of the history of the UI program. There have been overall assessments of the disincentive effect back to Dan Hamermesh (1977) in the 1970s and Paul Decker in the 1990s (Decker 1997). The conclusions in general have been that the disincentive effects are real but modest in size. Although there has been a range of published estimates as to the extent of the work disincentive effect (Decker 1997), the setting of UI benefit levels (i.e., the replacement rate for lost wages) is generally done to balance the adequacy of temporary income replacement against the disincentives that UI benefits create against the return to work.

### The UI Principle of the Unemployed Returning to Comparable (or "Suitable") Work

The UI program is designed to encourage UI recipients to accept an appropriate job match, not the fastest possible job match. Ever since the enactment of the UI program in 1935, a key concern of Congress and the UI program has been to return workers from unemployment to jobs that are comparable to their previous jobs in terms of wages and skill levels. In the UI statutes, this is called "suitable work." While in strong local economies there usually are a reasonable number of low-skilled, low-wage job openings, the UI suitable work provisions are designed to prevent UI recipients from having to take new work requiring significantly lower job skills and at significantly lower wages relative to their prior jobs. That was not the intent of Congress when it enacted the

Social Security Act in 1935, and it is not in the interest of individual workers or of the U.S. economy today for skilled, high-wage workers to take less productive minimum wage or near minimum wage jobs. Efficient job matching means the economy benefits by fully using the skills and abilities of workers when they move to new jobs. There is a loss in value to the economy when job matches are inefficient.

Thus, the design of the UI program is not to return UI recipients to work as quickly as possible, regardless of the wage and skill level of the new job relative to the workers' prior jobs. Rather, the goal is to return unemployed workers as soon as possible to "suitable work" at a wage and under conditions similar to their prior work.

This approach to reemployment is embedded in both federal and state UI law, even though policymakers have acknowledged decades of job search theory research that has demonstrated that UI claimants may delay their return to work as they set their job search intensity and their minimum acceptable (reservation) wage to maximize the present value of lifetime income. Thus, UI claimants may end their unemployment only when they receive a job offer that exceeds their minimum acceptable (reservation) wage (Mortenson 1977). UI recipients may somewhat delay their return to work relative to the wage they would accept if UI were not available. Nonetheless, Congress designed the program to promote return to "suitable work" even if pursuing suitable work somewhat delays the return to work.

## The Effects of UI Benefit Generosity on Job Search and Subsequent Employment

Many studies have shown that the generosity of UI benefits can influence the timing and extent of UI recipients' job search and their subsequent job finding. Furthermore, UI benefits can reduce the intensity of job search and still not improve the jobs and wages that workers find after their job search. From a public policy perspective, however, a key question is whether employee disincentive effects are large enough to suggest the need to statutorily change the generosity of benefits. In addition, the awareness over many decades of a disincentive effect has encouraged searching for ways to speed the return to work without changing benefit generosity. As a result, much of the effort since the 1970s (Ehrenberg and Oaxaca 1976; Feldstein 1974) to find ways to improve UI recipients' reemployment has focused on incentives to speed the return to work (see the discussion in Chapter 11 about re-employment bonuses) and to provide the tools to help accomplish that goal.

Krueger and Mueller (2010) find that job search intensity is inversely related to the generosity of UI benefits. Schmieder, von Wachter, and Bender (2016) find that extending the duration of UI benefits did not result in recipients finding better jobs when they return to employment. Card, Chetty, and Weber (2007) also find that longer unemployment durations for UI recipients did not lead to better job matches. However, given the shortage of in-person, effective reemployment services, most long-term unemployed workers do not receive effective reemployment services. Meyer (1995) finds that extending unemployment durations does not improve post job-loss wages. USDOL has funded evaluations of each of the congressionally enacted temporary emergency unemployment compensation programs, which have been proven to significantly reduce poverty while having small effects on extending unemployment durations during recessions.

It is precisely because of these findings that USDOL has conducted many UI experiments over the years to provide tools to improve and speed job matching, to provide workers with additional job skills, and to avoid unemployment in the first place (Benus et al. 1995; Corson et al. 1989; O'Leary, Decker, and Wandner 2005; Robins and Speigelman 2001; Wandner 2010). Federal and state legislation to enable these reemployment services and supply the resources to provide them, however, have mostly proved lacking.

**Disincentive and Benefit Duration**

Throughout most of the post–World War II period, research has shown that increased potential UI benefit durations result in longer durations of unemployment. While there is agreement that there is an effect, the key policy issue is, how large is the effect?

Many studies have examined the effect of benefit durations on UI recipient behavior throughout the business cycle. Schmieder, von Wachter, and Bender (2012) find that extended UI benefits are associated with longer unemployment durations but that this effect is smaller in recessions than in periods of expansion. Mulligan (2012) finds that expanded UI durations are associated with longer unemployment spells and thus higher unemployment levels. Looking at this issue from an international perspective, Ljungqvist and Sargent (1998) find that variation in UI generosity among nations is a major determinant of differences in unemployment levels across those nations and over time. It should be noted however, that the generosity of UI benefits varies vastly among nations, with many OECD studies finding that the United States has nearly the least generous UI programs among all the OECD industrial nations.

It has long been known that the disincentive effect of longer potential UI durations on UI recipients varies with the business cycle. During strong labor markets when job openings exceed job seekers, there is more concern about workers not taking available, suitable jobs if they are qualified to take comparable jobs to those that they have lost. Nonetheless, widespread worker dislocations occur during good times and bad.

For example, Schmieder, von Wachter, and Bender (2012) find that extended UI durations are associated with longer durations of benefits, although that effect is less so during periods of high unemployment. Thus, the disincentive effect of UI is less when unemployment is higher and there are fewer job openings relative to the number of unemployed workers. That relationship has been well known for many decades (Hamermesh 1977).[2]

Congress has long recognized the cyclical nature of unemployment and the need for modest numbers of weeks of UI benefits when the U.S. economy is strong but additional weeks when the economy weakens. USDOL has long advocated a maximum potential UI benefits duration of approximately 26 weeks during periods of low to moderate unemployment. Nonetheless, during every recession since 1958, Congress has enacted longer potential durations of benefits, paid from federal general revenue. Thus, Congress has recognized that the need for longer durations of benefits is greater during recessions, when the disincentive effect for workers is less. It also should be noted that for most of the temporary emergency benefit extensions, USDOL has conducted third-party evaluations, mostly by Mathematica Policy Research. Those evaluations have found only a modest increase in unemployment duration associated with the implementation of these programs at times of limited job openings.

The policy problem with extending UI benefits during periods of high unemployment has been that the Congress has not determined how to adjust the duration of benefits with variations in the unemployment rate and the availability of job openings. That issue—along with widespread agreement about how to respond to it—is discussed in Chapter 8. It also should be remembered that the large expenditures on UI benefits are made during recessions, when the disincentive effect is least and when UI benefits provide a substantial countercyclical macroeconomic effect.

**Disincentive as a Cyclical Issue: Increased Benefit Amounts**

Congress has increased the potential duration of UI benefits during every recession since 1958, deciding when such extensions are appropriate (Rangel 2008). However, other than one small program increasing UI benefit levels by a small amount during the 2007–2009 recession, Congress had never substantially increased weekly benefit amounts during recessions.

That changed dramatically in 2020–2021. What happened to the UI program during the year and a half after COVID-19 struck the United States is important to understanding the cyclical UI disincentive effect. As part of the response to the catastrophic shutdown of the U.S. economy in March 2020, Congress enacted legislation to provide unemployment compensation benefits (as social welfare programs, not as a social insurance program), including the Federal Pandemic Unemployment Compensation (FPUC) program, which significantly added to the basic UI benefits. All recipients—regardless of their prior wages—received an additional $600 per week in UI benefits, later reduced to $300 per week at the end of July 2020. Given the large supplement and subsequent reduction in benefits beyond the basic UI program benefit amount, it was possible to evaluate the effect of a large increase and cutback in benefits, making use of the "natural experiment" that occurred because of the large changes in benefit amounts. Economists looked for data to determine the effect of reducing the additional $600 per week to $300 and then eliminating the $300 add-on in June 2021 by some states and by all states in September 2021. They found a surprisingly small impact in the behavior of UI recipients given the large size of the benefit increase and the potential impact of its reduction and/or termination.

For example, one study examined the propensity of recipients to consume UI benefits as well as the disincentive effects on returning to work when receiving higher than usual UI benefits. Using J.P. Morgan bank data, the study showed that households spent the vast majority of their UI payments, and that despite the add-on benefits received during this period, there was little disincentive effect, with the job-finding rate remaining relatively steady (Ganong et al. 2021).

Dube et al. (2021) examined the effects of some states ending FPUC benefits early, in June 2021. Comparing the states that withdrew from FPUC with those that retained the program until it ended, the authors find that while UI receipt fell 36.3 percentage points, employment rose by only 6.8 percentage points by the time the FPUC program ended in early September 2021. While the number of UI recipients fell sharply, earnings increased only modestly. Thus, the return-to-work effect from the sharp decline in FPUC benefits expected by the states that withdrew from the program early was not realized.

## REEMPLOYMENT SERVICES AND REEMPLOYMENT INCENTIVES

In a U.S. economy in which the great majority of unemployed workers are permanently displaced, policies that aim to speed the return to productive work and reduce recipient disincentive effects should provide displaced unemployed workers with reemployment services and incentives for them to stay in the labor force and improve their job matches and speed their return to work. As shown in Chapter 11, and as discussed at length in Wandner (2010), several reemployment approaches that have been rigorously studied using randomized controlled trials provide causal evidence of effectiveness. These policies seek to prevent unemployment, provide reemployment services to facilitate the return of the unemployed to productive employment, and provide unemployed workers with incentives to speed their return to work. The main problems with making effective use of these approaches, however, are the lack of funding, federal legislation, and/or state enactment and usage.

Short-time compensation (STC) is a program to encourage employers to prevent layoffs by putting all workers on reduced hours—with

STC benefits providing partial income replacement for the reduced hours—rather than laying off a portion of workers. Federal UI legislation permits states to have STC programs, but just over half of all states have them and most make little use of them. Most other developed countries used STC programs to a much greater extent during the 2007–2009 recession (Cahuc 2014).

Using randomized controlled trials to evaluate job search assistance programs, this intervention has been shown to be cost effective in speeding the return to work (Wandner 2010). Job search assistance services provide displaced workers with the tools to improve their search for work. Most displaced workers have not searched for work for many years. Giving these workers the information and skills to do such things as prepare a resume, search for job openings, and successfully participate in job interviews does not create a disincentive to search for work. To the contrary, the services provide displaced workers with the information and skills that help them to search for work more effectively and return to work more rapidly.

Training services are essential to a small but significant percent of permanently separated UI recipients who lack the skills to return to a job with similar earnings and skills requirements. The USDOL-funded training programs include programs for dislocated workers, but those programs are grossly underfunded. While millions of American workers are displaced each year and many could benefit from career training, USDOL programs have tended to provide funds to train fewer than 200,000 unemployed dislocated workers per year from among the millions of workers who are displaced each year (Wandner 2010).

Reemployment bonuses also provide an incentive for permanently displaced UI recipients to speed their return to work, and several field experiments have shown that they do just that (Wandner 2010). An analysis of two field experiments suggests that targeting bonus offers to those most likely to have long UI receipt could be a cost-effective program design (O'Leary, Decker, and Wandner 2005).

## Policy Issues Relating to Disincentive Effects

The concern about employer and employee responses to the UI program has resulted in many policy proposals to counter employer and employee disincentive effects. The following list enumerates some of the many proposals to reduce the disincentive effects of the UI program. They include the following:

- changes to the UI experience rating system to reduce the confrontational relationship between employers and their former employees
- federal standards to reduce the power of employer organizations to reduce access to, the availability of, and the amount and duration of UI benefits to employees
- strengthening the UI work test to ensure that only eligible unemployed workers receive UI
- providing reemployment services that can improve job matching and speed the return to work
- providing monetary incentives to permanently separated UI recipients to speed their return to work
- encouraging employers to retain their workers using STC reduced hours rather than layoffs

UI exists to pay temporary partial income replacement during involuntary unemployment. While providing income replacement, UI creates some disincentive effects. Many of the UI reform proposals discussed in the following chapters can mitigate the disincentive effects of paying UI benefits. These proposals directly address negative employer and employee responses to the availability of UI benefits and to employer resistance to paying for legitimate claims for UI benefits.

## Notes

1. The UWC website states: "Many employers have found Unemployment Insurance cost management companies to be a cost-effective 'best practice,' in terms of administering UI claims and managing UI tax liabilities. Professional service organizations that can help you minimize your unemployment insurance taxes and exposure include members of the Association of Unemployment Tax Organizations" (UWC, n.d.).
2. Hamermesh (1977, p. 38) concludes that the impact of increases in potential durations "are much smaller, perhaps even zero, when the civilian unemployment rate is above 6 percent."

# 7
# Approaches to UI Reform

In response to the weaknesses of the UI program discussed in Part 2, many have called for comprehensive UI reform. Part 3 has discussed issues and approaches to UI reform. Part 4 will discuss a wide variety of possible components of such reform. Several of these reforms presently exist in some form in many states. Few are completely new, and most have been implemented only in those states with the most expansive state UI laws. The more restrictive state programs have very few of them.

Many of these reforms have been proposed by policymakers and analysts who have presented policy and empirical analysis to support the proposals. Those proposals have included new federal benefit standards, USDOL guidance to the states on a wide range of issues, and the recommendations of two national commissions. They also include proposals by the Brookings Institution, the National Employment Law Project, and the Century Foundation, as well as recent studies by Bivens et al. (2021); Dube (2021); O'Leary and Wandner (2018); Simonetta (2018); von Wachter (2020); and West et al. (2016). Senators Ron Wyden and Michael F. Bennet circulated a 2021 discussion draft of a comprehensive UI reform bill (hereafter the Wyden-Bennet proposal). Many of these proposals will be noted in the discussion of the reform options or proposals below. (See Chapter 5 for a brief history of past calls for UI reform.)

The reform option approaches discussed in this chapter could be implemented in a variety of ways, including through USDOL guidance, state legislation, the enactment of federal legislation, and incorporation into a new federal or national UI program, which would require an extensive congressional overhaul of the program.

Before turning to specific options and recommendations for UI reforms in Chapters 8–12, this chapter identifies four key issues for UI reform: 1) whether state financial incentives for reform are effective, 2) whether widespread adoption of employee contributions to program benefits could help improve the UI program by reducing the adversarial and political nature of the UI program, 3) the need to balance the benefit and tax sides of UI reform, and 4) how the UI program should be administered. Recommendations for each of these issues are presented here.[1]

## USING FINANCIAL INCENTIVES TO ENCOURAGE STATES TO REFORM THEIR PROGRAMS: HOW EFFECTIVE AND EQUITABLE ARE THEY?

The UI Modernization Program was a significant effort to reform the UI program using financial incentives to induce states to reform their UI programs. This program was part of the American Recovery and Reinvestment Act (ARRA) of 2009, enacted during the Great Recession to spur UI program reform. The UI Modernization Program offered states up to a total of $7 billion if they then had, or would adopt, several UI program components expanding UI benefits that the Obama administration considered desirable. The program required that states adopt or have in place the following criteria:

- alternative base periods
- dependents' allowances
- quitting for compelling family reasons: preventing the denial of benefits to individuals who leave work for compelling family reasons—domestic violence or sexual assault, caring for a sick family member, or moving because a spouse relocated to another location for employment
- part-time work: preventing the denial of benefits to individuals actively seeking part-time employment
- training benefit extension of UI benefits

The UI Modernization provisions represented a partial approach to UI reform that used federal financial incentives to induce states to reform their UI laws. Some states were unwilling to voluntarily enact any or all the proposed reforms and instead declined the financial incentives. Of the 53 UI jurisdictions in the federal-state UI partnership, 41 states enacted at least one UI reform, but the total distribution of incentive grants was $4.4 billion, only 63 percent of the total funds available.

Another problem was that there was the potential for backsliding as states could enact a provision, take the financial incentive, and then later revoke the provision (Wandner 2013).

But did the UI Modernization of state UI laws work? Its impact can be assessed by seeing how many states responded, how many states retained the provisions adopted to obtain the incentives, and whether there were systematic differences between the states that responded and those that did not.

Table 7.1 shows that the UI Modernization program had a significant effect on expanding the states' adoption of the modernization provisions, and continued to do so through 2020, even though it did not result in their nationwide adoption. The federal government did not require that states maintain the UI Modernization provisions for which they received incentive payments, and several states later repealed UI Modernization provisions, including Kansas, North Carolina, South Dakota, Tennessee, and Wisconsin.

**Table 7.1  UI Modernization Enacted in 2009: States with Provisions before and after ARRA**

| UI modernization provisions | No. of states with provisions before ARRA | No. of states with provisions in 2011 | No. of states with provisions in 2020 |
|---|---|---|---|
| Alternative base period | 19 | 41 | 40 |
| Part-time work | 6 | 28 | 30 |
| Compelling family reasons | 0 | 21 | 45 |
| Dependents' allowances | 4 | 7 | 11 |
| Training extension | 0 | 16 | 16 |

SOURCE: Wandner (2013) and USDOL, ETA (2022).

The use of financial incentives improved the program overall but did not achieve interstate equity across the United States. Rather, they made the difference between the adopting and nonadopting states more extreme. For example, in 2020, 40 states had an alternative base period. All but two of the remaining states that did not have an alternative base period were in the bottom half of states listed by recipiency rates as indicated in Figure 3.4. Thus, those states that did not adopt an alternative base period were the least likely to provide easy access to the UI program.

It appears that financial incentives can be moderately effective in encouraging states to adopt more expansive benefit payment provisions. The federal government has also used an incentive approach in other policy efforts, such as the 2014 incentive to forward fund UI benefits by issuing standards for 0 percent borrowing from Federal Unemployment Tax Account (FUTA) for state UI trust fund accounts that meet average high-cost multiple standards. To date, however, the adopting states mostly have been those that already have provided unemployed workers easier access to the UI program. Therefore, it is likely that only through the imposition of a federal mandate will all states provide easier access to the UI program, including adopting the provisions contained in the UI Modernization Act.

**Recommendation**

While financial incentives can induce some states to improve their UI programs, experience shows that not all states participate. As a result, program improvements are made without ensuring interstate and demographic equity. Federal requirements are needed to have fully adequate and equitable UI programs for all Americans in all states. Since financial incentives don't necessarily result in permanent changes to a state UI program, achieving reforms requires statutory changes to federal law accompanied by regulatory conformity requirements to ensure the changes are implemented nationwide. Also, because federal incentives may not result in permanent changes in state UI programs, new federal legislative standards are needed that can be translated into federal regulatory requirements that allow USDOL to impose variable penalties for nonconformance, rather than the current single blunt instrument of a total loss of a 90 percent reduction (from the 6.0 percent tax) in the federal tax paid by employers.

## EMPLOYEE CONTRIBUTIONS: A WAY TO REDUCE THE POLITICIZATION OF UI?

Most decisions about the design and levels of UI benefits and taxes are made by governors and state legislators. State governments, in turn, are lobbied by employer and employee organizations. In general, this lobbying effort is quite unequal because of the decline in the strength of labor unions. Nonetheless, unions are much more powerful in some parts of the country than in others. The unions in states that are more unionized have been able to exert greater influence on the robustness of the state UI programs. As a result, in states with a higher percentage of unionized workers, the structure of the UI programs results in higher levels of UI recipiency (Figure 3.7).

Over time, political processes have determined the adequacy of UI benefits and the sufficiency of taxes to pay for those benefits. In all but three states, employers directly pay the full cost of the UI program, and generally employers have been successful in keeping benefit costs and taxes low if they do not face a strong voice of organized labor (Anderson and Meyer 2000).

In the interview discussed in Chapter 4 with Robert Asaro-Angelo, the New Jersey Commissioner of Labor and Workforce Development, he and his senior staff expressed the belief that the New Jersey employees' contribution to their benefits has a significant effect on giving employees a sense of ownership of their UI program and encouraging workers to apply for benefits when they become unemployed. That sense of ownership is real because, as shown in Table 7.2, employees in New Jersey pay a large percentage of the UI taxes that fund the program—34 percent of the tax in 2019.[2]

If enacted nationwide, an employee contribution could improve the acceptance of comprehensive national UI reforms in the areas of benefit access and adequacy, as employees would be paying a substantial percentage of the costs. The cost of comprehensive UI reform could be financed in part or in whole with the introduction of an employee tax as a federal conformity requirement for states.

An employee contribution rate could be set such that it covers some designated percentage of the cost of a comprehensive UI reform proposal. To allow employees to have a substantial voice in the making

**Table 7.2  New Jersey UI Taxes as a Percent of Taxable Wages, 2019**

| Employer tax | Employee tax | Employee tax/Total tax |
|---|---|---|
| 0.72 | 0.3825 | 0.347 |

SOURCE: Employer tax: https://oui.doleta.gov/unemploy/docs/aetr-2019.pdf
Employee tax: *2019 Comparison of State Unemployment Insurance Laws.*

of UI state and local UI policy, the employee tax would probably need to be set at a rate at least as great as the New Jersey rates. If a shared employer/employee tax does not fully cover the cost of comprehensive reform, a substantial increase in the federal taxable wage base would ensure that the UI tax is more progressive and that the average tax rate on lower wage-paying employers and lower-wage receiving employees would decline after implementation of the reforms. Thus, while an increase in the federal taxable wage base might otherwise be fully offset by a decline in tax rates, the increase in the base could be used to reduce the employer tax rate, making reform more palatable to employer groups.

One might ask why employees should be asked to bear the cost of UI reform, both by paying a UI tax and by increasing the wage base upon which they would be taxed. One reason for employees to accept paying a new employee contribution is that employers already shift the costs of the UI tax that employers pay onto employees in the form of lower wages (Anderson and Meyer 2000). A new employee contribution thus might not cause a significant decline in employees' total compensation compared to a similar tax increase on their employers. Another reason for employees to support employee contributions is that by paying into the program, they would "own" a piece of it, and they or their representatives are likely to have more of a voice in future UI public policy. As a result, in many states employees could expect enhanced benefits if they become unemployed during an economic downturn.

Employee contributions would not, of course, resolve all issues between employers and employees. Under a federal-state program, even with UI reform, state governments will continue to make changes in state UI laws. However, employee funding of a portion of the total UI tax would tend to increase the power of employees and lessen the adversarial relationship between the employees and employers, while providing more adequate benefits and fully funding program costs.

## Recommendation

Employee contributions should be required in all states and should be between one-third and one-half of total UI taxes. Implementation of employee contributions would increase political support for the UI program and reduce the adversarial relationship between employer and employee organizations.

## BALANCING BENEFIT AND FINANCING REFORM:
## LESSONS FROM THE SOCIAL SECURITY PROGRAM

It is impossible to consider either UI benefits reform or UI financing reform separately. Benefits reform generally results in an increase in benefit costs that cannot be paid without increased financing. Similarly, financing reform by itself is meaningless. The issue is this: What needs to be financed? Furthermore, benefit and financing reform are not a one-time occurrence. Adequate benefits with sufficient financing today may be insufficient tomorrow. As the cost of living increases every year, benefits must similarly increase, and financing will have to pay for that increase. This tandem approach to benefits and financing, however, is in effect only in a small number of states, but not in the great majority.

Similarly, federal UI funding must accommodate rising costs. The federal government pays for UI and ES administration, but most of the costs of administration are for federal and state staff. Each year, the wages of state UI staff increase, and an effective UI program would have to pay those increasing costs. Instead, UI administrative funding has long been constrained while ES funding has declined. The result has been a steady decline in UI and ES staffing across the country.

This issue can be understood by comparing the failure of UI reforms to the relatively superior approach of Social Security old-age pension reforms. While Social Security program policy is far from perfect, it demonstrates that a strong social insurance program requires an ongoing balance of program benefits and costs.

The UI program and the Social Security old-age pension programs started on the same path when they were enacted, but they have diverged widely over the past eight decades with respect to both benefit adequacy and financing sufficiency. The development of the Social Security program after 1935 shows the need for automatic, balanced, and synchronized increases in benefits and taxes with periodic legislative adjustments to bring the system back into balance. The UI program could have reduced or avoided many of its current problems if it had followed the path of the Social Security program.

Unlike for Social Security, there has been no steady, balanced process of increasing benefit payments and revenues in the UI program. States set their own benefit levels and tax rates, and the state taxable wage base must only be as high as the federal taxable wage base. Balanced increases in benefits and funding are not possible without the enactment of federal benefit payment standards, especially since the federal taxable wage base has been frozen at a ridiculously low $7,000 level since 1983.

In fact, one early change to the UI federal taxable wage base initiated the process of keeping the UI taxable wage base low. The 1939 amendments to the Federal Unemployment Tax Act reduced the wage base from total wages to $3,000, in part so that it would be the same as what the Social Security wage base was at that time (Haber and Murray 1966). As Haber and Murray explain, that change "was not considered to be important. . . . The change has grown in significance, however, as wages have increased over the years."

Once the UI federal taxable wage base was set at $3,000, congressional neglect left it there until 1972, when it was raised to $4,200. The fact that the UI taxable wage base has been increased only three times over the life of the program and has remained at $7,000 since 1983 has greatly exacerbated both state and federal UI funding problems.

By contrast, Congress enacted an amendment to the Social Security program that raised both benefits and revenues and attempted to bring them into balance by tying both to the annual cost of living increase. In almost all years since 1975, the Social Security taxable wage base has been indexed to some measure of wage growth, and the indexing formula has been adjusted several times (Whitman and Shoffner 2011). In 2023, the Social Security taxable wage base rose to $160,200—over 20 times the UI taxable wage base.

On the benefits side, Congress also began to enact major increases in Social Security benefits in the 1950s. The 1950 Social Security amendments significantly increased benefits by 77 percent. Finally, the 1972 amendments eliminated the need for regular congressional action to increase Social Security benefits by tying benefits to the cost of living and increasing benefits by 20 percent. In 1977, Congress made a similar change in the Social Security taxable wage base, also having it automatically increase each year as average earnings rise (Ball 1985).

Thus, by the end of the 1970s, Congress determined that Social Security benefits and taxes should be brought into balance every year. That balance was based on automatic annual increases in both Social Security benefits and taxes, with periodic rebalancing made by congressional action. This critical decision helped create a sounder Social Security expenditure and financial system—an approach that still has not been enacted for the UI program.[3]

Thus, the key to having a sustainable Social Security or UI program is automatic adjustment and balancing of benefits and taxes, as well as periodic legislative reforms of the system when the system gets out of balance. Today, the UI program is greatly in need of federal legislative reform and rebalancing because nationwide it has neither automatic adjustments of benefits and taxes nor even moderately comprehensive legislative structural reform since 1976.

### Recommendation

Both UI benefits and taxes should be adequate to provide a strong UI program throughout the United States. Once adequate levels of benefits and taxes have been achieved, benefits and taxes should be indexed so that they remain in balance at a level sufficient to fund a robust UI program.

## THREE OPTIONS FOR UI PROGRAM ADMINISTRATION

In 1934, while the Committee on Economic Security considered whether the new UI program would be a "federal-state" program or a "national" program, the Social Security Act of 1935 opted to make UI a federal-state program. It is worthwhile, however, to consider what UI reform would look like under these two alternatives, as well as under an intermediate approach—a "federal" program.[4] Below is a brief discussion of each of three possible approaches that bear further consideration.

### Federal-State Partnership

A reformed federal-state UI program would continue to be administered by the states. The states also would administer the program under individual state UI laws and administrative procedures, although an increased number of federal standards would direct the states to enact legislation that yields more interstate uniformity in the program. These standards could cover a wide range of issues, including benefit access, eligibility, and payments; tax bases, tax rates and procedures; and program administration and processes, information technology, data systems, and research and evaluation.

The wider the range of federal standards, the more likely the UI program would pay adequate benefits and raise sufficient revenue to fund benefits nationwide, and the more each state program would look like that of the states. Program outcomes also would become more similar. Nonetheless, because of divergent state goals and interests, reforming the UI program under a federal-state framework is still likely to result in substantial interstate differences and thus continue to present administrative and equity issues.

Some of the results of such a federal-state system might include the following:

- States would continue to have separate UI laws and administration, with substantial differences between states, although benefit adequacy and tax sufficiency would increase by imposing federal minimum standards.

- Interstate and demographic equity would be increased, but some differences would remain.

- UI reform under the federal-state approach would be the least administratively difficult to implement of the three possible approaches.

- Given the resistance of some states to expand their UI programs, increased USDOL oversight and enforcement would be critical.

### Federal Program

A federal UI (and ES) program would be administered by the states as agents of the U.S. Secretary of Labor. There would be a single set of laws and administrative procedures that states would implement. A new federal law would incorporate the best practices from existing state UI laws plus additional reforms.

- Because all states would be administering the same laws and procedures, processes and outcomes for the states' unemployed workers and covered employers would be more consistent than under federal-state administration.

- States would continue to administer the UI program from state and local workforce offices.

- Because of differences in the methods of administration between states, however, some interstate outcomes would still differ. Nonetheless, there would be greater interstate and demographic equity than under a federal-state UI system.

- This approach would be more administratively and legislatively difficult to implement than under the current federal-state system because of the greatly increased need for the national UI office to provide guidance, direction, and enforcement to the states, resulting from the significant changes in UI administration by the states and the need for coordination between states.

- The administrative burden on the national and regional UI staff would increase substantially and require much more oversight and funding than in the current program.

## National Program

A national program would be administered by a federal agency, probably the SSA because of its experience with paying benefits and collecting taxes, actions that would become centralized and result in greater efficiency. Many claimant and tax services provided to unemployed workers and employers could be centralized or regionalized—such as communications, adjudication, and appeals services—resulting in increased administrative efficiency.

- There would be a single federal UI law that would shape all aspects of the UI program.

- In a national system, processes and outcomes would be the same throughout the United States. Interstate and demographic differences between states would be eliminated.

- UI and ES staff would be placed in local offices around the United States, either in existing offices or newly created ones. All UI and ES state staff would become federal employees.

- In the short run, this approach would be most difficult and expensive to implement because it would require establishing an entirely new UI system.

- The administrative burden for the national operating organization would initially increase dramatically with the need to establish an entirely new UI program. Once established, however, the program would be simpler and less costly to administer, taking advantage of centralization and, perhaps, regionalization.

Pavosevich (2020) finds that a national UI system with increased costs from legislative reforms could be funded with reasonable tax rates and an increased and indexed taxable wage base. Dube (2021) recommends a national program. A more detailed discussion of the options for administration is presented in Appendix A, and Pavosevich's cost estimates are found in Appendix B.

### Recommendation

The administration of the UI program, both nationally and by state, needs to be greatly strengthened. While a strong program throughout the country and for all workers nationwide might be best served by a national UI program, such a major change is not likely to be politically feasible. A federal program would be a second-best solution. If neither of these are feasible, the current federal-state UI program should be greatly strengthened by enacting strong federal requirements and significantly strengthening state and national UI oversight.

## WYDEN-BENNET PROPOSAL

In 2021, Senators Michael Bennet and Ron Wyden were the first members of Congress in recent years to undertake a serious effort at comprehensively reforming the UI program. Their proposal was circulated in April 2021 (Wyden and Bennet 2021) and included many UI reform proposals. The April 2021 proposal was never introduced as legislation. A more limited bill, the Unemployment Insurance Improvement Act (Senate Bill 2685) was introduced on September 28, 2021, but it was not enacted. It was more limited in scope than their original proposal and covered fewer UI benefit issues, eliminating a Jobseeker's Allowance proposal, and, like the April 2021 proposal, lacked financing provisions (Wyden, Bennet, and Brown 2021).[5] The original proposal contained many important reforms to the UI benefit payment system. Some of those proposals are discussed below as part of the discussion of individual UI issues and reform options. The original Wyden-Bennet proposal, however, was not fully comprehensive, and it did not include many of the benefit payment proposals discussed below. The following are major omissions:

- Implementing a minimum benefit amount.

- Dependents' allowances: requiring states to provide a minimum allowance (e.g., $25 per dependent) with subsequent indexing.

- Employee contributions: Every state would have an employee contribution flat rate that would pay up to half of each state's UI benefit costs.

- Extended base periods: Permitting the use of earlier quarters of earnings beyond the normal UI benefit year to allow more re-entrants to the labor force to qualify for benefits.

- Balancing benefits and taxes: To keep the UI system in equilibrium over time would require adequate UI benefits that are indexed annually. To pay for these benefits, tax receipts would have to be sufficient and increase each year. This could be accomplished in part by raising and indexing the state and federal taxable wage bases.

- Jobseeker's Allowance: This proposal is a social welfare program, not a social insurance program. Nonetheless, if enacted, reasonably accurate administration would require that USDOL receive participant earnings data to administer the program and prevent fraud, particularly for contract workers. To accomplish this, IRS and USDOL would have to work together to create a searchable database available to state UI agencies to collect income data for contract employees and the self-employed.

While the Wyden-Bennet April 2021 proposal did not include benefit financing provisions that are critical to a system that balances benefit and tax provisions, with amendments and the addition of financing provisions, it could be a useful starting point for considering comprehensive reform.

# Notes

1. A more comprehensive list of proposed reforms to the UI program can be found in Appendix A.
2. In New Jersey, there may be rebates on taxes paid by multiple job holders and other factors that cause differences in total percentages. In Pennsylvania, the employee tax is much lower than in New Jersey—between 0.00 and 0.08 percent of gross covered wages. Thus, only New Jersey and Alaska have significant employee taxes.
3. While automatic increases in Social Security taxes and benefits might be sufficient to address Social Security's solvency problem in the short term, periodic interventions have still been needed (Ball in NCSW 1985). Similarly, implementing automatic increases in UI benefits and taxes would likely also require periodic congressional adjustments.
4. These options are discussed in greater detail in Wandner (2020).
5. The press release for Senate Bill 2865 stated that the bill was a "down payment on reforming the nation's unemployment insurance system" (U.S. Senate Committee on Finance 2021).

# Part 4

# Recommendations for UI Reform

# 8
# Regular UI Benefits
## Improving Access, Eligibility, and Benefits

This chapter and successive chapters in Part 4 address UI reform by describing each issue and presenting alternative possible solutions and recommendations.

There has been a decline in access to benefits and the amount and duration of benefits over time as measured by benefit recipiency (see Figure 3.4), although benefit recipiency varies widely by state (see Figure 3.5). The enormous variation among states has been illustrated by differences in the most generous states (e.g., New Jersey) and the least generous (e.g., North Carolina and Florida) that were discussed in Chapter 4. The discussion below analyzes how public policy can counter both the decline in benefits over time and the wide disparities among states.

## ACCESS TO BENEFITS

Access to the UI program refers to the extent to which experienced workers in covered employment receive UI benefits when they experience involuntary job loss. The recipiency rate is the best single measure of the ability of unemployed workers to access the UI program. It is measured as the percentage of all unemployed workers who apply for and receive UI benefits. There are vast differences among the states in the ability of unemployed workers to receive UI benefits, as shown in Figure 3.4. With 2019 recipiency rates varying between 57 percent in New Jersey and 9 percent in North Carolina, it is not surprising that the components of the state programs are vastly different. Indeed, it is not clear that states with the lowest recipiency rates can be said to be operating a reasonable social insurance program for the unemployed.

At least five factors determine access to benefits for experienced workers who are unemployed:

1) the availability of information about how to file claims for benefits

2) the ease or difficulty of completing and submitting an initial and continued claims for benefits application

3) the ability of applicants/recipients to communicate with the state UI agency

4) state administration that either encourages or discourages participation in the program

5) the state UI law's provisions regarding initial and continuing eligibility

While UI monetary and nonmonetary eligibility criteria are addressed separately later, what follows is a discussion of each of the other factors that impact access to benefits and what we know about them.

## INFORMATION ABOUT THE AVAILABILITY OF BENEFITS

### Issue

Many workers who are separated from employment know little about UI benefits or how to apply for them. Some workers obtain general information about the application process through their separating employers, through informal social networks, or by searching online. Unionized workers are commonly informed of their rights to apply for UI benefits by their unions, but unionized workers are a small and declining part of the labor force. For others, the U.S. system may work for laid off workers who are well educated and computer savvy, but for other unemployed workers—including many low-wage workers—finding out how to file a claim, the eligibility requirements for benefits, and where to apply is more difficult.

Today, there is no widely available uniform and easy to understand source of information for most U.S. workers. A more equitable approach would be to provide all separated workers with information about four aspects of the UI system:

- How to apply
    - call center telephone number, online URL address, and in-person at an American Job Center (AJC) (with address and telephone number)
- Information required when applying for benefits
    - Social Security number
    - name, payroll address, and telephone number of separated worker's last employer
    - start and end dates of separated worker's last job
    - whether or not separated worker will receive vacation pay, severance pay, etc.
    - alien registration number, if applicable
    - form DD-214 military release form, if served in the U.S. military during the last 18 months
    - standard Form 8 (SF-8) release form, if worked for the federal government in the last 18 months
    - name(s), date(s) of birth, and Social Security number(s) of any dependents
- Eligibility requirements for unemployment benefits
    - how to demonstrate that separated worker is able to work, available for work, and actively seeking work
- Work registration
    - separated workers must register for work at a local workforce office (provide the address and telephone number) or online URL address

Further, all communications must use plain language—preferably, pretested on claimants for comprehensibility—in all online and paper applications, letters, alerts, and notices.

**Provider Options**

Workers who become unemployed usually have limited information about how to apply for UI benefits unless they belong to unions
that encourage them to apply. Increasing the access to UI benefits for
other workers can be assisted by the state UI agencies or by the private
sector. States and their UI agencies can reach out to potential claimants
and explain how and where to apply (e.g., at the time of layoff to laid off
workers or later through public service announcements). There are two
ways the private sector could provide information at the time of layoff.

1) Mass Media: In general, it is not particularly efficient to provide information through the mass media. The target audience
   (those workers who are about to be or who have recently been
   separated from their jobs) is only a small segment of the total
   audience. Nonetheless, during the COVID-19 pandemic there
   were examples of successful media campaigns to alert the public to the availability of unemployment benefits. For example,
   a 2020–2021 public service announcement campaign was
   sponsored by the Maryland Department of Labor and broad-
   cast by Maryland public television.

   As part of a statewide effort to encourage participation in
   short-time compensation, the announcement encouraged both
   unemployed workers and employers to apply to participate in
   the program. Another smaller but still effective approach used
   by states and advocacy organizations has been to use social
   media sites to inform unemployed workers how to successfully apply for UI benefits.

2) Record of Employment: A broader approach to providing information about the availability of UI benefits and how to apply
   for them would be for the federal government to require all
   states and employers to provide workers with what the Cana-
   dians call a record of employment (ROE) at the time of separation. The Canadian ROE is an official Employment and Social
   Development Canada (ESDC) form that an employer can submit to a federal government agency either electronically or
   manually. Almost all employers produce ROEs electronically
   from their payroll systems. The form includes employer and

employee names and contact information, employee occupation, dates of employment, hours worked, earnings, and the reason for separation (ESDC 2014).

If adopted in the United States, UI applicants could submit an ROE to their state UI agency when applying for UI benefits. This form would give the separated workers information about whether they are likely to receive benefits and would provide the state UI agency with much of the information it needs to determine monetary and nonmonetary eligibility. In the case of electronic ROEs, they could be given to the separating employee in paper form but also be transmitted directly to the state UI agency or to a national clearing house agency.

Manual ROEs would have to be accepted from some small firms. U.S. adoption of an ROE would help to increase knowledge about and initial applications to the UI program.[1] Employers already must submit employment and wage information quarterly on their covered employees, and they submit other information when their employees apply for UI benefits. Thus, it should not be burdensome for employers to submit an ROE with a final quarterly wage record to separating employees and to state UI agencies.

**Recommendation**

An ROE should be made a requirement for all state UI programs. The layoff employer should be required to provide each separated worker and the state UI program with a copy of the ROE. The use of ROEs should increase benefit recipiency by making it easier for claimants to apply for and state UI agencies to process benefits. Later discussion will show how the use of an ROE could also reduce fraudulent applications.

# INITIAL CLAIMS APPLICATION

## Issue

The design and administration of the initial claims application can make a vast difference in the percentage of initial applicants who are able to properly complete the application. The discussion regarding Florida and New Jersey in Chapter 4 shows sharp differences in the ease of navigating the application process. Florida's system is not old: it was built in 2013, but it was difficult for UI applicants to understand and complete. In April 2020, when Florida's online application system crashed, Floridians waited in long car lines to file paper applications because the Florida agency had eliminated its telephone service to assist unemployed workers seeking benefits, and their electronic application had been found to be faulty by the Florida auditor in 2015 but had not been fixed (Ghosh 2021; Lee et al. 2021; Mower 2020; State of Florida 2019). By contrast, the New Jersey application was carefully developed, tested, and retested to ensure that it is easy for applicants to understand and complete.

## Options

1) Assess state applications: All state benefit applications should be easy to understand and complete, but they vary greatly. To improve the current process, it is necessary to learn what makes state UI applications different. One proposal is to have USDOL conduct studies on the ease or difficulty of completing applications, the results of which would reveal the states that need to improve their UI application procedures to make the program accessible to all qualified unemployed workers. Similar studies could assess the entire application process.

2) Standardize applications: USDOL could develop new model application software, which would strive for uniformity across states. Survey design experts would develop and test new initial and continued claims questionnaires to eliminate any phrasing that might have a negative disparate impact on certain groups. That products would be provided to state UI agen-

cies with technical assistance on how to implement the new and improved applications.

3) Employer filing: Encouraging employers to file on behalf of separating employees could increase completion of applications. Employers could submit the workers' application for benefits not only for the short-time compensation program, as is currently done in several states, but also for other temporary layoffs (West et al. 2016).

4) Rapid response filing: As part of the Workforce Innovation and Opportunity Act (WIOA) program, statewide Rapid Response teams are sent to worksites that are about to conduct mass layoffs. Experienced state merit-based UI staff could be sent out with these teams to take UI claims before the large scale layoffs take place, whether or not the soon to be unemployed workers are covered by the WARN Act.[2] They, along with state employment service staff, funded under the Wagner-Peyser Act, would directly assist displaced workers being laid off in filing their UI initial claims applications, work registrations, and, if the layoffs were to be permanent, obtaining placement services and potential referrals to WIOA training.

**Recommendation**

To increase UI recipiency for separated workers who have difficulty applying for and receiving UI, initial applications should be simplified, tested, and standardized. They should be reviewed, assessed, and approved by the national UI office. For large layoffs, employer filing and Rapid Response teams filing, and assistance should be encouraged.

## COMMUNICATIONS

**Issue**

The unprecedented 2020 pandemic, which resulted in the largest number of benefit applications in the UI program's history, has shown the need for much better communication and the flexibility to rapidly expand and field questions from vastly more unemployed workers during severe economic downturns. When UI applicants needed to obtain more information during the pandemic to help them apply for benefits, to determine why they had not yet received benefit, or had other questions, they were frequently stymied. Often, their calls were not answered, even after being held in a queue for long periods of time. The need was for states to rapidly increase their ability to communicate beyond what they could do with their own limited staff. One promising and unusual approach was implemented by New Jersey that handled the crush of calls by setting up a dual call center system: they hired a private contractor to take the easy calls and provide quick answers, and the contractor's employees were instructed to transfer the more difficult questions to the state UI agency's call centers where experienced staff would provide answers.

**Option**

Employers could better communicate with employees and provide the answers to frequently asked questions if they were required to provide employees, at the point of separation, with written information on how and where to apply for UI benefits. This information would be contained on the worker's ROE, like the ESDC document discussed above.

**Recommendation**

Employers should be required to provide separating employees and state UI agencies with ROEs. This would increase recipiency by ensuring that separating employees have information about whether they are likely to be eligible for UI benefits and how and where to apply. It would also facilitate the state agency's accurate processing of claims.

## PROGRAM ADMINISTRATION

### Issue

It is difficult to measure the expansiveness or restrictiveness of a state program's administration. It is clear, however, that some states use their methods of administration to either encourage or discourage successful UI applications and the provision of reemployment services. The New Jersey agency makes extensive efforts to help UI applicants successfully apply for and receive UI benefits, as the interview with Commissioner Asaro-Angelo, presented in Chapter 4, makes clear (see Note 3 on p. 76). At the same time, the collapse of the Florida initial claims application process and former Governor Scott's bragging about being responsible for large reductions in the number of Floridians receiving UI benefits while he was governor make clear that Florida has a restrictive approach to UI program administration that was developed while Scott was governor and continues to this day (Oliver 2021). The effect of the different approaches is shown in the fact that New Jersey had the highest recipiency rate in the nation in 2019 while Florida had the second lowest.

### Recommendation

Having more consistent and equitable program administration could be facilitated if USDOL were to greatly increase federal monitoring of state program administration to ensure equitable treatment for UI applicants and recipients.

## REFORM OPTIONS TO IMPROVE UI PROGRAM ACCESS AND PROGRAM ADMINISTRATION

### Issue

Reforming UI benefit levels and potential durations is meaningless if unemployed workers cannot enter the program. Yet issues about the ability of unemployed workers to access the UI program and work with state UI staff to resolve eligibility issues exists throughout the United States. Many potential administrative and legislative reforms could improve access, and many options have been suggested. Below are several options that lawmakers, policymakers, and analysts have advanced. Improvements to access by their nature overlap with other UI reforms:

1)  In Maryland, State Delegate Lorig Charkoudian carefully examined the UI access and program administration problem. In her Maryland House Bill 1002, she made extensive proposals to improve access by imposing a wide range of requirements on the Maryland agency (Charkoudian 2021), including requiring the Maryland agency to

- develop a call-back system for callers
- develop better voicemail messages that would make applicants' options clear
- ensure adequate call center staffing
- ensure adequate access to language and interpretive services
- develop a system to have all agency calls show the agency caller ID
- periodically reassess and improve public communications
- enable claimants to track claims
- fill all open state UI agency positions
- develop a plan to invest in technology
- establish state standards for the timely processing of claims

Charkoudian's proposal points to some of the many ways that states can make changes that would improve and speed up the claims process.[3] Some of the proposals would cost money and might be facilitated by increased federal funding for UI administration. USDOL also could develop model approaches for implementing some of these recommendations.

2)  West et al. (2016) suggest that increased access could be facilitated by requiring state UI agencies to contact the separated employees of private firms and public agencies, notify them of the potential availability of UI benefits, and provide informa-

tion on how to apply for them. They also suggest that USDOL explore the possibility of developing a federal performance standard requiring states to maintain a specified application rate for separated employees. By increasing the expected application rate, that performance measure would attempt to raise the recipiency rate, since the rate of completed applications is low in many states.

3) The Century Foundation (2020) proposes improving access and administration by improving the timeliness of benefit payments. They would have USDOL "launch a new initiative focused on timely payment of benefits, including a review of challenges facing the states, the positioning of accessibility enforcement staff through the Employment and Training Administration (ETA) regional offices, stronger regulations, and new performance standards on the performance of online systems." This recommendation aims to ensure the timelier payment of benefits for UI applicants who have been found eligible for UI benefits.

4) Sec. 304 of the Wyden-Bennet proposal (Wyden and Bennet 2021) also sought to improve access with four provisions: 1) require employers to provide information about claims-filing to all workers at their time of separation, 2) have employers inform state UI agencies of each separating employee who might apply for UI, 3) improve online claims-filing systems, and 4) ensure that there are alternative approaches for filing UI claims by workers who are unable to file online.

5) The most comprehensive and equitable policy might be to have USDOL develop a single, improved initial and continuing claims process and ensure that all states adopt and administer it. Such a process would be easy to administer in a federal or national UI system with a single, uniform, and carefully tested set of data elements and questions collected across states, with perhaps a single agency administering the program. Within the current federal-state administrative system, states could be encouraged (or required) to adopt a model system developed by USDOL with supplemental UI administrative funds to aid the transition.

6) Access to the UI program might also be improved by developing a federal access goal or standard. States could be encouraged or required to raise their recipiency rate to some minimum level. Given that the average recipiency rate has fallen below 30 percent, a minimum rate could be set at perhaps 30, 40, or even 50 percent.

7) Access might also be improved by having USDOL monitor access by assessing applications, communication systems, state UI legislation, and other factors that affect the level of UI access.

### Recommendation

Because access to the UI program is so limited, and because there are numerous issues preventing U.S. workers from entering the program, many of the above options should be considered and tried. The current low UI recipiency rate in most states demonstrates the need for increased access to UI benefits by separated workers by trying a variety of approaches to have a fair, equitable, and robust UI program.

## MONETARY ELIGIBILITY: BENEFIT AMOUNTS AND DURATION

### Issue

The oldest UI reform proposals are federal benefit standards. They date back to 1939 and were proposed by Presidents Roosevelt, Truman, Kennedy, and Johnson (Haber and Murray 1966). National benefit standards also were proposed by the ACUC in the 1990s. More recently, there have been renewed calls for benefit standards. To recap, the three traditionally proposed standards are

1) a replacement rate of 50 percent of prior wage

2) a maximum weekly benefit amount of two-thirds the state average weekly wage

3)  potential benefit durations of at least 26 weeks

While these have been the proposed standards for eight decades, recently more generous standards also have been proposed, including minimum weekly benefit amounts. The next section sets out several options for minimum weekly benefit amounts, replacement rates, maximum weekly benefit amounts, and maximum durations.

Missing from some proposals is a fourth benefit standard. It would create a minimum weekly benefit amount set as a percentage of the worker's average weekly wage or as a percentage of the maximum weekly benefit amount. Such a federal standard would counter some states' low minimum benefit amounts that have not increased over time. These low minimums disproportionately adversely affect low-wage workers who can receive only low weekly benefit payments.

## Options

A minimum benefit amount federal standard would raise the minimum in some states and, by annual indexing, would ensure that the minimum does not decline in real terms over time. Eight states currently set the minimum in this manner. Kansas is the most generous, setting the minimum at 25 percent of the state's average weekly wage.

USDOL advocated in the Kennedy administration for a minimum weekly benefit amount tied to states' average weekly wages (USDOL 1962). The Wyden-Bennet proposal, however, did not include a minimum weekly benefit amount. Bivens et al. (2021) would set the minimum weekly benefit amount at 30 percent the state average weekly wage.

## Recommendation

A minimum benefit standard also should be set at perhaps 25–30 percent of the state's average weekly wage. Alternatively, although no states currently tie minimum benefits to the current maximum, a minimum standard could be between 25 and 30 percent of the maximum.

## REPLACEMENT RATE

### Issue

The UI program replaces a portion of a UI recipient's lost wages, expressed as a percentage of the worker's prior wages, generally 50 percent. Most states, however, pay a higher replacement rate for low-wage workers.

### Options

1) 50 percent: The consensus at around a 50 percent replacement rate has been based on past benefit adequacy and consumption smoothing studies (East and Kuka 2015; Gruber 1997; O'Leary 1998) that have found that level to be sufficient to maintain consumption during a short period of unemployment.

2) Other than 50 percent: With declines in temporary layoffs, laid-off workers now are likely to be permanently displaced and need to find a new job. Increasing displacement is related to an upward trend in long-term unemployment. These labor market changes call into question the adequacy of a 50 percent replacement rate during longer spells of unemployment.

The Wyden-Bennet's proposal's response to the perceived inadequacy of a 50 percent replacement rate for longer spells of unemployment was to propose a 75 percent replacement rate, while for Bivens et al. (2021), the replacement rate would vary with past wages, with high replacement rates for lower-wage workers.

The Wyden-Bennet proposal would have created the three traditional federal standards discussed above, but it also would have raised the replacement rate to 75 percent in normal times and 100 percent during public health emergencies or other major disasters or emergencies.

Biven et al. (2021) also would provide for more generous benefit standards. The replacement rate would depend on need and would decline from 85 percent for the lowest-income workers to 50 percent for the highest-income workers. The maximum weekly benefit amount would be set at 150 percent of the states' average weekly wage. The potential duration for the regular program would be 26 weeks and would have a wage-based replacement rate. This proposal would move the UI program from a social insurance program to a social welfare program.

During past recessions, while Congress has extended the duration of benefits, it has never increased the replacement rate. There was the expectation that workers could search for and find work reasonably quickly such that higher replacement rates were not required.

The COVID-19 pandemic changed that assumption, as seen in research cited in Chapter 6. Because whole sectors of the U.S. economy were shut down to protect the health of the country, some members of Congress wanted to increase the replacement rate. State UI agencies, however, informed Congress that their inflexible IT systems could not be programmed to make such a change in their UI benefit payment systems, and the result was a benefit payment supplement that was initially $600 per week, but later reduced to $300. It seems clear that in planning for the future, state UI benefit payment systems should be improved such that states can flexibly and temporarily raise the wage replacement rate.

## Recommendation

The UI replacement rate during periods of low unemployment should remain at 50 percent. Consideration should be given to raising that replacement rate during periods of high, long-term unemployment if UI recipients are unlikely to find new jobs in the near term. Based on benefit adequacy studies, a 50 percent replacement rate is likely to be adequate during good economic times or during mild recessions.

## MAXIMUM WEEKLY BENEFIT AMOUNT

### Issue

While the maximum weekly benefit amount must be limited, the ceiling for high-wage workers varies widely among states. Some states have high maximums and others low. Some states infrequently raise the state maximum, while other states increase the maximum annually by tying the maximum to a percent of the states' average weekly wage.

## Options

1) The long-standing proposal for a maximum benefit standard that has been included in most UI reform proposals would set the maximum at two-thirds of the state average weekly wages. At present, 14 states have met or nearly meet that standard with maximums of 63 percent or greater, not counting dependents' allowances.[4] USDOL policy could encourage other states to adopt the two-thirds of the state average weekly wage maximum weekly benefit amount.

2) Alternatively, a federal requirement for the maximum weekly benefit amount could be enacted and would increase the maximum each year along with the increase in average state wages. A state-based indexed taxable wage base would not be a uniform wage base across the United States. Rather, it would result in different taxable wages between states as determined by variation in their average wages. This would be a dramatic change. Today most states do not have high maximums, although 31 states currently have some form of automatic annual increase.

## Recommendation

Congress should set the maximum weekly benefit in all states at a minimum of two-thirds of each state's average weekly wage. States should not be permitted to override these annual increases. The current maximum in many states results in most recipients being cut off by the maximum and receiving a very small percentage of their prior wage.

## MAXIMUM POTENTIAL DURATION OF REGULAR BENEFITS

## Issue

In 1935, the Committee on Economic Security's actuaries suggested that the initial maximum duration of benefits should be approximately 15 weeks. This low maximum was set because it was expected that there would be high levels of unemployment resulting in a very large demand for UI benefits from the Unemployment Trust Fund. That high level of demand, however, never materialized. By the late 1940s, President Truman proposed that every state provide benefits for 26 weeks to all eligible workers at all benefit levels, with additional benefits for dependents. Based upon program experience in the United States, policymakers determined that under normal conditions a six-month duration was sufficient to provide income for nondeferrable expenses—such as food, rent/mortgage, car payments, and medical bills—through temporary spells of unemployment (Harry S. Truman Presidential Library & Museum 1950; USDOL 1962). After the recession of 1974–1975, the National Commission on Unemployment Compensation (NCUC) reexamined the question of benefit duration, and in 1980 it once again recommended that states provide potential durations of 26 weeks (NCUC 1980).

Despite the failure of successive administrations to obtain from Congress a compulsory federal UI duration standard, USDOL policymakers encouraged states to increase their maximum potential durations, and by the mid-1970s, the standard became at least 26 weeks in all states (see Table 4.2). What appeared to be a state consensus of a 26-week maximum remained for nearly four decades but ended in 2010, when some states began reducing their maximum durations, sharply in some cases, in response to the 2007–2009 recession. These states opted to reduce benefits rather than to replenish their state trust fund account balances with tax increases. Today eight states have durations of less than 26 weeks (AL, AR, FL, GA, MI, MO, NC, SC), and that number has been increasing since the pandemic crisis has ended (Gwyn 2022; USDOL 2020). Conversely, two states (Illinois and Kansas) that had reduced their durations below 26 weeks after the Great Recession reversed course and now again provide 26 weeks of benefits.

## Options

There are several proposals for setting maximum potential durations.

1)  Congressional action: Requiring all states to establish and maintain a maximum potential duration of 26 weeks would require an amendment to federal law requiring a standard for benefit duration. The Obama administration FY 2017 budget

legislative proposal that was not enacted would have required all states to offer at least 26 weeks of benefits.

2)  USDOL action: Alternatively, USDOL could encourage states to amend their own state laws and provide model language to help them to do so.

3)  Uniform maximum duration at 26 weeks: In most states, the potential duration of benefits varies with the past earnings of new UI beneficiaries. Some states, however, have uniform durations such that all UI recipients are eligible for up to 26 weeks. West et al. (2016, p. 60) recommend a uniform maximum duration in all states, which would help low-wage workers who are likely to be eligible for less than 26 weeks of benefits. However, unless recipients' total benefit entitlement were increased, a uniform duration of 26 weeks could mean that low-wage workers' weekly benefit amounts might be lower over the duration period compared to the weekly benefit amounts under a variable duration.

4)  Increased maximum duration: Bivens et al. (2021, p. 6) would increase maximum benefit duration in normal economic times to 30 weeks, arguing that increasing the duration provides benefits that last long enough to alleviate economic insecurity until workers can secure jobs at decent wages.

## Recommendation

Congress should require all states to have a maximum potential duration of at least 26 weeks. Durations should uniformly be 26 weeks, regardless of the past wages of the recipients, aiding low-wage workers during periods of unemployment. All states had at least that maximum until 2010. The reductions below that level were enacted to keep taxes low rather than to take care of the needs of UI recipients.

## DEPENDENTS' ALLOWANCES

### Issue

As a form of social insurance, UI covers and pays individual workers. Benefits are based on the individual's prior wages, not on the size of the household in which the worker lives. As a result, additional benefit amounts for dependents are a form of *unemployment assistance* and are not based on insurance principles. Dependents' allowances are an aspect of an expansive UI program, with the allowances added to the worker's UI regular benefit amount. The formula for dependents' allowances is generally independent of the formula for regular benefits. In the late 1950s, USDOL studied benefit adequacy and found that heads of households with dependent families who received UI benefits needed to have their weekly benefits increased by one-third to meet their nondeferrable expenditures (Becker 1960). As a historical matter, USDOL has supported dependency allowances, and those allowances have been paid in some state UI programs for many years. Such an allowance reflects the states' concern about the unemployed worker's entire household, not just the unemployed worker him or herself.

Congress encouraged states to adopt dependents' allowances in 2009 with the enactment of the American Recovery and Reinvestment Act (ARRA), which made $7 billion in incentive grants available to states to modernize their unemployment insurance programs, including by adding dependents' allowances. Seven states had dependents' allowances in place in 2010, and since then the program has expanded to 13 states, mostly in higher recipiency rate states. The states that currently have dependents' allowances are Alaska, Connecticut, Illinois, Iowa, Maine, Maryland, Massachusetts, Michigan, New Jersey, New Mexico, Ohio, Pennsylvania, and Rhode Island.

### Options

1) Given the limited state adoption to date, the Wyden-Bennet proposal would have required all states to pay dependents' allowances of $25 per dependent per week. A dependents' allowance would be indexed to the increase in the Consumer

Price Index. The federal government, rather than state UI trust funds, would pay for the allowances.

2) Bivens et al. (2021) would support a dependent allowance indexed from $35 per week per dependent.

**Recommendation**

States should be encouraged to establish dependents' allowances as part of their regular state UI programs. If they do so, the dependents' allowance should be set at $25 or more per dependent per week and that payment should then be indexed over time to keep up with inflation. Consideration should be given to limiting the total number of permitted allowances per household.

## QUALIFYING FOR UI BENEFITS

**Issue**

For claimants to qualify for benefits they must demonstrate sufficient labor force attachment. In almost all states, this is accomplished by having a certain level of earnings in a year-long (base) period before applying for UI benefits. Most states require work in two calendar quarters and focus on the amount earned in the two highest earnings quarters of the base period—because this most closely reflects full-time work. These requirements put low-wage workers at a disadvantage, especially restaurant workers and others who may be earning a sub-minimum wage. An alternative that would be more equitable to low-wage workers, especially in low-wage states, would be to have an hours-worked requirement instead of an earnings requirement. Two states use hours worked to demonstrate labor force attachment: in Washington, workers with 680 hours and earnings of at least one dollar in base period earnings qualify, while Oregon uses two qualifying methods, one based on earnings and an alternative qualifying requirement of 500 hours.

## Options

Congress could increase equity in qualifying for UI benefits by requiring states to collect, in addition to earnings, quarterly hours worked within a certain period, for example, several years from the federal statute's effective date as part of the employer's quarterly wage report to the states. Bivens et al. (2021) support an hours-worked requirement.

## Recommendation

Following the Washington or Oregon approaches, states should be required to either 1) use an hours-worked requirement or 2) use an hours-worked requirement as an alternative to their earning-based qualifying requirement.

## BASE PERIOD

### Issue

The traditional state UI base period is a lagging four-quarter period, calculated as the first four of the last five completed quarters. This base period can lag for up to six months prior to an unemployed worker's application for UI benefits. Such a base period is sufficient for unemployed workers who had a steady, long period of employment before being laid off.

The rigid traditional base period was developed before modern computerized data systems were developed. Other approaches can be used today that can better accommodate current labor force behavior. Specifically, the traditional base period does not work well for relatively new entrants to the labor force who may have had much of their work experience during the lag period. It also may not work for reentrants to the labor force who may have had their last employment prior to the traditional base period.

An "alternative base period" exists in 40 states. It generally is used to compute a more recent base period—the last four completed quarters.

Its wide adoption indicates that states believe that experienced workers with only recent earnings should be able to collect UI (Vroman 1995).

An "extended base period" exists in nearly half of the states. It allows the UI applicant to use more distant quarters of wages. It is only permitted if unemployed workers do not have sufficient wages in the traditional base period. Currently this option is only available to workers who were injured on the job and could not work during the traditional base period.

## Options

If the extended base period were expanded to permit reentrants to the labor force to use wages from periods before they left the labor force, eligibility for returnees to the labor force—who historically have been mostly women—would increase. Several base period proposals have recently been made.

1) The Wyden-Bennet proposal would have created both an alternate base period and an extended base period of an additional four prior quarters for workers who were not physically capable of work or took family leave.

2) West et al. (2016) suggest extending the base period back 18 months for individuals with erratic work histories.

3) Bivens et al. (2021) suggest using a six-quarter base period. An extended base period also could be offered to any reentrant to the labor force, regardless of their reason for exiting the labor force.

## Recommendation

An alternative base period and an extended base period should be required for all state UI programs under the Social Security Act, making them a conformity requirement. It exists in most states, and it helps separated workers who have entered the labor force reasonably recently. States with alternative base periods have been found to administer it without difficulty.

## WAITING WEEKS

### Issue

Waiting weeks delay payment to eligible workers for one or more weeks after their filing an initial claim for UI benefits and are designed to reduce UI benefit costs. In 1935, the Committee on Economic Security recommended a four-week waiting period based on their concern for UI solvency rather than for any programmatic reason. Thereafter, waiting weeks declined as it became clear that they were not needed to keep state trust fund accounts solvent. In the early 1980s, however, cost saving reductions in the UI program mandated by federal law included a requirement of at least one noncompensated waiting week. The penalty imposed in federal law for state noncompliance is that there is no Federal share reimbursement to states for the first week of EB for all EB recipients.[5] All but seven states (CT, GA, IA, MD, MI, NJ, WY) continue to impose a one-week waiting week for the regular UI program.

### Option

Today, other than cost savings to state trust funds, there is no programmatic reason for maintaining waiting weeks. The Wyden-Bennet proposal would have required all states to eliminate waiting weeks.

### Recommendation

Waiting weeks should be eliminated in all states. They primarily have been cost reduction efforts, delaying and reducing adequate benefits. Waiting weeks should not be needed as a cost cutting effort in an adequately funded state UI program.

## PENSION OFFSET

### Issue

Pension offset provisions were first enacted in the 1976 UI amendments. The offsets were enacted out of concern that older workers were collecting UI benefits after retiring and permanently leaving the labor force. The provisions were to prevent "double dipping," such that fully retired workers would collect their pensions at the same time as collecting UI benefits (Hamermesh 1980). In their final reports, both the NCUC (1980) and the ACUC (1996) recommended repealing these provisions.

### Recommendation

A federal requirement that states repeal any pension offset, including those for Social Security benefits, is even more compelling today given the substantial increase in the labor force participation rate of workers over 55 since the mid-1990s. With virtually no defined benefit pension plans in place in the United States, as well as low Social Security benefits and low savings rates, many older workers cannot survive on Social Security alone and will have to search for new career or bridge jobs after they become unemployed. It makes little sense to deprive older workers of UI benefits when they remain attached to the labor force.

## PARTIAL EARNINGS DISREGARD

### Issue

While the goals of the UI program itself are both to provide temporary, partial income support to workers and to be an automatic stabilizer to the U.S. economy, it is equally important to the UI program to help UI recipients return to work. One way to encourage the return to work is to provide incentives for individuals to return to work part-time while they search for work that will provide them with greater income.[6]

**Options**

1) One incentive to return to work is to disregard a portion of the individual's part-time earnings, so that the individual can collect the full amount of his/her weekly UI benefits while also working part-time. Earnings disregards are set by states in three ways: as a dollar amount, a percentage of the individual's weekly benefit amount (20–60 percent), or a fraction of their wage (one-fourth to one-third of wages). Setting the disregard as a percentage of the average weekly benefit amount (or of prior wages) prevents the development of low dollar disregards that can discourage the return to work. The higher the earnings disregard, the greater the incentive to return to work and to seek more hours of work.

2) West et al. (2016) recommend a federal requirement setting the earnings disregard at 50 percent or greater of the average weekly benefit amount. In this way, allowing claimants to disregard a higher percentage of their part-time earnings, the UI program encourages work and allows claimants to be rewarded for searching for work opportunities.

3) Bivens et al. (2021) would allow part-time workers to keep up to 110 percent of their pre-layoff average weekly wage from combined UI benefits and earnings from part-time work. In May 2021, the Biden administration announced that USDOL would be encouraging states to raise the income threshold on partial earnings so that workers can both work and receive a higher percentage of their regular UI benefits (White House 2021).

In addition, studies have shown that an additional incentive to work more is to not have a fixed maximum disregard after which earnings are taxed dollar for dollar. Greater work effort can be encouraged by taxing further earnings at less than 100 percent.

## Recommendation

A partial earnings disregard should be set nationally as a percent of the recipient's weekly benefit amount, perhaps at 50 percent. Earning disregards encourage UI recipients to return to work, even if they can only find part-time work.

## NONMONETARY ELIGIBILITY

### Issue

There are a wide range of nonmonetary issues, divided into those relating to job separation and nonseparation. Many of them are not controversial and are basic to the operation of the UI program as a social insurance program. Others present potential reform issues that have been implemented in some states.

What most of the potential reform issues have in common is that they reflect a perceived need to adjust eligibility to reflect the many changes in the U.S. economy and labor force that have occurred over time. These reforms tend to be related to issues such as the large-scale entry of women into the labor force, the continued employment of older workers beyond age 65, the increase in part-time work, the widespread existence of multi-earner households, worker and household mobility, transportation issues related to work in geographically large labor markets, and the need for many workers to provide child, elder, and sick care.

Some states have chosen to accommodate aspects of the changed workforce. Others have not. When these changes have been accommodated by the UI program, it has been with the understanding that many of these separation and nonseparation issues are beyond the control of workers, and that accommodation can help to keep workers attached to the labor force, improve long-term labor market outcomes, or encourage the return to work. For example, dual-earner couples moving to new jobs can increase employment rates and earnings of both partners (Venator 2021) by allowing the "following spouse" or partner to collect UI while looking for new work after their relocation, while the transition of older workers from full-time career jobs to part-time "bridge" jobs can keep these workers productively in the labor force (Wandner et al. 2015).

Disputes regarding the entitlement to benefits when an employee separates from a job can be divided into 1) voluntarily leaving work, and 2) discharge for misconduct connected with work. For the most part, misconduct issues have not been of reform concern, because it is generally accepted that UI is paid to workers unemployed through no fault of their own. On the other hand, the scope of eligibility for voluntarily leaving a job has been expanding in state UI programs and has been proposed as a subject of federal reform. Some of the separation issues that are presently taken into consideration by states or considered for further UI reform include voluntarily leaving a job for compelling reasons such as

- domestic violence
- sexual harassment
- domestic obligations to care for the illness or disability of a family member
- relocation of an individual's workplace or that of the individual's spouse
- loss of child care
- unusual risk to health or safety
- irregular work schedules or unpredictable pay
- transportation issues

Nonseparation issues are divided into whether the recipient is able, available, and actively seeking work and whether the recipient has refused suitable work. Some of those key issues are

- lack of availability because of illness or disability
- search for only part-time employment
- refusal of work for person/family reasons
- lack of availability while in training
- refusal of referrals to job openings or refusals of suitable work
- work search requirement

The able-to-work and available-for-work requirements are designed to demonstrate that the claimant is currently attached to the labor force. And, federal and state laws/rules explicitly state that claimants must be available for suitable work for any given week.[7] As a policy matter, USDOL has long held that an active search is a necessary component of availability, and that states should include it in their laws, though there is no specific number of federal work search contacts required for the regular UI program.[8] Traditionally, states have required that claimants who are permanently separated from employment should be active candidates for jobs as a condition for receiving benefits. The test of availability, however, is tempered by taking economic conditions into consideration, for example, business conditions and the availability of jobs in the local area. Most states require claimants who are job-ready and permanently separated from employment to engage in two or more work search activities or job contacts each week,[9] unless the requirement is waived. In addition, state agencies are required to give claimants necessary and appropriate assistance in finding suitable employment by providing job finding, placement, and other employment services.[10]

During the last two decades, USDOL has instituted the Worker Profiling and Reemployment Services and Reemployment Service and Eligibility Assessment programs, which have been shown to effectively assist claimants in obtaining suitable employment and reduce UI benefit durations through proactive job-finding and placement services. Unfortunately, these programs are underfunded, and sufficient funding likely is dependent upon an increase in revenues from the FUTA Employment Security Administration Account, requiring an increase in the federal taxable wage base. According to West et al. (2016) and Balducchi and O'Leary (2018), the effectiveness of these programs underscores why adequate funding of the Wagner-Peyser Act Employment Service is vital. The program aids claimants, particularly unemployed low-wage workers, in their job search activities, including providing staff-assisted interviewing, testing, counseling and referral to suitable job openings.

## Options

Many individual state UI laws reflect the reality of the changing labor force by taking the above issues into consideration and encouraging a more flexible approach to UI eligibility. Policymakers, thus, have recommended expanding eligibility with respect to many or all those bases. Optional reforms include the following:

1) USDOL could encourage expansion of the reasons for voluntary quits for compelling reasons in all states.

2) Congress could require the states to implement many of the compelling need voluntary quit eligibility provisions discussed above.

3) Congress could offer states financial incentives to enact improved eligibility provisions, similar to the incentives offered by the UI Modernization provision of the ARRA (von Wachter 2020).

4) Bivens et al. (2021) would extend eligibility to separating employees who leave work for several reasons beyond compelling personal or family reasons including: seasonal, temporary, and home health care workers whose work ends; workers participating in strikes or other "concerted activities"; and workers whose rights are violated in the workplace or whose safety is threatened. They also would consider extending eligibility to undocumented workers.

5) The Wyden-Bennet proposal would have addressed a range of these issues with federal requirements. It would have: 1) prohibited states from denying workers benefits because they worked part-time or were seeking part-time work; 2) prohibited states from denying benefits to workers who quit for compelling personal reasons including domestic violence, illness or disability of a family member, sexual harassment, relocation of the worker's workplace or the worker's spouse's workplace, loss of child care, unusual risk to health or safety, irregular hours, or unpredictable pay; and 3) expanded eligibility to certain student workers.

## Recommendation

State UI programs should be required to 1) significantly expand eligibility for workers separated for compelling personal reasons, 2) permit eligibility for workers previously working part-time work and seeking part-time work. These requirements would significantly improve access to UI benefits, especially for women and older workers.

## Notes

1. Recently, Wisconsin has instituted an ROE similar to Canada's. "Beginning Nov. 2, 2020, all employers covered by Wisconsin's Unemployment Insurance (UI) law must provide employees with written notice regarding the availability of UI benefits upon separation from employment. The notice must include specific information summarized below" (Godfrey & Kahn 2020).
2. The WARN Act requires employers with 100 or more full-time employees (not counting workers who have fewer than six months on the job) to provide at least 60 calendar days advance written notice of a worksite closing affecting 50 or more employees, or a mass layoff affecting at least 50 employees. A WARN Act notice must be given when there is an employment loss, and a temporary layoff or furlough that lasts longer than six months is considered an employment loss.
3. The bill also calls for the Maryland Department of Labor to "examine and consider any report or recommendations made by the National Academy of Social Insurance Unemployment Insurance Task Force of 2021."
4. Having a statutory maximum weekly benefit amount at or near two-thirds of the state average weekly wage does not mean that the actual maximum is at that level. Several states, like Louisiana with a maximum of around $200 have an override based on their state trust fund reserves, and their stringent financing systems frequently constrain the level of their reserves.
5. Section 204 of the Extended Unemployment Compensation Act provides that a state shall not receive reimbursement for the first week of EB if its state UI law does not include a waiting week. However, Section 4105 of the Emergency Unemployment Insurance Stabilization and Access Act of 2020 provides 100 percent funding of the first week of EB in states with no waiting week. This provision was initially in place through December 31, 2020, but it was extended by both the Continued Assistance for Unemployed Workers Act of 2020 and the American Rescue Plan Act of 2021 (which expired on September 6, 2021).
6. Lee et al. (2021) show that it is more efficient to raise the UI disregard than to lower a partial benefit earnings reduction rate. It can be an incentive for part-time work if a state availability for work rule allows part-time work and seeking part-time work.
7. Under the Middle Class Tax Relief and Job Creation Act of 2012 (Public Law 112-96), an individual must be able to work in any given week. Specifically, section 303(a)(12) of the SSA also requires an applicant to actively seek work as a condition of eligibility for benefits.
8. P.L. 96-499 (1980) created a "sustained and systematic" search for work requirement only in the Federal-State extended benefits program (see 20 CFR Part 604, Unemployment Compensation – Eligibility; Final Rule, January 16, 2007).

9. In most states, the job contacts can be made in-person, online, by mail, or by fax.

10. A USDOL-sponsored demonstration project (2004–2005) in Wisconsin, the precursor of the Reemployment Services and Eligibility Assessment program, demonstrated the effectiveness of reemployment services. During the demonstration, UI and ES staff jointly assisted UI claimants, conducted eligibility reviews, and provided extra employment services and staff-assisted referrals to suitable jobs. They also urged claimants to make additional job contacts per week. The great majority of claimants made additional work search contacts beyond the two required per week and returned to work sooner than the control group (Almandsmith, Adams, and Bos 2006).

# 9

# UI Benefit Coverage, Taxation of Benefits, and Extended Benefits

While nearly all wage and salary workers are covered under UI, the COVID-19 pandemic made clear that during a recession as severe as the 2020 pandemic recession, other workers will need financial protection when they become unemployed, even if not as part of the regular UI program. The Pandemic Unemployment Assistance (PUA) program covered gig workers, contract workers, and the self-employed. Under the regular UI program, however, these workers are not covered. Policymakers must decide whether to permanently cover these workers under some social welfare program or to cover them only during periods of extreme economic conditions.

## GIG WORKERS/CONTRACTORS

### Issue

UI coverage for gig/contract workers is a highly political issue.[1] Employers have been increasing the number of workers they classify as contract workers, while employee organizations have pushed back. Nonetheless, gig work has increased rapidly rapidly—between 2005 and 2015, employment in independent contracting grew 30 percent (BLS 2017; Katz and Krueger 2017). The politics of the coverage issue first became clear with the promulgation of a regulation during the Trump administration excluding gig workers from the definition of "employees" potentially entitled to UI benefits (USDOL 2022a). The Biden administration then rescinded the rule in May 2021.

States also have become involved in the issue of whether to treat the increasing number of contract and gig workers as employees, and thus are covered by and eligible for UI benefits. A small number of states have sought to deem them covered by the UI program. California,

Washington State, New York, and New Jersey are among the states that have attempted to cover these workers.

Large companies that use the majority of these workers, however, have resisted. In 2017, in response to California enacting legislation covering gig workers, Uber, Lyft, and other gig employers responded by committing $200 million to develop a ballot initiative, Proposition 22, that excluded ride-hail and gig workers from state UI program coverage. The proposition was approved in 2020.

Nevertheless, gig workers and many other Form IRS-1099 workers would be considered employees under the "ABC" test that is already used in some states and is generally considered to be a better measure of employee attachment to the labor force. Under the three-part ABC test, a worker is considered to be an employee, and not an independent contractor, unless the hiring entity satisfies all three of the following conditions:

1)  The worker is free from the day-to-day control and direction of the hiring entity in connection with the performance of the work, both under the contract for the performance of the work and in fact.

2)  The worker performs work that is outside the usual course of the hiring entity's business.

3)  The worker is customarily engaged in an independently established trade, occupation, or business of the same nature as that involved in the work performed.

New Jersey uses the ABC test to determine employment status. In 2019, the New Jersey Department of Labor and Workforce demanded that Uber pay UI and disability insurance back taxes for 2014–2018, the first time a state agency had made such a demand. While Uber continues to insist that its workers are independent contractors, in 2022, the New Jersey agency announced that Uber paid $100 million in back taxes for those five years (Metz 2022). Clearly, the battle over UI coverage for gig workers will continue.

## Options

Many gig and other contract employees are not employees under current state laws, although they would be if the states used the ABC test. While some states will likely continue to press for UI coverage for these workers, the issue may have to be resolved by broader, more comprehensive federal legislation. Some analysts have suggested fully treating gig workers as employees.

1) Krueger and Harris (2015) suggest an intermediate solution. They would create a new class of independent workers who would receive some, but not all, of the protections and benefits of employees. Independent workers would include a broad group of online and "offline" (e.g., taxi drivers) workers, especially those who use intermediaries to identify customers to whom they provide services.

    Like the Kreuger-Harris proposal, in 2021 the British determined that Uber drivers are "workers," an employee status that gives Uber drivers some but not all the benefits of "employees." In response, there have been calls for federal legislation in the U.S. to recognize gig workers as employees. International pressure by other countries on gig companies may put further pressure on the United States to take action to recognize gig workers as employees.

2) Biven et al. (2021) would require the application of the ABC test, which has been adopted in several states, and, according to the authors, is a simpler and more protective legal test for ensuring employee rights as it presumes that a worker providing a service to a business is an employee.

3) The Wyden-Bennet proposal also would have amended Section 3304(a) of the Internal Revenue Code such that all states would be required to apply the ABC test to determine whether workers are employees covered under UI law.

4) The proposed Protecting the Right to Organize Act (H.R. 842 in the 117th Congress) would have made the ABC test universal through its definition of an employee for purposes of federal labor law, although its goal was to better protect workers' rights to organize and collectively bargain.

## Recommendation

Congress should adopt the ABC test to determine whether workers are employees for federal employment purposes, including for UI coverage, because such a requirement would provide a strong legal test for determining employee status. In the meantime, states should legislate or enforce the ABC test as the determination of UI coverage to gradually have gig workers covered by the UI program.

## SELF-EMPLOYED WORKERS

### Issue

Over the history of UI, state programs have failed to find an effective way to cover self-employed workers. Only California provides optional coverage for the self-employed. Its method of coverage is to have the self-employed be "reimbursing employers."[2] This approach, however, provides little real protection to the self-employed as it is essentially only a short-term loan. Although self-employment coverage has been part of California law for many years, it has been little used.

### Options

While the California experience suggests that a reimbursable self-employment program is impractical, the United States could develop a self-financing self-employment UI program, either optional or required, that would pay UI benefits to the self-employed after they make contributions of a requisite dollar amount to the Unemployment Trust Fund.

1) A self-employment UI program could provide coverage to the self-employed if they paid into the system for a requisite period of time, paying a specified amount of taxes. Requiring the self-employed to pay into the system for a significant number of quarters would reduce any adverse selection if participation in the program were optional. The potential benefits paid, however, likely would be relatively low in both amount and duration because of the relatively short history of low contributions.

For example, Canada has a small, voluntary self-employment UI program. In 2020, to be eligible, self-employed workers had to have earned at least $7,279 in the prior year (2019) and paid UI taxes on those earnings at the same rate as employers of salaried employees for at least one year. The self-employment UI benefit, however, was lower than that for wage and salary workers. In 2020, there were only about 30,000 people registered in the self-employment program. Nonetheless, it is an attempt, albeit weak, at a social insurance program that provides future protection to self-employed workers who enroll in the program (Canada Employment Insurance 2021). The United States could adopt a voluntary system like Canada's. Alternatively, it could create a stronger program that would be a true social insurance program by making participation mandatory, covering all self-employed workers, and requiring all self-employed workers to pay into it.

2) Alternatively, self-employed and other independent workers could participate in a private UI program organized by an intermediary (von Wachter 2020).

3) Conceptually, Whittaker (2021) suggests the following options for financing a program for the self-employed (and contract) workers:

- tax self-employed workers as if they were employers (analogous to their treatment under Social Security)

- set the tax rate on self-employed workers as if they were reimbursable employers by requiring self-employed workers to repay benefits after periods of unemployment

- federal-state-worker cost share

- tax advantage individual unemployment accounts

Based on the experience in California, it seems unlikely that a voluntary repayment/reimbursable approach would work for most self-employed workers. The tax-advantaged individual unemployment account would be more of a private savings account than a social insurance program, paying benefit amounts and durations that would make the program self-financing but not necessarily equal to the prior contribution. Thus, to create a program that is more like social insurance, the choice for financing a self-employment program appears to be a flat-rate tax (as in Canada) or an experience-rated finance program that looks like a modified UI program.

## Recommendation

Congress should enact a nationwide, voluntary self-employment program like the Canadian program. It would be funded by contributions from the self-employed and would be available only to self-employed workers who have made sufficient contributions to qualify for benefits when they become unemployed. Because this program is unproven in the United States, if enacted, it should be evaluated within five years, and a report should be submitted to Congress for possible changes. While coverage for all self-employed workers is desirable, it's hard to enact and implement a mandatory program, so it would be worthwhile to devise a feasible voluntary program.

## NEW ENTRANTS AND REENTRANTS TO THE LABOR FORCE

### Issue

Unemployed individuals who have not recently worked in covered UI unemployment are not eligible to receive UI benefits. Nonetheless, there has been a public policy effort to devise a new program to try to provide some of these workers with UI (social insurance) or unemployment assistance outside of the UI program. There are limitations that prevent most of these workers from receiving UI as a social insurance program. There may be ways to revise the UI program to allow some of these workers to receive UI. Others could only receive benefits from a new social assistance program that is not part of UI.

New entrants are workers who enter the labor force but have not previously worked in covered employment. As such, they have no base period earnings in a recent four-quarter period. They cannot be eligible for UI benefits under a social insurance framework.

Reentrants are workers returning to the workforce who have had previous covered employment, but even if they had worked in covered employment before, their prior employment may not have been during either the state UI base period or alternative base period.

Both types of workers are in the labor force, but they either have not yet found employment or have worked for such a short time during their base period—even if that work was in covered employment—that they would not be eligible for benefits under state UI laws. Under the current rules of the UI program, neither new entrants nor most reentrants would be eligible for UI benefits. Some reentrants, however, would become eligible for benefits if states adopted a new extended base period that includes prior wages reaching back to earlier base periods.

## Option

New entrants have not worked in covered employment and cannot receive UI as part of a social insurance program. They could only become eligible for a social assistance program such as the proposed Jobseeker's Allowance.

Some reentrants, however, could receive UI benefits if Congress or the states enacted a time-extended base period that considered wages older than the regular UI base period of the first 4 of the last 5 completed calendar quarters. Thus, workers with older experience working in covered employment might be eligible for UI if an extended base period could go back more than 5 or perhaps 8 or 10 quarters. Because states collect and store quarterly wage records, they could be required to store records for at least 8 or 10 quarters, and they could look back more than the current 5 quarters if unemployed workers did not qualify for UI benefits using first 4 of the 5 five calendar quarters of wage records.

## Recommendation

Congress should enact an extended base period to encourage workers who move in and out of the labor force, especially women, to return to the labor force and to assist them during their period of job search.

## PREPARATION FOR ANOTHER EMERGENCY EXPANSION IN COVERAGE: CREATING A SEARCHABLE DATA SYSTEM

Under the PUA program, contract workers were able to receive PUA benefits, but the UI state agencies had difficulty verifying the earnings of applicants to this program. In the event of another program like PUA, the UI program should be better prepared to pay benefits rapidly and more accurately.

Thus, if nonwage and salary workers, such as contract workers who receive the IRS Form 1099, do not otherwise become covered by the UI program, state UI agencies could prepare for a possible future temporary extension of coverage to these workers by obtaining access to their earnings data. The reason to make these preparations is to make timely, accurate payments and to avoid future fraud or erroneous payments. The PUA program was rife with integrity problems, sometimes because of the applicants' unfamiliarity with program requirements, resulting in non-fraud errors and overpayments, especially for unemployed workers who were not previously covered by the UI program. Frequently, however, PUA was subject to widespread fraud, particularly by criminal enterprise groups that obtained access to stolen identification information through large-scale hacking. One way to limit such fraud in the future would be to provide state UI programs with access to the latest wages of uncovered workers.

Data from SSA or IRS could be used to create a searchable database that only the state UI staff could search. It could work like the UI Interstate Connection Network (ICON), which allows states' UI agencies to request applicants' interstate wages. To verify that they are making a legitimate claim, applicants would be required to provide earnings information that legitimate applicants would have but that individuals making fraudulent claims likely would not.

Whether there are policy initiatives for recessionary coverage of the uncovered, as in the PUA program, or a permanent program such as Jobseeker's Allowance that covers gig, contractors, and self-employed workers, a searchable data system that would collect earnings data of these workers would be essential if a benefit assistance program were going to be administered with minimal amounts of fraud. For such programs, the eligibility of nonwage and salary workers could be determined on a calendar year basis using their 1099 or tax data. As discussed above, another approach that could reduce fraudulent UI claims would be for the United States to require that all employers issue Canadian-like records of employment for all separating employees, whether W-2 wage and salary employees or IRS Form 1099 contractors.

## JOBSEEKER'S ALLOWANCE

### Issue

A Jobseeker's Allowance has been proposed since 2016. Such allowances would vastly increase the coverage of the UI program to include workers who are not currently covered when they become unemployed. Newly covered workers would include the self-employed and contract workers. It also would include workers who have little or no recent employment. As such, the program would not be a social *insurance* program. Rather, it would have to be an unemployment *assistance* program funded by federal general revenue with benefits paid out by state UI programs. Implementing a Jobseeker's Allowance program, however, could provide a further impetus for states averse to paying UI benefits to further reduce their own state UI program.

### Options

There have been several recent proposals for creating a Jobseeker's Allowance program, including federal legislation.

1) West et al. (2016) advocate for Jobseeker's Allowance as a method to permanently expand UI coverage beyond experienced wage and salary workers who are normally the only workers covered by the UI program. This expanded coverage would be offered to a variety of unemployed workers who otherwise would not be covered under even the most expansive UI eligibility requirements. These workers would include

   • workers entering the labor force for the first time (new entrants)

- reentrants to the labor force who are searching for work but whose previous work history may be prior to the UI base period that usually reaches back no more than the last year to year and a half
- contract and self-employed workers who have not worked in UI-covered employment
- intermittent workers and UI exhaustees

These authors urge a means-tested unemployment assistance benefit in the fixed amount of $170 (indexed), available for 13 weeks but for longer during periods of high unemployment. Both benefits and program administrative costs would be funded from appropriated federal general revenue. Participants would be required to engage in employment services, with options for career training and subsidized employment. The estimated annual cost of the program in 2016 was $18.9 billion per year (West et al. 2016).

2) The Century Foundation (2020) recommends a similar Jobseeker's Allowance program. They suggest the enactment of a program that would provide basic benefits and employment services to those who are looking for work but are not eligible for UI benefits. The allowance, financed through federal appropriations, would be equal to one-half of the regular UI benefit and would be available to gig workers and new entrants not covered by the regular UI program.

3) Bivens et al. (2021) also support a broad Jobseeker's Allowance program that would support job seekers newly entering or reentering the labor force but with a fixed allowance of $200 per week or 20 percent of the state's average weekly wage.

4) The Wyden-Bennet proposal also advocates a Jobseeker's Allowance. Under their proposal, the program would provide a federal weekly benefit to unemployed workers who are seeking work but are not covered by UI or are eligible for only a small UI payment. This would include coverage for workers newly entering the labor force and self-employed workers.

Under their proposal, the allowances would be 100 percent federally financed. To be eligible, workers would have to

- be unemployed or partially unemployed
- have no right to regular unemployment compensation or be eligible for unemployment compensation in an amount less than the amount of the Jobseeker's Allowance
- be able to work, be available to work, and be actively seeking work
- be at least 19 years of age (or at least 18 in the case of foster youth) or have earned a high school diploma or the equivalent
- have an adjusted gross income less than the Social Security taxable wage base

The amount of a Jobseeker's Allowance under the Wyden-Bennet plan would be $250 per week (indexed annually for inflation), minus any weekly unemployment benefit for which the individual is eligible. For individuals seeking work for less than 20 hours per week, the maximum amount of the weekly allowance would be reduced by 50 percent. Individuals would be entitled to 26 times the weekly benefit amount (meaning most individuals would qualify for 26 weeks of payments). The number of weeks for which the Jobseeker's Allowance would be available could increase in times of high unemployment, like Extended Benefits. When unemployment is above 7.5 percent, a narrower group of individuals claiming an allowance—only those who have a documented history of self-employment—could claim a supplement to their weekly allowance such that their total allowance would replace roughly 75 percent of their average weekly earned income in the most recently completed tax year (Wyden and Bennet 2021).

**Recommendation**

A Jobseeker's Allowance program should not be considered as part of UI reform. Rather, it should instead be considered on its merits as a new, separate social welfare program. It also has the potential negative effect of providing an incentive to states, especially those with weak UI programs, to further cut their regular UI program with the Jobseeker's

Allowance program taking up the slack. Such a program would be difficult to enact.

## FEDERAL TAXATION OF UI BENEFITS

### Issue

UI benefits have been fully subject to federal income taxation since the enactment of the Tax Reform Act of 1986. The taxation of UI benefits by federal and state governments, however, has had the effect of reducing the recipient's benefits at a time of low wage replacement rates (Whittaker 2015). Congress recently excluded a portion of UI benefits from taxation as part of the American Rescue Act of 2021. For tax year 2020, the first $10,200 of UI benefits was excluded for taxpayers with incomes less than $150,000. It has been argued that income from leisure (i.e., unemployment) should not be taxed at a lower rate than from work (Feldstein 1978), but the concept of unemployment as leisure has less cogency for permanently dislocated workers, especially in an era of low and declining UI wage replacement rates.

During the COVID-19 pandemic, the adverse effect of taxation became apparent when the number of UI claimants increased enormously, many of whom had never collected UI benefits before. Not understanding that UI benefits are taxable, many UI claimants did not voluntarily have the state UI programs withhold taxes on their benefits. Near the end of 2020, many UI claimants suddenly faced a large tax liability that had to be paid to the IRS.

As the tax year 2020 tax preparation season began, the media explained to the public that a $1,200 stimulus check was not taxable but one's UI benefits were (Carrns 2021). The news about the taxation of UI benefits for tax year 2020 was not received well. The result was that Congress enacted a one-time exclusion from the taxation of some benefits for some workers. Some journalists took a closer look at the history of the taxation of UI benefits, and at least one recommended the permanent end to the taxation of UI benefits (Singletary 2021).

## Options

There are several potential approaches to taxing UI benefits.

1) The Advisory Council on Unemployment Compensation (1996) recommended ending the taxation of UI benefits. Congress could follow the ACUC's recommendation and stop taxing benefits altogether. The effect would raise the net value of the UI benefits that claimants receive.

2) Since the federal taxation of benefits is effectively a reduction in net benefits, the taxation could be retained, but recipients could receive an offsetting increase in weekly benefits.

3) Bivens et al. (2021) recommend eliminating the tax on benefits for low-wage workers but retaining it for high-wage workers.

From a policy perspective, the political advantage of eliminating the federal tax on benefits is that it would invisibly reduce general revenues without raising the ire of employers by directly raising their UI tax costs. By contrast, raising benefits for UI recipients would require raising UI taxes across the United States and would be resisted by employers.

## Recommendation

UI benefits should not be subject to federal taxation. Taxation of UI benefits was introduced for the first time in the 1980s as a method of reducing net UI benefits that were already inadequate at that time. To make UI benefits more adequate, UI benefits should not be subject to federal taxation.

## EXTENDED BENEFITS AND TEMPORARY EMERGENCY BENEFITS

## Issue

Extending UI benefits during recessions has been a key component of U.S. countercyclical macroeconomic policy since 1958, but it has not worked well. Nonetheless, after much research, there is broad agreement about the general structure of a new and improved UI recessionary policy. The discussion below fleshes out the need for reform and options for implementing it. Chapter 6 considers the behavioral effects of extending UI benefit durations.

Beginning with the 1958 recession, Congress recognized that 26 weeks of UI benefits were inadequate when the unemployment rate was high. Accordingly, Congress enacted a temporary emergency unemployment compensation program, and it has continued to do so in every recession since then.

Believing that temporary emergency programs should be eliminated and replaced by a program that is more responsive to increases and decreases in unemployment rates, Congress enacted the permanent Extended Benefits (EB) program in 1970, effective January 1, 1972. From the beginning, EB did not work effectively in recessions with respect to either timeliness or sufficiency. It has been a triggered program that originally triggered on and off based on measures of the insured unemployment rate (IUR)—that is, the number of insured unemployed workers divided by the number of workers in covered employment—with both state and national triggers, although the latter was eliminated in the 1980s. The IUR triggers have been shown to be nonresponsive to changes in overall unemployment, and because there has been a downward trend in UI recipiency, the IUR has been trending downward for decades, making it an even worse EB triggering mechanism.

To address the nonresponsive IUR trigger, Congress offered the states an optional, more responsive triggering mechanism that uses the BLS total unemployment rates (TURs). Adopting the TUR trigger, however, increases the UI costs to the states because they have to pay half of the costs of the extended benefits that are paid after the first 26 weeks of regular UI benefits. Instead, most states have chosen not to enact the optional trigger and rather wait for Congress to enact temporary legislation in which the federal government pays 100 percent of the benefits beyond week 26. As a result, today only about one-third of the states have adopted the TUR trigger. Because of its low adoption rate, in recent recessionary extensions of UI benefits, Congress has federalized EB benefits and paid for them out of federal general revenue.

During recent recessions, the United States has had three duration levels: the regular UI program, EB, and a temporary emergency compensation program. The system has not worked well over time, and it still does not work well. With most states not adopting TUR triggers, when recessions occur, many states do not pay extended benefits until Congress federalizes the EB program. While Congress eventually enacts a temporary emergency benefit program, enactment often is considerably delayed such that many workers exhaust their UI benefits, remain unemployed, and do not receive additional benefits until Congress acts. Further, when a temporary emergency program is finally enacted, it tends to expire after a short period. Congress must enact further extensions, and gaps frequently occur between extensions. This means that UI beneficiaries have gaps in their receipt of benefits while state UI agencies must deal with the administrative burden of turning the program on and off multiple times.

## Options

Because of dissatisfaction with the current program, analysts have generally agreed that the EB program needs to be reformed. Such reforms might include

- restoring a national trigger
- adopting the more responsive TUR trigger
- phased increases in EB benefits, with multiple phases
- triggering on benefit phases using TUR rates from 5 to 10 percent
- additional weeks of EB benefits as unemployment increases, generally in 13-week increments
- federal funding of all UI benefits after week 26

Table 9.1 shows six recent proposals. They tend to be similar in their goals, but they use different numbers of phased increases, different levels/ranges of weeks of benefits paid, and different trigger rates to trigger each phase.

Thus, there is agreement among many analysts that there should be an EB program with a responsive TUR trigger that pays increasing durations of benefits up to at least 52 weeks. There also is general agreement that a national trigger should be restored such that when a recession is nationwide, EB benefits also should be paid throughout the United States.

**Table 9.1  Extended Benefits Reform Proposals**

| Proposer | Number of phased increases | Range of extended benefits reform durations (weeks) | Range of rates (%) | National trigger |
|---|---|---|---|---|
| Wyden-Bennet | 4 | 13–52 | 5.5–8.5 | Yes |
| Obama | 4 | 13–52 | 6.5–9.5 | Yes |
| West et al. | 4 | 13–52 | 6.5–9.5 | Yes |
| Dube | 6 | 8–72 | 5–10 | Yes |
| Bivens et al. | 6 | 3–68 | 5–10 | Yes |
| O'Leary and Wandner | 5 | 7–52 | 6.5–10 | Yes |

SOURCE: Wyden-Bennet UI reform discussion draft bill (April 2021); President Obama, 2017 budget in Simonetta (2018); West et al. (2016); Dube (2021); Bivens et al. (2021); O'Leary and Wandner (2018).

While strengthening the permanent EB program with one of these proposals, Congress could still later intervene during an individual recession and provide new or modified benefits. In addition, Congress would remain able to create new temporary emergency programs whenever it sees fit. The advantage of the above EB proposals is that they would provide timely and proportionate benefits, depending on the nature and depth of each recession.

## Recommendation

Congress should enact a tiered EB program with increasing durations as unemployment rates rise. It should be similar in design to one of the recent proposals presented above after simulating the likely outcome of each proposal. A tiered program is needed largely because recessions often occur rapidly, and it is necessary to adjust the number of additional weeks of benefits upward as recessions become more severe.

# Notes

1. Gig workers enter into formal agreements with on-demand companies to provide services to the company's clients. They are generally treated as a subset of contract workers who receive federal 1099s at the end of the year rather than W-2s.
2. Nonprofit and state and local government agencies were brought under UI coverage in 1972 with the option of being either contributing or reimbursing employers. As contributing employers, they face the same experience-rated tax rates as other employers in the state. As reimbursing employers, they must repay benefit charges dollar-for-dollar in the calendar quarter following the benefit charges.

# 10
# Improving Financing

## Options and Recommendations

UI taxes have not been sufficient to fund benefits for at least five decades. The funding shortfall is a result of federal and state policy that stems from weak federal and state law and policy. The problem can be seen from the discussion of Figures 3.1, 3.2, and 3.3.

From a public policy perspective, UI taxes must be sufficient to pay for UI benefits. While it is hard to define "sufficiency" because UI finance is a dynamic process over many business cycles, Vroman et al. (2018, p. 212) provide a definition: "While there is no single universally accepted definition of successful funding, we have taken it to mean maintenance of a healthy trust fund balance and avoidance of prolonged and large-scale indebtedness to the U.S. Treasury following a recession." Unfortunately, very few states engage in successful funding of adequate benefits largely because of the prevalence of the low taxable wage bases and low tax rates that hamper the accumulation of adequate reserves during good times to allow sufficient funds to pay benefits in bad times (forward funding). On the other hand, funding is not "successful" from a policy perspective if it does not fund a reasonable UI program. Some states have reduced benefits enough through some combination of restrictive access, low maximum benefit amounts, and shortened durations that they can "successfully fund" only very low levels of benefits.

Benefit financing issues include

- taxable wage bases: level and indexing
- tax rates
- experience rating
- forward funding
- employee contributions
- reinsurance

Each is addressed in turn.

## TAXABLE WAGE BASE: LEVEL AND INDEXING

### Issue

The taxable wage base is the level of annual earnings on which UI taxes are levied. Initially, the UI taxable wage base was total wages. In 1939, it was reduced to $3,000. Since then, the federal UI taxable wage base has been increased only three times in the history of the UI program. It has remained at $7,000 since 1983. The federal taxable wage base determines the ability of the federal UI reserve accounts to fund the federal portion of UI benefits and UI and benefit administration. It also affects state UI financing by setting a floor on the state taxable wage base. Thus, if UI benefits and UI and ES administrative funding are to be made adequate, UI financing reform must start by significantly increasing the federal taxable wage base and then increase it each year, with annual increases calculated in a manner like the annual increments in the Social Security annual taxable wage base. While UI is a federal-state program and Social Security is federally funded, public finance principles require both programs to have tax rates and a taxable wage base adequate to fund the benefits paid out. In addition, Congress originally set the taxable wage base for both programs at the same level. It then has responsibly increased the Social Security taxable wage base annually but failed to do so for the UI program for the past four decades.

The UI tax is intended to fully fund the payment of UI benefits. Vroman (2016) and Lachowska, Vroman, and Woodbury (2020) find that state UI benefits are more likely to be fully funded if states have an indexed taxable wage base.

The lesson learned from comparing the UI program with Social Security is that a social insurance program cannot pay benefits that keep pace with the cost of living unless revenue also increases frequently over time (see discussion in Chapter 5). While Social Security payments and revenues have not remained in balance without occasional legislative revisions—and such a revision is needed now—the Social Security program has performed vastly better than the UI program.

At present, few states have an indexed taxable wage base as high as any of the options presented below, although nearly half the states index their bases annually.

As a new federal requirement, the federal and state taxable wage bases do not have to be the same. One option is to establish two different indexed tax bases so that the state taxable wage base would yield revenues sufficient to pay for benefits under a reformed state UI system, while the Federal Unemployment Tax Account (FUTA) taxable wage base would yield revenues sufficient to pay the federal cost of both extended benefits and UI and ES administration.

Most analysts recommend a partial or total offsetting of any increase in the federal taxable wage base by adjusting the federal tax rate to raise sufficient federal funding without having revenues become excessive. Full offsetting might be possible without major UI reform, but if major UI reform increases the administrative role of the UI program and increased reemployment services and the UI work test responsibilities of the ES, the result would be sharply increased benefit costs, and responsible financing would only partially offset the tax base increase.

## Options

An increase in the taxable wage base and indexing could be accomplished either, in part, through USDOL encouraging states to raise their taxable wage bases, or, more realistically, by setting a federal standard both for the taxable base and indexing the base. Most recent proposals call for both a higher federal taxable wage base and indexing, such that the taxable wage base increases each year, adjusted by a factor such as the increase in wages. Increasing the federal taxable wage base also affects the range of state UI rates that states must have.

1) West et al. (2016) call for raising the taxable wage base in six annual increments to 50 percent of the Social Security wage base.

2) O'Leary and Wandner (2018) recommend a base of 33.33 percent of the Social Security wage base, although they offer an alternative measure of 26 times the national average weekly wage in covered employment.

3) Bivens et al. (2021) support a taxable wage base of 100 percent of the Social Security taxable wage base.

4) The Obama administration FY 2017 budget proposal would have raised the taxable wage base to $40,000 in 2018 and then indexed each year after that (Simonetta 2018).

5) The Wyden-Bennet proposal did not spell out its FUTA taxable wage base provisions, but it also indicated that the taxable wage base would increase and be indexed for inflation, while the FUTA tax rate would decline to keep the federal tax take unchanged.

6) In 1980, the NCUC was concerned about the decline of the federal taxable wage base as a percent of the U.S. average annual wage in UI covered employment. Despite a significant number of objections by a minority of members, the NCUC proposed increasing the taxable wage base as a percentage of the average annual wage in four steps between 1984 and 1990 to 50, 55, 60, and 65 percent. That increase would have resulted in a 1990 taxable wage base of $16,100. Today, 65 percent of the U.S. average annual wage would yield a taxable wage base of approximately $40,000.

**Recommendation**

The taxable wage base should be indexed such that it increases each year. Indexing could be accomplished by having the taxable wage base set at 50 percent or more of the Social Security taxable wage base. Alternatively, the taxable wage base could be indexed to wage growth in covered employment. The higher wage base should be phased in over a period of approximately five years. To finance an adequate UI benefit program, tax rates need to be higher than they are today and must keep up with benefit amounts that also should be adjusted upward each year.

**STATE TAX RATES**

**Issue**

Given their taxable wage bases, the tax rates in many states are inadequate to fund their state programs. Some state UI financing systems appear to be designed to underfund their UI programs with low minimum and maximum rates and an insufficient number of tax rates in each of their tax schedules. For example, see the case studies of Florida and North Carolina in Chapter 4.

## Options

Some of the options for raising sufficient state UI revenues through tax rates in the states include

- requiring a nonzero minimum tax rate
- raising the lowest state maximum tax rate above the current 5.4 percent by raising the federal tax above 6.0 percent
- ending the practice of states overriding their own tax laws and not allowing their UI program to move to a higher tax rate schedule when the state of their trust fund would require it under state law

Below, three options are examined for minimum and maximum tax rates and for state legislatures overriding statutory state tax provisions.

### Minimum tax rates

Although many states have low or zero minimum tax rates, higher minimum rates can be critical for paying for UI socialized costs—that is, costs not assigned to individual employers—and improving the solvency of the states' trust fund accounts.

Recent research indicates the need for a higher minimum rate. Thus, in states that experience rate with a benefit-ratio system (benefits charged divided by employer's payroll), most employers are at the minimum rate in most years because of zero benefit charges against them in the preceding three or four years, while a large percentage of employers in reserve ratio states (taxes minus benefits charged divided by payroll) are also at the minimum rate in most years (Vroman et al. 2017). Minimum taxes need to take into consideration that experience rating does not cover all charges assigned to employers. As a result, all employers must pay "solvency" or "socialized" taxes due to ineffective charges (employers consistently paying the maximum tax) and inactive accounts (firms that close without paying the benefit charges to their account).

## Options

1) The NCUC (1980, p. 93) concluded that zero rates are "not appropriate" for the UI program and that every state should have a minimum rate of greater than zero.

2) The Obama administration's FY 2017 Budget proposal would have required all states to have a minimum UI tax of at least 0.175 percent (Simonetta 2018).

3) Jeff Robinson, manager of labor force statistics at the Washington Employment Security Department, partially attributes Washington State's UI financing success to imposing a 0.5 percent "social cost factor" on all employers, as well as having the highest taxable wage base in the country (Robinson 2021). Having more (or all) states adopt such a social cost factor would end zero rates, have all firms pay for socialized costs, and contribute to trust fund solvency. States could be encouraged to enact minimum nonzero rates by USDOL, or Congress could require all states to have some specified nonzero minimum rate.[1]

### Maximum tax rates

Under federal UI law, states must have a tax rate in all their tax schedules that is at least as high as 5.4 percent. For many states, however, that floor has become a ceiling, and states sometimes do not have rates higher than 5.4 percent. That is because if states did not have UI laws, all their employers would have to pay a 6.0 percent tax. Since all states have "voluntarily" adopted a UI law, all employers must pay a 0.6 percent federal tax plus an experience-rated state tax that must be set by the states at between a minimum employer tax of zero and a maximum tax of at least 5.4 percent.

## Options

1) In response to rate problem, West et al. (2016, pp. 32–33) recommend that federal law raise the lowest maximum rate that states must charge from 5.4 percent to 7.0 percent to increase the effectiveness of experience rating.

2) Congress could mandate some other rate that is higher than 5.4 percent. States, of course, can raise their maximum tax rates above 5.4 percent on their own initiative. Thus, an alternative to a federal requirement would be to have USDOL encourage states to impose higher maximum rates, but that is likely to be less effective.

## Ending state overrides

As state UI trust fund accounts decline or become negative and the state must borrow from the U.S. Treasury, state UI laws have tax tables with triggers that raise more taxes by moving to a higher tax schedule. Resistance by employers frequently means that the state legislature overrides the statutory tax mechanism and keeps the state at a lower tax schedule than called for by state law. This issue could be resolved by enacting federal legislation that makes it a conformity requirement to have tax schedules meet certain criteria and prohibiting those tax schedules from being overridden.

## Options

Federal law could require that state UI programs have reasonable and responsible tax tables and that, once established and approved by USDOL, cannot be overridden by changing state UI laws.

## Recommendation

State UI tax rates should be made sufficient by having provisions with respect to the issues discussed above to ensure sufficient funding for the program.

1) All employers should be required to pay a minimum, nonzero tax.

2) While the federal tax rate should be adjusted downward to provide sufficient funds for federal UI purposes when combined with a much higher federal tax base, nonetheless, states should be required to set their maximum tax rate at a level considerably higher than the current requirement of a maximum of at least 5.4 percent. Thus, the federal required setting of states'

maximum tax rates should be set independently of the federal tax rate.

3) States should be required to establish reasonable tax tables approved by USDOL, and they should move to higher and lower schedules, depending on state economic conditions, without the ability to override the movement to new schedules.

## EXPERIENCE RATING

### Issue

States finance their UI programs by having employers assigned to tax rates that vary depending on employers' layoff experience. Within each tax schedule, there are multiple rates to which employers are assigned. State laws contain multiple tax schedules that raise varying amounts of revenue, and state UI tax systems move to higher tax schedules as their trust fund reserves decline.

Assigning employer tax rates based on employers' past layoff experience is mandated by federal law. The purpose of experience rating is to allocate costs to employers who engage in layoffs and to incentivize employers to minimize layoffs. Research has found that experience rating helps to stabilize employment when states have tax systems that are responsive to benefit charges, especially in the case of temporary cyclical and seasonal layoffs (Levine 1997; Woodbury 2014). For example, many firms that hire workers seasonally and lay them off at the end of the season are encouraged by experience rating to revise their human resources policy to try to limit seasonal hires and, therefore, to control their UI costs. There are other factors that determine the effectiveness of experience rating of benefit financing beyond having an appropriate range of state tax rates and the effectiveness of charging UI benefits to individual employers. Lachowska, Vroman, and Woodbury (2020) find that having an indexed taxable wage base is important, since states with flexible wage bases have approximately twice the reserves of states that do not. Vroman (2016) finds that, to have their systems in balance, indexing the taxable wage base is needed in states that also index their maximum benefits. Thus, while having high indexed taxable wage bases leads to a less regressive method of taxation, indexing alone helps to maintain the solvency of state trust fund accounts.

There are two main experience rating approaches: reserve ratio and benefit ratio systems. Reserve ratio systems measure reserves (cumulative contributions minus cumulative benefits) divided by the average taxable payroll over the history of the firm. Benefit ratio systems measure benefit charges over the previous three-year period divided by taxable payroll over the same period. Because it only looks at a firm's more recent history, the benefit ratio system has been found to be more responsive in helping depleted trust funds recover quickly after a recession (Lachowska, Vroman, and Woodbury 2020). The benefit ratio system could be made less disruptive to state UI financing after a recession if the ratio were based on four or five previous years rather than just three. Miller and Pavosevich (2019) find weaknesses in both systems and are concerned that both approaches create an adversarial relationship between employers and employees as employers try to minimize their UI costs.

## Options

It is important to have a range of rates in every tax schedule that finely reflects differences in employers' past layoff experiences. Some states have strayed far from this approach, frequently having few rates. Maintaining only a small number of rates is not real experience rating.

1) O'Leary and Wandner (2018, p. 153) recommend requiring states to have at least 10 rates in every state tax schedule. Some larger number of rates also could be considered. States could either be required or encouraged to adopt such a system.

2) Miller and Pavosevich (2019) recommend abandoning both reserve ratio and benefit ratio systems and replacing them with one of two methods that end the adversarial relationship between employers and employees. These alternative methods would not consider layoff behavior but rather variations in either employment or payrolls, rewarding employers that have the highest growth rates with the lowest taxes.

3) Bivens et al. (2021) would experience rate based on hours worked. States could either be required or encouraged to

develop such experience rating systems. One problem with these alternative rating methods is that they could greatly impact small employers from year to year because, based on these measures, a small change in employment or payrolls could have very large increases or decreases in UI tax rates.

4) While employers should be charged for costs related to the layoffs they conduct, should they be charged for separations beyond their control? Many good-cause separations for personal reasons are beyond the control of an employer. West et al. (2016, pp. 32–33) recommend that non-job-related good-cause separations should not be charged to employers. Non-charging, however, results in socialized costs that must be paid by all employers. That is why there would have to be a "social cost factor" noted above to fund benefits that are noncharged.

5) West et al. (2016) are concerned about the wide differences in experience rating systems among states because some systems are inadequate for providing the program with sufficient funding. They recommend the enactment of a federal standard that would harmonize experience rating provisions across the states.

6) Vroman et al. (2017) examined alternative methods of experience rating and reported extreme tax rate volatility for small employers.

7) While no other industrial country has experience rating by firm, some countries vary contribution rates by industry. Such an approach would tend to allocate UI costs to individual employers by using the broader measure of UI costs of their industry. Such industry experience rating would be far simpler to administer than the U.S. system, which currently assigns new individual tax rates to each employer every year, and it would reduce the confrontational relationship between employers and their former employees.

**Recommendation**

The current experience rating system needs to change. It does not work well, and it creates an adversarial relationship between employees and employers because more benefit payments to former employees result in higher tax rates for the employer. A comprehensive study should be conducted that analyzes and compares the proposals considered here to help design an alternative system.

## FORWARD FUNDING

### Issue

The UI program is intended to be forward funded, to collect taxes from firms when they can most afford to pay them, and to minimize UI tax contributions during and immediately after recessions, when firms can least afford them. A forward-funded system would accumulate reserves in each state UI account in the U.S. Treasury's Unemployment Trust Fund such that the accounts generally would be sufficient to allow the states to pay benefits through each normal recession without having to raise taxes quickly at the start of the recession's recovery.

To encourage forward funding, before the onset of a recession, states are supposed to have reserves sufficient to pay 12 months of benefits, measured as a percentage of their highest past annual cost—a "high-cost multiple" of 1.0.[2] An earlier measure of state trust fund account sufficiency set a goal of a high-cost multiple of 1.5, such that states could withstand an 18-month recession as severe as the highest past recessionary cost they had experienced. Because many states are reactive and do not build up their state trust fund account balances, most states at the onset of recent recessions do not meet the 1.0 target, much less the earlier 1.5 target.

The NCUC (1980, p. 93) supported the concept of forward funding by states such that they "provide adequate reserves and sufficient replenishment capability without neglecting countercyclical considerations."

### Options

To encourage state forward funding, most policy recommendations have consisted of either positive or negative incentives to states to maintain adequate reserves before the onset of a recession.

1) The Obama administration's FY 2017 budget proposal (Simonetta 2018) would have imposed a financial penalty on states for not meeting a minimum standard of solvency.

2) Other analysts also have suggested imposing penalties for having insufficient trust fund balances during expansions (von Wachter 2020; West et al. 2016).

3) The ACUC (1996) recommended that the federal government provide financial incentives to encourage forward funding. They proposed that an interest premium be paid to states for the excess funds that they have in their state trust fund accounts above a measure of past high benefit costs. They also recommended that short-term interest free loans to states with negative balances and preferential interest rates on loans be restricted to states making satisfactory progress toward forward funding. Other analysts also have recommended providing financial incentives to states to create forward-funding tax systems.

### Recommendation

States should be encouraged to forward fund their UI programs by a combination of substantial financial incentives to achieve trust fund adequacy and substantial financial penalties for not doing so. At the same time, states should be encouraged to provide adequate UI benefit programs with respect to program access, benefit levels, and durations.

## EMPLOYEE CONTRIBUTIONS

### Issue

In 1935, a Committee on Economic Security report indicated that states could pay for UI benefits by employer and/or employee contributions. In fact, employee contributions have not played an important role in state UI programs, and today UI benefits are funded almost exclusively by employers. Only three states (Alaska, New Jersey, and Pennsylvania) have employee contributions, while only in Alaska and New Jersey do employees pay a significant percentage of benefits.

What is the effect of employee contributions? The New Jersey agency says that state employees are aware of their contribution to the UI program. They can see what they are paying on their pay stubs right next to their contribution to Social Security. As a result, employees feel a sense of ownership of the program. The New Jersey agency believes that a sense of ownership encourages an expansive UI program and is one of the reasons why New Jersey has the highest recipiency rate in the United States. See the summary of an interview with Commissioner Asaro-Angelo in Chapter 4. Bivens et al. (2021) raise the potential of a phased-in employee tax that would both increase worker awareness of the UI program and create a sense of program ownership by workers.

In most other industrial nations, employee taxes are an important part of UI revenue. In those countries, like in New Jersey, employee contributions give employees a significant voice in the governance of their countries' program through their employee representatives, and their UI programs are generally far more generous than that of the United States.

## Options

1) To increase the use of employee contributions, USDOL could encourage wider state adoption of employee contributions and provide technical assistance about how to implement this new form of UI taxation.

2) Alternatively, employee contributions could be made a federal requirement. Dube (2021) recommends joint funding by employers and employees.

## Recommendation

All states should be required to impose employee contributions set at approximately 50 percent of the employer contribution. Employee contributions would make it easier to raise sufficient funds to finance an adequate UI program. They also would tend to depoliticize the UI program by making employees an equal partner in the making of UI public policy decisions. Politically, however, such a large employee contribution may not be politically feasible.

## ADMINISTRATIVE FINANCE: FUNDING FEDERAL FUNCTIONS

### Issue

While states pay for their regular programs with funds from their state unemployment trust fund accounts, the federal tax is used to pay for three functions and are paid into three separate accounts—the Employment Security Administrative Account, the Extended Unemployment Compensation Account, and the Federal Unemployment Account—that pay for the following services, respectively:

- administration of the UI and ES program, mandated by the Social Security Act and the Wagner-Peyser Act, respectively, and other functions such as funding for labor market information

- extended benefits

- loans to states when they become insolvent

Federal functions are paid for by a flat 0.6 percent tax on all employers on the first $7,000 of their employees' wages. While the 0.6 percent tax may have been sufficient in the past, it is inadequate today, especially for funding UI and ES administration.

The federal tax is essentially a head tax of $42 per worker per year $(0.06 \times \$7,000 = \$42)$. It is highly regressive as a fixed percentage on a very low taxable wage base. Since the federal tax base sets the minimum for state tax bases, most state UI taxable wage bases are low and state benefit financing is often very regressive. Insufficient UI state administrative funding is due both to inadequate annual congressional appropriations and the structural difficulty under the Reed Act of transferring excess federal trust fund monies to the states that could be used for administrative and other purposes (Balducchi and O'Leary 2018).

### Options

1) The regressiveness of the federal UI tax on the first $7,000 of wages and salaries each year could be reduced by increasing the federal taxable wage base and reducing the federal tax rate by a fully offsetting amount, resulting in no increase in tax revenues.

2) Alternatively, if, as part of a reform proposal, the increase in the taxable wage base were not fully offset by a decrease in the federal rate, administrative funding for UI and ES could be increased from the federal tax. Thus, the partial offset (reduction) in the federal rate could accommodate the increase in administrative costs, and the reduction would not fully offset the increase in the taxable wage base.

If a federal administrative capital account were created to pay for improvements in and replacement of state UI hardware and software, a federal tax increase would have to accommodate the creation of such an account.

## Recommendation

Federal UI administrative funding should be substantially increased for 1) ongoing increases in federal, regional, and local UI and ES staffing; 2) funds to pay for an enhanced extended benefits program during recessionary periods; and 3) funds for loans to states. These functions have been severely underfunded, and a reformed UI program cannot operate without substantial increases. An adjusted federal tax rate and increased taxable wage base should be used to pay for these administrative needs. These tax increases should also be used to create a federal administrative capital account.

## REINSURANCE

### Issue

Reinsurance is widely used in supporting the primary insurance markets in housing, life, auto, property, and financial instruments.[3] In a typical reinsurance plan, each member of a group of insurers contributes, through an assigned premium, to a central fund that is used to support the needs of any member that is having an extraordinarily unfavorable experience. Reinsurance relieves all the participant insurers of the necessity to maintain excessively large reserves sufficient to meet an occasional catastrophic event. In essence, the reinsurer aggregates a larger number of participants, which allows the financing (primarily of the riskiest participants) to be broken into small affordable portions.

A reinsurance program could be adopted for the UI program. Individual states would still be the active insurers of individual employees, while the federal reinsurer would become the insurer of a portion of each individual state's UI benefits. The application of reinsurance principles would act as protection for the states against recessionary periods or other periods of high unemployment.

If states were covered by a UI reinsurance plan, each state would not have to maintain as large a reserve balance against the possibility of the worst economic conditions. Reinsurance decreases the possibility of having to borrow large amounts of funds during the worst economic times. Reinsurance also increases the overall underwriting capacity by freeing up the capital of the primary insurers. In the case of the UI program, reinsurance could allow a state to provide more benefits to more claimants.

To obtain reinsurance, states would have to pay an annual premium into a reinsurance fund that is separate from their state UI trust fund reserves in the federal Unemployment Trust Fund. Premiums would vary depending on the likelihood of future state financing crises. If adopted, an issue that would have to be resolved is the extent to which reinsurance would replace the current Unemployment Trust Fund loan fund and repayment system.

From the early 1960s to the early 1980s, there was substantial support for the adoption of reinsurance in many fields, including UI. Proposals were offered as congressional bills during that period. Interest in adopting a new reinsurance program arose, in part, because of the 1973–1975 recession that at the time was the worst in the history of the UI program and resulted in very high levels of state indebtedness.

## Options

1) Proposals during the late 1970s were structured to pay benefits when the state reached a specified level of unemployment (or benefit payments), with the funds coming from the FUTA. Employers could pay for reinsurance as a flat federal UI tax in a newly created Reinsurance Account.

2) More recently, Rob Pavosevich, former chief actuary of the national Office of Unemployment Insurance, offered a plan that—rather than insuring a portion of the UI benefit payments—would have the federal government insure a state's UI trust fund account above a specified amount. That is, if a state used up its entire reserve during a specified period, the federal government would pay all the amount that would otherwise have to be borrowed to pay benefits. The NCUC (1980) reviewed four UI reinsurance plans and recommended the federal enactment of a new reinsurance program.

## Recommendation

Before establishing a reinsurance program for UI, proposals should be subject to a comprehensive study to better understand their implications. A report should be sent to Congress for its consideration.

## Notes

1. Socialized costs accrue mainly from ineffectively charged benefits (employers at maximum tax rates for successive years) and inactive accounts (employers go out of business).
2. The high-cost multiple is a ratio of two ratios. It is the end-of-year state trust fund balance divided by covered wages for the year, then divided by the highest cost benefit payout period payout for a year as a percentage of covered wages for the same period.
3. Rob Pavosevich, former chief actuary for the Office of Unemployment Insurance at USDOL, developed this reinsurance proposal.

# 11
# Special Programs

## Options and Recommendations

### SHORT-TIME COMPENSATION

### Issue

Short-time compensation (STC), often referred to as work sharing or shared work, is a program that allows firms to reduce workers' hours of employment rather than lay them off. Employees who are placed on reduced hours receive a pro rata share of their weekly UI benefit payments for the reduction in hours worked.

STC began in Europe and exists there as a program to prevent unemployment. In Europe, it is a form of unemployment assistance, not paid from unemployment compensation taxes. The program is available to firms in lieu of layoffs and is used most heavily during recessionary periods. However, it also has been used to prevent more structural types of unemployment, such as when Germany used it in Eastern Germany in the 1990s after reunification (Wandner 2010). With the onset of the COVID-19 shutdowns, much of Europe again used STC or wage supplements to prevent unemployment (Birnbaum 2020).

A small program in the United States, STC is treated as an optional UI program, with 28 current state programs. Even in states with programs, STC is little used. The incentives for firms and workers to participate is limited because, unlike in Europe, employers in the United States pay for STC benefits just as they do for UI. Employers who do participate in the program do so because it is frequently difficult to replace skilled workers after a recession, a significant problem after the pandemic layoffs. STC benefits also reduce participating workers' future eligibility for UI benefits.[1] In addition, STC is administratively cumbersome. An attraction for participating workers is that they continue to receive fringe benefits, which they would not if unemployed.

The COVID-19 recession has shown the sharp differences between the United States and European STC programs. In the United States, the size of the program has been small, but employers who have used STC like it and have high repeat usage (Balducchi et al. 2015). Nonetheless, most employers lay off workers rather than place them on STC. In Europe, by contrast, STC use has been widespread.

Williams (2020), in an article in the *Economist*, contrasted the approaches in the United States, Canada, and Ireland with that of most of Europe and Australia. Williams calls the first group "Protectors," who engage in layoffs and then provide UI and other stimulus payments to protect unemployed workers. The second group is "Preservers," who extensively use STC and other wage supplements that prevent workers from losing their jobs. During the pandemic, the *Economist*'s writers tended to endorse the Preservers' policy, but they worried about the negative effect on labor mobility, since STC might discourage workers from looking for new, more productive jobs. In editorials about STC in recent years, the *Economist* has supported STC in the short run as superior to the Protector approach but was concerned that, once implemented as a countercyclical policy instrument during a recession, STC should not remain in place for long periods of time. Although its role as a Preserver has been limited, STC in the United States did contribute to reducing unemployment during the 2007–2009 recession (Abraham and Houseman 2014).

The United States must determine what its policy should be in future recessions. Does it want to remain a Protector or does it want to become a Preserver? To become more of a Preserver, the United States would have to enact a much more robust, national STC program, requiring states to implement an STC program and encourage employers and workers to participate in the program. This approach would have the advantage that employers retain their workers and do not have to train new employees when the economy rebounds.

## Options

Potential changes in the STC program could include integrating STC into the state UI benefit payment programs, simplifying employers' initial applications and weekly filing for benefits, and eliminating the charging of STC benefits against employers such that they do not pay a UI tax for their program participation. Similarly, employees would be encouraged to participate by not charging their STC benefits against their total entitlement to benefits during their benefit year. Alternatively, STC could become a national program separate from the UI program, like the European approach. Below are five studies that offer suggestions for improving STC participation and administrative simplicity:

1) Dube (2021) recommends streamlining the STC program by allowing employers to submit online applications and using employer payroll records to determine payments.

2) Both Dube (2021) and von Wachter (2020) recommend that employers pay STC benefits directly to their employees, with government reimbursement for the program costs.

3) Dube (2021) and Houseman et al. (2017) recommend a major information campaign to encourage participation.

4) West et al. (2016) recommend that STC become a mandatory program in all states, with the federal government fully funding the program. While federal funding would incentivize employers to participate, employee participation would be encouraged by having STC benefits not reduce their future total entitlement to benefits during their benefit year. States could simplify STC administration by automating the program with federal grants and making STC part of their automated UI benefits system.

5) O'Leary and Wandner (2018) recommend requiring every state to have an STC program and giving states initial implementation funding to relieve employers of the cost of STC.

## Recommendation

The STC program should be a federal requirement for all state UI programs because it can help many firms and workers weather recessions without layoffs. STC should be automated and integrated into the state UI benefit payment system. To encourage employer participation, STC benefits should not be charged to employers using the program whenever unemployment is high, such as when the state is using the EB program.

## SELF-EMPLOYMENT ASSISTANCE

### Issue

Self-Employment Assistance (SEA) is a program that allows targeted UI recipients to receive self-employment allowances in the same amount as their UI weekly benefits while they work to establish their own small businesses. Participants must engage in entrepreneurial training while they are establishing their businesses to increase the likelihood of business success.

SEA is a small program, authorized in only eight states—Delaware, Pennsylvania, New Hampshire, New Jersey, New York, Maine, Oregon, and Rhode Island (USDOL 2022a). Because of staffing and funding limitations, the program is only active in the latter four. Like STC, SEA originated in Europe and is widely available there.

In 1994, SEA was enacted into federal law as an optional UI program after experimental testing found the program to be cost effective, and especially effective for older workers (Benus et al. 1991, 1995).[2]

### Options

SEA could be expanded if the program were better integrated into and supported by the UI and federal training programs and if administration of the program could be simplified. This improvement in the SEA program would require increased funding for entrepreneurial training, the lack of which has proved to be a key roadblock to bringing the program to scale in the eight SEA states (Wandner 2010, Chapter 8).

1) West et al. (2016) recommend expanding SEA by requiring all states to participate in the program.

2) O'Leary and Wandner (2018) recommend a nationwide program with entrepreneurial training funded by USDOL and provided by the national Small Business Development Center network at locations around the United States. All workers would be able to participate in the program after filing their UI claims, and the work search requirement for obtaining UI benefits would be waived.

## Recommendation

SEA should be a required program in every state. The WIOA program should pay for the entrepreneurial training, but the SEA program should have its own performance measurement system, separate from other training programs. This is a valuable program for getting unemployed workers back to work, and it is particularly helpful for older workers who have difficulty finding new wage and salary employment.

## REEMPLOYMENT BONUSES

### Issue

For over four decades, policymakers have experimented with providing reemployment bonuses to unemployed workers as a method of speeding the return to work for permanently separated UI claimants. The experiments assumed that dislocated workers were searching for work but that a cash incentive might help speed up their return and prevent a decline in wages in their new job. Several randomized controlled studies were conducted and evaluated. An analysis of the experimental results found that a bonus of approximately three times the individual's weekly benefit amount offered for reemployment within 12 weeks of job loss was the bonus offer most likely to be cost effective. It was found to speed the return to work without reducing the earnings of bonus recipients (O'Leary, Decker, and Wandner 2005).

Reemployment bonuses, much like those recommended by O'Leary, Decker, and Wandner (2005), based on estimates of hypothetical targeted reemployment bonuses using data from Pennsylvania and Washington State experiments, were included as an optional state program in the proposed Reemployment Act of 1994. That bill, however, was not enacted (Wandner 2010).

In response to concerns about the potential work disincentive effects of federal pandemic UI benefits, several states, including Montana, sought early termination of their agreements with USDOL to continue federally funded supplementary UI benefits that Congress extended into September 2021. As an alternative to federal benefits, however,

Montana Governor Greg Gianforte announced that his state would offer UI recipients a Return-to-Work Bonus of $1,200. Thus, Montana would offer a reemployment bonus to workers in approximately the amount that researchers consider optimal. The governor ended the $300 weekly Federal Pandemic Unemployment Compensation payment and offered the $1,200 Montana employment bonus after four weeks on the job.

However, Montana's Return-to-Work Bonus is different from the experimental reemployment bonuses conducted four decades ago. Those experiments offered bonuses to dislocated workers early in their spells of unemployment with the hope that it would speed their search for and return to work. The Return-to-Work Bonuses assume that UI recipients are not searching for work and need to have their UI benefits reduced or eliminated to encourage them to look for work, and that only then would a bonus act as an incentive to search for and find employment. Nonetheless, this new effort should remind policymakers that the older bonus experiments worked and deserve consideration as part of a UI reform effort.

## Options

1) Congress could enact legislation that either offers states the option or requires them to provide reemployment bonuses as a method of speeding UI recipients' return to work.

2) O'Leary and Wandner (2018) recommend that the United States enact an optional state reemployment bonus program targeted to the UI recipients most likely to exhaust their UI benefits.

## Recommendation

Congress should enact a reemployment bonus as an optional program for state UI programs. While the program has been shown to speed the return to work in rigorously evaluated demonstration studies, public policy should ensure that it works as a national program. An evaluation of the new program should be federally funded with a report due to Congress within five years. Congress could then use the evaluation to determine whether to enact a mandatory, permanent program.

## WAGE INSURANCE

### Issue

Permanently displaced workers often suffer earnings losses because they lose the value of their firm-specific human capital. Sometimes they also are forced to change industry and/or occupation, such that, when they return to work, they are at the bottom rung of a new job ladder. One potential response to this wage loss is a proposal called "wage insurance," which actually is a social welfare program rather than a social insurance program. It is designed to encourage workers to take a job even if the wage is below their previous wage level by having the federal government pay for a portion of those workers' wage losses for a fixed period while they build new firm-specific human capital. Analysts at the Brookings Institution have promoted wage insurance for many years in many publications (Wandner 2016). Wage insurance currently exists in the United States only as a small federal program, called Reemployment Trade Adjustment Assistance, that is part of the overall Trade Adjustment Assistance (TAA) program. Like the TAA program, this wage insurance program is a social welfare program paid for by the federal government. The federal government pays workers aged 50 and older a wage supplement out of federal general revenue. Since its inception in 2002, participation has been low; in 2020, only 13.9 percent of TAA participants received Reemployment Trade Adjustment Assistance benefits. Because of the low take-up rate, this program has not been evaluated (Wandner 2016).

### Options

1) To better understand whether to proceed with wage insurance as a public policy initiative, the United States could conduct a rigorous randomized controlled trial experiment to better understand the net impact of such a program on displaced workers.

2) West et al. (2016) argue that wage insurance should be considered as an option, but only in combination with a broader effort to protect working families.

3) The Obama administration FY 2017 budget proposal included a wage insurance program to encourage the return to work (Wandner 2018). It would have provided benefits to workers who had been employed by their prior employers for at least three years. If their new job paid less than $50,000 per year, they could receive payments of up to half of the difference between their new and prior wage, up to a maximum of $10,000 over a period of two years.

**Recommendation**

Because no U.S. wage insurance program has been run as a large-scale program and provided to a wider group of dislocated workers, its effectiveness is unproven. Thus, USDOL should initiate a major experimental wage insurance demonstration project to determine the benefits and cost of an ongoing program. USDOL should submit this evaluation report to Congress.

## THE EMPLOYMENT SERVICE AND REEMPLOYMENT SERVICES

**Issue**

Throughout the history of the UI program, the Employment Service (ES) has been the main provider of reemployment services to a significant percentage of UI claimants. For example, in 2014, ES staff registered 5.4 million UI claimants and provided 1.8 million of them with job search activities (USDOL 2014). While high-wage dislocated workers (and employed workers) may find jobs either on their own or through private search firms that list job openings, lower wage workers who need reemployment services to assist their return to work mostly cannot turn to private firms to provide that assistance.

As documented by biannual BLS dislocated worker surveys since the 1970s, in recent decades, UI recipients' need for these services has increased as a much larger percentage of them have become permanently displaced, have been subject to long periods of unemployment, and have needed job search assistance to return to work. Rigorous research has shown that such job search assistance is highly effective in helping workers speed their return to work without any decline in wage and salary levels (Wandner 2010, Chapter 5). Based on this research, Congress in 1993 enacted, as amendments to Title III of the Social Security Act, the Worker Profiling and Reemployment Services program and the Reemployment Services and Eligibility Assessment program in 2018. Both programs are designed to provide intensive reemployment services to UI claimants.

Over the past four decades, UI claimants have experienced an increased need for employment services, while overall funding for the ES has declined sharply. Although ES grants to states have been relatively stable in nominal terms at roughly between $600 and $800 million since 1984 (Wandner 2015), most of ES's costs are for staffing, and staffing has plummeted as indicated by the decline in real ES grants (O'Leary and Wandner 2018). The decline in funding has resulted in a sharp decrease in effective in-person, one-on-one services by ES staff. Instead, when job seekers go to a local job center for help with finding a job, they tend to be referred to a resource room where they sit at a computer terminal and use programs to conduct self-assessments, develop resumes, and access labor market information. While these automated tools may be useful for the computer-savvy, they are less so for less-educated and English-as-a-second-language job seekers. Nonetheless, state UI agencies report that automation of employment services accelerated sharply after the 2007–2009 recession (Wandner 2013) and continues today. The decline in funding also has resulted in a sharp, steady decline in the number of local job centers where job seekers can go to receive job search assistance from 3,582 at the end of 2003 to 2,287 on May 16, 2023.[3] Most of the declines in the availability of services have been in less populated areas of the United States, a geographic inequity.

From the enactment of the Wagner-Peyser Act of 1933 until the 1990s, all state ES staff were merit staffed (Balducchi, Eberts, and O'Leary 2004). The decline in ES merit staffing has not had a positive effect (Jacobson et al. 2004). In April 2022, USDOL issued a Notice of Proposed Rule Making to permanently reinstate ES merit staffing nationwide (*Federal Register* 2022). Merit staffing is discussed in more detail in Chapter 12.

**Options**

The sharp decline in real ES funding since the 1980s (see Figure 3.9) and the corresponding decline in the provision of services have resulted in calls for more in-person, one-on-one services that will require increased funding. Increasing the provision of ES services in local workforce offices would enhance coordination of the of UI and ES programs through improved reemployment services and UI work test integrity (Balducchi, Eberts, and O'Leary 2004; Balducchi and O'Leary in Wandner 2018).

1) One option is to resurrect the USDOL national office organization, the United States Employment Services (USES), which was eliminated in the early 2000s. It would have to be reestablished to provide coordination with the UI program's national office in the provision of reemployment services and payment of UI benefits. This coordination would be enhanced if USES and the national UI program were either administered together under an organizational arrangement like the defunct Bureau of Economic Security (1939–1969) or their administration were otherwise closely coordinated. The reestablished USES also would require an administrator and must be fully staffed.

2) Another option is to restore the ES within local workforce offices such that the ES could provide similar but updated types of services as it did in the early 1980s. Achieving that goal would require substantially increased ES funding to restore the real funding levels it had four decades ago. Balducchi and O'Leary (2018) recommend restoring ES funding to its real 1984 funding level; in FY 2015, that would have required funding of $1.5 billion instead of the congressionally appropriated $600 to 700 million, an increase of approximately $800 million. West et al. (2016) recommended adding $1.0 billion to the then-existing $680 million appropriation to bring the total appropriation to $1.68 billion.

Providing UI recipients with reemployment services is relatively inexpensive, costing only a small fraction of the cost of career training, yet it can return workers to productive employment. A report from the Brookings Institution (Jacobson 2009) estimated that, in 2009, providing staff-assisted assessment and job search assistance services to UI claimants would cost $360 per claimant. Thus, if the ES budget were increased by $1 billion adjusted upward for inflation, at approximately $500 per claimant in current dollars, two million UI claimants could receive intensive job search assistance services.

## Recommendations

Reestablish USES within USDOL. Increase the overall ES budget to approximately $1.5 billion and then adjust for inflation to pay for the increases in wages over time. While the ES program should serve all workers seeking assistance in finding a job, it should target assisting UI beneficiaries return to work. In addition, all state ES staff should be merit staffed.

## Notes

1. Nonetheless, in a 2012 tax statute, the CARES Act, and the American Recovery Act, the federal government temporarily funded STC benefits. This temporary effort might indicate Congress's willingness to permanently fund the STC program.
2. SEA was enacted temporarily as part of the North American Free Trade Agreement Act (P.L. 103-182) and was made permanent in 1998 by P.L.105-306.
3. www.servicelocator.org (accessed May 16, 2023).

# 12
# Modernizing Information Technology

## BACKGROUND

The history of the automation of the federal-state UI system has been rocky and has resulted in vast differences in the effectiveness of state UI application, benefit payment, and tax collection systems. The reporting and data systems associated with UI program operations also have tended to be seriously neglected.

During the early years of the UI program in the late 1930s, benefit payment and employer account processing were primarily manual tasks. By the mid-1950s, many states had migrated to the extensive use of automatic business machines for most UI functions. In the 1960s, mainframe computers were introduced, and in the early 1970s, states used computer punch cards to process benefit payments and microfiche readers to assess the status of benefit payments, first in administrative offices, and later in local offices.

Technology advances and the severe 1973–1975 recession drove policymakers to support new methods of state administration that incorporated high speed computer systems to upgrade states' UI benefit and tax processing systems. In 1975, USDOL launched a $3 million project to develop a model online benefit payment system. The goal of the system was to make possible a computerized claims-taking and adjudication procedure in all states, drawing on the experiences of four pilot states.

In 1976, the Employment and Training Administration announced an ambitious five-year Employment Security Automation Project (ESAP). The objective was to coordinate the development, implementation, and operation nationwide of automated employment security systems, both UI and ES programs. ESAP was designed to implement several systems—job service matching systems, UI online benefit and tax systems, and the consolidation of nationwide UI data systems. ESAP's final estimated cost was $250 million, with projected UI operational costs of $134 million, scheduled for completion in 1984. However, in

1981 the incoming Reagan administration halted project implementation. The program expired, incomplete and without full funding.

Since the early 1980s, financial support for IT at USDOL has been episodic and limited. By 1985, a budgetary UI Automation Support Account had been established to upgrade the technology of existing state UI benefit and tax systems. Thereafter, under different federal technology priorities, annual budgetary appropriations, and ETA solicitations, states have submitted proposals to compete for limited technology funds to expand or redesign their mainframe-based UI tax and benefit systems architectures or link them to statewide local-based computer networks.

Until the 1990s, filing initial and continued UI claims was an in-person process, with claims submitted in local workforce offices. In 1995, the UI program rapidly began leaving local workforce offices. This move occurred after the 1994 creation of One-Stop Centers, which would house all agencies in workforce centers. This decision aimed to prevent the UI program from becoming the principal funder of the local One-Stop Centers across the country. The move began with state UI staff taking initial and continued claims from call centers. Soon after, computer claims-taking began. The UI national office provided grants to states to assist with the transition to telephone and computer claims-taking. The effort, however, was rushed and not well organized. The new claims-taking processes varied greatly by state. With few UI staff remaining in the local workforce offices, UI became a "telephone on the wall" at local workforce offices. UI claimants were forced to adapt to the new technology (Wandner 2010), and many were unsuccessful because often there were no UI staff to help them apply for benefits. In addition, the number of local workforce offices declined sharply, particularly in rural areas where workers could not easily drive to local workforce offices and did not have ready access to computers (Dunham et al. 2005; Wandner 2015).

With the sharp decline in staffing in the UI national office, the number of staff devoted to IT dropped from an inadequate 28 full-time equivalent in 1976 to a totally inadequate 17 in 2015 (see also Table 2.3). Given the IT needs at the state UI agencies, USDOL now out-sources almost all its IT work, funding the National Association of State Workforce Agencies to operate the UI Information Technology Support Center and more recently the Interstate Connection Network. The

Information Technology Support Center provides states with a variety of IT services, including information, software tools and products, and consultation. The Interstate Connection Network system allows state UI agencies to request and receive data for use in the filing and processing of UI claims and related information. The system provides for the exchange of data between state workforce agencies and their federal partners. Despite requests by researchers over many years for similar access to interstate data for research purposes, states have been unwilling to provide the data for those purposes.

## Issue

IT systems vary greatly among states. With limited funding, many states have not updated their systems for decades, and some that have upgraded did so in a way that is not claimant-friendly. One study indicates that only 22 states modernized their UI IT systems between 2001 and 2018 (Simon-Mishel et al. 2020). More recently, as part of their UI benefit systems IT modernization projects, 24 states have completed a modernization, 10 are under development, 9 are working on acquisition, and 10 are still in the planning stage. The American Rescue Plan Act of 2021 provided $2 billion to ensure timely, accurate, and equitable UI payments, including provision of IT funding (USDOL 2020b).

Some states have been forthright about the problems they face. For example, in 2017, Pennsylvania's Secretary of Labor stated: "Our current 50-year-old computer system is working, but it's held together with chewing gum and duct tape" (Ghosh 2021). Problems with UI IT systems are not only related to their age. Even some newer systems have significant problems. In 2019, Florida's state auditors informed Governor Ron DeSantis that its UI applicant website, updated in 2013, had major problems, including more than 600 system errors that needed to be fixed. The auditors had previously pointed to the same problems in 2015, but the state had not fixed them. By the end of March 2020, when the COVID pandemic began, the Florida system was failing under an unprecedented level of UI claims, and many of Florida's unemployed were unable to apply because the site kept crashing. For a while, Florida UI staff were forced to hand out paper claims forms to unemployed workers lining up in their cars in front of Florida workforce offices (Ghosh 2021; Mower 2020; State of Florida 2019).

**Options**

1) Adopting states' best practices. A major study of state UI IT calls for updating systems using best practices from the states that have already modernized (Simon-Mishel et al. 2020). The authors call for a customer-centered design and user-experience testing as the core of systems that serve unemployed workers well. They find that less than half of states had modernized or were in the process of modernizing. They provide best practices from the modernizing states they studied, as well as advice about how to conduct the modernization at the planning, design, and implementation stage. They also point to several things that all states can do in the short run and give advice for the design and implementation of system improvements. They recommend replacing old, slow, and ineffective IT systems—often on mainframe computers—with modern systems using cloud computing. The enormous delays in paying state UI benefits and federal COVID-19 UI assistance which began in 2020 has renewed the call for modernizing UI IT systems.

2) Proposals for IT modernization. Modernizing state UI IT systems across the country would be expensive. The Century Foundation (2020) has called for a $2 billion investment in UI IT. The Wyden-Bennet proposal would update state UI IT systems using a modular approach that could be adopted by any state that wishes to participate. The proposal would be to appropriate $500 million for USDOL to create a modular set of components to modernize state UI technology. States would be able to choose which pieces to implement, ranging from components focused on claims filing, eligibility determinations, and tax systems. The proposal would require a study to identify the states' current technology needs, including ensuring program accessibility and addressing equity issues (Ghosh 2021).

3) Components of UI modernization. Most efforts to modernize state UI IT systems have dealt with the back end of the system: the benefit payment and tax collection systems. Frequently neglected have been the front-end systems that include not

only initial claims and continued claims-taking, but also providing information to claimants, communication by telephone and email, and the availability of UI staff to assist claimants in workforce local offices. In addition, almost always neglected in the updating of UI benefit and tax systems are the data and reporting systems to be used for reporting, performance measurement, and research and evaluation purposes. An important contribution to improving the UI programs and increasing UI recipiency rates would be front-end quality control and the standardization of information, communication, and application systems, as well as improved reporting and standardization of data systems.

4)  Sharing of interstate data for research and evaluation purposes. In addition to program administration, UI data are valuable for both UI research and other types of research. Because states have resisted this expansion in the use of interstate data, federal legislation is required if deidentified interstate data is to be shared with USDOL and researchers and evaluators.

5)  Updating and improving modernization projects. Another problem with past efforts to update UI IT systems has been that they frequently were built by for-profit firms that had limited knowledge of the UI program and its administration. These firms generally do not continue to update and improve the new systems once they are built. An alternative could be to use one or more nonprofit organizations under long-term contracts that would learn the UI system, build new systems, and continue to improve those systems over time.

An alternative to the use of for-profit IT firms could be the establishment of a new USDOL federally funded research and development center (FFRDC), such as the Rand Corporation, using a long-term contract. FFRDCs are used by many federal agencies, but not by USDOL's ETA. An FFRDC could not only develop and maintain IT systems, but it could also be a repository for UI and other workforce development agency data, ensuring the quality of the data, and conducting research and analysis that would be useful for the state agencies and for the federal government (Lane 2020).

6) IT support. Over the years, the UI national office staff has been decimated and needs to be rebuilt and greatly expanded. Especially since most of the IT software and hardware development is provided by for-profit firms, USDOL must ensure that its federal IT funds are well spent. USDOL should hire more IT knowledgeable staff. Better contracting out should avoid past weak products and lack of ongoing support from for-profit firms. Consideration might be given to having a nonprofit organization support the UI national office. This support could be given by an FFRDC, other nonprofit organizations, or state research universities.

**Recommendation**

The UI computer system desperately needs to be modernized and maintained and improved over time. Many of the options suggested above should be adopted to deal with woefully out-of-date systems. These new and improved systems should be done efficiently and effectively by providing funding, but only with rigorous oversight and management.

## NATIONAL UI DATA STANDARDS: CREATING CONSISTENT DEFINITIONS

This section considers four ways of improving the UI data systems:

1) Create national UI data standards with a single set of definitions that are consistent between states.

2) Increase data collection for programmatic, economic, and research uses.

3) Expand the use of state longitudinal data to improve and evaluate the UI program.

4) Improve state data systems and reporting to the UI national office.

## Issue

Currently each state UI law defines covered employment, employment and wages, and unemployment in its own way. The lack of consistency creates problems for employers, employees, USDOL, statistical agencies, and researchers and analysts:

- For multistate employers, inconsistent and idiosyncratic definitions mean that employers must treat each state as a separate unique program with respect to the benefit and tax sides of the program.
- Employees and UI claimants have difficulty navigating each state's unique program and definitions, especially if they become UI claimants with wages in more than one state.
- USDOL has difficulty evaluating state program performance and individual state programs compared to other states.
- Researchers and analysts have difficulty conducting interstate research and evaluations.

Lack of consistency has been a concern throughout the history of the UI program, but little has been done about it. For example, in 1996, the ACUC recommended that the UI national office, with advice from BLS, "design the elements of a comprehensive information system of UI data that are comparable in definition and format for all states" (ACUC 1996, p. 36). The ACUC gave a long list of data elements that should be rigorously defined, including coverage and eligibility; labor market attachment; levels and duration of benefits paid; the extent and cause of nonmonetary determinations; labor market information at the federal, state, and local levels; and federal and state program administration. The ACUC recommended that "(e)ach state should maintain its database in accordance with U.S. Department of Labor requirements so that statistical standards, definitional comparability, and easy computer access for all users can be maintained" (ACUC 1996, pp. 34–37).

In response to the adverse effect on employers of the continuing lack of national UI data standards, the U.S. Chamber of Commerce Foundation and the T3 Innovation Network conducted a study (2021) that developed proposed employment and earnings records standards (including data elements, definitions, and reporting guidelines) and recommended that state agencies adopt these standards for use in collecting quarterly wage and earnings data from employers and for improving federal and state data collection and labor market information. This comprehensive report includes a conceptual model, a data dictionary, and more detailed technical specifications and other documentation to implement the standards.

The report demonstrates employers' concerns regarding UI data and especially pertaining to state UI quarterly wage records. Employers use these records for their business planning and management of human resources. Employers also report the data required by each state. The lack of consistency between states imposes a large cost on multistate employers, which must adapt their UI reports to each state's requirements, and the resulting data for all the states in which they operate are not consistent. The goal of the Chamber's effort is to reduce employers' reporting and data collection costs and improve data quality in a manner that it thinks would provide substantial benefits to employers, government, and other stakeholders. Another objective of the Chamber's recommendations is to improve labor market information used by employers, job seekers, policymakers, and the public. In the Chamber's view, better data can be provided more economically by reducing the number of reports while still improving labor market information.

## Options

Improvements suggested by the ACUC, the U.S. Chamber of Commerce Foundation, and others could be accomplished in several ways.

1) Under the current federal-state UI system, states could voluntarily work together to develop quarterly wage records and other UI data systems with common definitions. This is the approach the Chamber is currently undertaking as it works with the National Association of State Workforce Agencies to encourage state cooperation.

2) Congress could enact common definitions and specify the content and format of quarterly wage records.

3) As the ACUC recommended, USDOL could promulgate regulations specifying data definitions and data collection and maintenance methods that states would be required to use.

4) Under a national UI system, wage reporting would be conducted using a single national format and definitions. In the case of a national system, not only would employers use common definitions, but they would report wage and employment data only once to the federal government, rather than separately to each state UI agency.

## Recommendation

Congress should mandate common definitions, and USDOL should be given the authority and resources to develop the standardized definitions and oversee their accuracy and consistency. The use of consistent definitions and a common data system across states would not only help the UI program assess state performance, it would benefit other public data systems that use UI data for research and private employers for whom it would be more economical to work with a single system rather than 53.

## INCREASED DATA COLLECTION AND DATA INTEGRITY

### Issue

UI data are critical for the UI program, but also for many other purposes. The U.S. Department of Commerce uses UI wage data as an important factor in calculating the wage and salary component of the U.S. national income accounts (e.g., GDP). UI data also are important indicators about the health of the U.S. economy. For example, the Commerce Department considers UI initial claims to be a leading economic indicator, while UI continued claims are a concurrent indicator. Because of the importance of this information, the weekly initial claims data are reported to chair of the Federal Reserve System and to the Council of Economic Advisors at 8:30 a.m. on Wednesday mornings, a full 24 hours before the data are released publicly, so that economic policymakers can make an early assessment of what is happening in U.S. labor markets.

UI data systems could be an even more important source of economic data. For many decades, data analysts and researchers have called for improved labor market data by increasing the data collected with UI quarterly wage records. Recently, the BLS Workforce Information Advisory Council (2020) also expressed eagerness for more UI data for labor market information.

While USDOL provides guidance about definitions of UI data elements, there is little oversight to ensure that definitions are consistent within and between states over time. Researchers and policy analysts find inconsistencies in UI data that make it difficult to oversee the program, measure performance, and evaluate the effectiveness of programs. Thus, the quality and integrity of UI data need to be enhanced.

**Options**

1) With respect to the sensitive economic data produced by the UI program, USDOL could provide greater oversight over the quality of many key UI data elements and better maintain the security of these data before they are released publicly.

2) With respect to labor market information data, the USDOL Workforce Information Advisory Council (2020) recommends adding the following items to the quarterly wage report:

   - hours worked, allowing for the calculation of hourly earnings and changes in hours worked

   - job title, which BLS could use to improve occupational data by converting job titles to a Standard Occupational Classification via text analysis

   - work location, because some employers' accounts cover multiple work sites

   - demographics, such as race, ethnicity, sex, education, and age to promote inclusion

State UI agencies and many employers and employer organizations have traditionally opposed the addition of labor market information elements to the data they collect. They have been interested in minimizing the burden on the UI system, even if additional data might improve the UI program and provide important labor market information. Hours

worked, however, could be used by UI agencies to determine monetary eligibility in a manner that would more accurately measure labor
force attachment and be more equitable to low-wage workers. Job title
and work location also would be useful for improving labor market
policy and not too difficult to collect. A standardized auto coder could
be used to add an occupation code to the data reported. Demographic
data already are collected on the UI initial claims form, but the data are
not uniform. Standardizing initial claims data, demographic definitions,
and formats, and making the data available for labor market information purposes would increase data quality and uniformity. Demographic
data are already collected from the state UI agencies and reported on
the federal ES-203 report. The current report is not reliable, but it could
be improved significantly with reporting changes and increased federal
monitoring (O'Leary, Spriggs, and Wandner 2021).

**Recommendation**

USDOL should require increased UI data collection, including
hours worked and other key variables for UI and labor market information purposes. These data could be used to monitor and evaluate the
UI system and help to make it more equitable for low-wage workers,
improve labor market information, and be useful in a variety of ways to
private sector employers.

## MAKING USE OF STATE LONGITUDINAL
## DATA SYSTEMS

**Issue**

For many decades, the UI program has recognized that state UI
aggregate reporting data are insufficient for many purposes, including
program measurement and management, economic data analysis, labor
market information, and research and evaluation. USDOL has supported several efforts to make use of UI program administrative microdata. The first effort was launched in the 1960s, followed by three major
efforts:

1) Continuous Wage and Benefit History was a 1970s project funded by the national UI office providing grants and technical assistance to 16 states as they assembled longitudinal administrative databases consisting of UI benefit and wage data. The program was cancelled in the early 1980s. Of the 16 states, only Washington State maintained and expanded its Continuous Wage and Benefit History program. Washington currently maintains a longitudinal administrative data system that includes many programs other than UI.

2) The Administrative Data and Research and Evaluation Project (ADARE) began in 1998, when USDOL brought together researchers from state research universities (and the W.E. Upjohn Institute for Employment Research) who already had access to state microdata, consisting of UI and other workforce data, to conduct research and evaluation for their states. The original participating states were Florida, Georgia, Maryland, Michigan, Missouri, and Texas, later joined by Illinois, Washington, California, and Ohio. The partners produced many research papers (Stevens 2012) and two books (King and Mueser 2005; O'Leary et al. 2019). Most of the participating research institutions are still active. While ADARE federal funding ended, all but one former ADARE state, Georgia, has received one or more Workforce Data Quality Initiative grants that have substituted for ADARE funding.

3) The Workforce Data Quality Initiative was an initiative that began in 2010 and gave its eighth set of grants to states in 2021. It was designed to help states create, improve, and make use of the workforce longitudinal databases in conjunction with the Department of Education's State Longitudinal Administrative Data System. Together the two systems follow individuals from school through their work lives.

The problem with creating and using state UI and other workforce data is the unevenness in states' ability to create and maintain these longitudinal data systems, which makes it difficult to use them for administrative, research, and evaluation purposes. As a result, most states do not have active, useful data systems, and those that do are mostly dependent on outside researchers—usually at state universities—to analyze the data and use it for research and evaluation purposes.

## Options

Solutions to these problems vary.

1) USDOL could establish an FFRDC like those established by many other federal agencies (Lane 2020). As discussed earlier in this chapter, an FFRDC could serve many purposes with respect to improved IT and data systems. In addition, it could create, improve, and maintain state longitudinal data systems as well as analyze data and provide findings to individual states and to the federal government. It also could make deidentified data available to outside researchers. Using an FFDRC would result in the creation of a nationwide system of state longitudinal data sets, with an organization that could use the data for analysis, research, and evaluation providing for the needs of both individual states and the federal government.

2) A system of regional data centers could be created. Since a relatively small number of states have the capacity to develop strong longitudinal data systems and conduct their analyses, a smaller number of states could work with other states in their region to gather and organize state data and conduct analyses. Most of this work could be done by 1) state research universities, 2) one or more FFRDCs, or 3) other nonprofit research institutions. One nonprofit, the Coleridge Initiative (Lane 2020), is already working with several state workforce agencies to use their microdata for program and policy purposes.

3) The perceived failure of the state data systems available in 2020 to inform COVID policy making has been raised as one reason to improve UI data systems. Sean Simone (2021) calls for the creation of such state systems and making them available to the federal government. To accomplish this, he makes the following recommendations:

   • Enact federal or uniform state legislation permitting research and analysis using deidentified state data.

- Conduct a review of all federal laws that limit the sharing of data across program areas and states.
- Encourage activities that increase research capacity within state governments.

The critical issue for creating state longitudinal data systems is whether the systems created should be state specific, regional, or national. State systems are strong in some states but weak or nonexistent in others. Regional systems could ensure that all states have access to their own state longitudinal data and the capacity for its analysis. For some national public policy purposes, however, a national data system would be needed.

### Recommendation

USDOL should ensure that all states have consistent longitudinal data systems for program management and research and evaluation purposes. States should be encouraged to develop, maintain, and use their own systems. USDOL also should fund an FFRDC to house, clean, and make use of the data systems for use by the states and the federal government. The improved data and analysis can be used to better understand the UI system and other public workforce systems. They also can be used for evaluation and analysis purposes.

## IMPROVED NATIONAL DATA AND REPORTING SYSTEMS AND STAFFING

### Issue

The national UI reporting and data team at USDOL operates with only a small staff. Those staff issue reporting instructions to the state UI agencies, receive state data, produce and analyze state and national data, and protect and provide the data used as economic indicators that are used as inputs to the U.S. national income accounts. While the staff are highly professional and are known for the high quality of their work, the resources available to them are inadequate, limiting data analysis and risking the security of sensitive information.

UI data are needed for purposes beyond UI program administration and performance measurement. UI data are used to develop labor market information used by state and national governments. The Department of Commerce's economic indicator series, for example, uses initial claims as a leading indicator and continued claims as a concurrent indicator. Because of the importance of initial claims as a leading indicator, the USDOL chief economist, the chairman of the Federal Reserve, and the macroeconomist at the Council of Economic Advisors receive initial claims data 24 hours in advance of its release each Thursday at 8:30 a.m. The national income accounts uses UI wage data as an important input.

With increased resources, the UI data reporting teams could improve the quality of UI data, better monitor the data, provide more data for program administration and performance measurement purposes, strengthen data security, and better support other federal agencies that use the data. At present, there are significant weaknesses in the UI data systems and innovation is limited.

## Options

1) An increase in reporting and IT staff and resources would greatly improve national data and reporting systems. With greater resources, state data could be made more secure, qualitatively improved, further analyzed, and be more productively utilized.

2) The UI national office data development and data analysis capacity also could be improved with outside assistance, such as with support from the BLS, a new federally funded research and development center, or a research university.

## Recommendation

The UI national office should be given the staff and other resources to oversee and maintain UI data and reporting systems to allow for improved data and data analysis for the UI programs as well as for other private and public uses.

## RESEARCH, DEMONSTRATION, AND EVALUATIONS

### Issue

For a large social insurance program that pays billions of dollars in benefits to millions of unemployed workers each year, the national research budget is tiny, especially compared to funding for other social insurance programs administered by the SSA. Funding for UI research at the federal and state levels has been declining for decades. Indeed, there is no line item in the USDOL budget for UI research.

There are no longer dedicated UI research staff at USDOL. The already small national UI research unit was eliminated in the mid-1990s. Their numbers declined steadily from nearly 30 individuals in the early 1970s to just a few staff members. The remaining staff were transferred to the ETA research office into which they were absorbed and assigned research dealing mostly with issues other than UI. Then the ETA research budget also was eliminated, so that the only research budget in all of USDOL that can be used to fund UI research is in the department-wide Office of the Chief Evaluation Officer. Thus, the UI program must now compete for limited research funds with all the other USDOL subagencies.

In the 1980s and early 1990s, the national UI office ran a series of 11 rigorously evaluated reemployment demonstration projects that searched for cost-effective ways to help permanently separated UI recipients return to work. Some of these experiments had positive outcomes and resulted in the enactment of two new federal programs, the Worker Profiling and Reemployment Services initiative and Self-Employment Assistance (Wandner 2010). By the mid-1990s, however, the demonstrations were ended, and staff were transferred to other functions. No new demonstration projects have been initiated in three decades.

The state workforce agencies also can conduct only limited research—it is so limited that the state workforce agency research offices are, in fact, called labor market information offices, because their main source of funding is from BLS to create labor market information data. While state agency research staff would like to conduct more research, they not only have insufficient funds, but they frequently have no access to statistical or database software packages. They also typically do not have easy access to UI administrative microdata either. Responding to a 2012 nationwide survey, state research directors asked USDOL to provide a wide variety of assistance, including software, database management systems, and training in research methods (Wandner 2013).

**Options for State UI Research**

There are several alternative models for reinvigorating state UI and state workforce research.

1) Internal research by the state workforce agency. Washington State is the premier example of a state that conducts its own research and evaluations internally, mostly using state funds rather than federal grants. Having built on and expanded its Continuous Wage and Benefit History data efforts of the 1970s with a longitudinal data system, Washington makes its data available to analysts in three state agencies: the workforce development agency, a research and evaluation group in the state treasurer's office, and a program performance measurement agency. Each organization maintains its own capability to conduct research and analysis. The state also contracts out some research (Chocolaad and Wandner 2017).

2) Long-term contracts with a state university. Ohio's state workforce agency has had a successful relationship with Ohio State University's Center for Human Resource Research. It shares its data with the Center, and the Center organizes, maintains, and ensures the quality of the data. Center staff regularly conduct analyses for the agency, as well as research on selected topics. Under tight confidentiality arrangements, outside researchers are given access to deidentified Ohio data. Other state agencies also have contractual arrangements with the Center (Chocolaad and Wandner 2017).

3) Sharing data with a state university. This approach is an extension of the ADARE approach where microdata is shared, generally with a single state university, and university researchers conduct analysis, research, and evaluations for the state workforce agency. The state university is generally a research university in the state. California has broadened this approach

through its working relationship with the California Policy Lab located at the University of California at Los Angeles. The lab conducts research and analysis for California state and local governments dealing with many policy areas, making use of experts throughout the University of California system.

4) National research center or regional research centers. Another option for all states, but particularly useful for states with limited resources, is to share data with a national research organization that would conduct research and analysis for the individual states and for the federal government. A national research center also would have access to data from all states, allowing national research to be conducted with state administrative data. One option for creating a national research center is for USDOL to establish a new FFRDC, like other cabinet department FFRDCs that provide research services. Alternatively, USDOL could fund several regional research centers that might be located at state research universities.

These and other models for research centers and other resources to support the state agencies also would require that states dedicate their own resources to conducting state research, either using their own funds or funds provided by USDOL. Having additional state agency research staff, training for those staff, and research funds would be necessary to expand this effort. State agency research directors expressed their eagerness to participate in research if they had more resources (Chocolaad and Wandner 2017).

5) Reemployment Services and Eligibility Assessment (RESEA) evaluations. States must conduct annual evaluations of their own RESEA programs, and those that are effective as judged by causal evidence are eligible for a grant from USDOL. While all states conduct evaluations to one degree or another, the quality of these evaluations could be improved. To do so, USDOL could provide technical support to individual states and convene regions or other groupings of states to discuss evidence from evaluation studies. Several studied interventions could be evaluated, including behavioral nudges to encourage participation in reemployment services.

**Options for Federal UI Research**

1) The national UI office could reestablish a research office with substantial staff and funding. As in the past, it could contract out research, demonstration, and evaluation projects. It also could resume testing new approaches for helping the unemployed return to work.

2) It is difficult for USDOL to secure data to conduct federal research and evaluation projects. Conducting these projects would be greatly enhanced if Congress enacted federal legislation that permits the use of deidentified UI data for research purposes and requires states to make their data available for research purposes. Receipt of and ensuring data confidentiality could be the responsibility of USDOL, a federal statistical or research agency, or a national UI research organization, such as an FFRDC.

3) One function of a national UI research office could be to help states with their research efforts. USDOL could provide funding to states for specific research projects or for a series of projects.

4) USDOL could resume funding of the Workforce Data Quality Initiative effort, with increasing emphasis on funding research and evaluation projects as longitudinal administrative databases are better established.

5) Not all states are likely to establish strong systems of state longitudinal databases and internal research capacity. Given economies of scale and issues with small state research capacity, USDOL might consider funding regional research data centers at research universities or an FFRDC that could serve many states, especially for those states that do not have substantial research capacity. Regional or national research data centers could encourage expanded research by making deidentified state longitudinal data available to academic or other researchers for reviewed and approved projects.

## Recommendation

UI research and evaluation should be supported at the state and national levels. States should be encouraged to conduct research by themselves and by sharing their data with state research universities. At the federal level, USDOL should conduct research and evaluation, making use of an FFRDC, state research universities, and contract research organizations. Such research and evaluation could be used to improve the UI program and other government programs.

## FEDERAL AND STATE UI STAFFING

### Issue

Understaffing of the UI program exists at the local, state, regional and national levels. If the federal government is to once again become a strong and effective federal partner in rejuvenating the federal-state UI program, staffing and other resources would have to be greatly increased.

### Options

1) National office. The national UI office has been working with sharply declining staff for over four decades. As a result, federal leadership of the UI program has greatly diminished. The national UI office cannot provide effective leadership and guidance unless it has more staff. While national office staffing has always been inadequate, full-time equivalent staffing declined from 325 in 1980 to 66 in 2015, and it continued to decline until recently (see Figure 2.1 and Table 2.3). The current staffing level of well under 100 cannot perform national office functions for a multibillion-dollar program.

   To create a more effective national office, USDOL must substantially increase the number of staff, regardless of how the UI program is administered. Staffing needs would increase much more sharply, however, if the UI program were to become a federal or national program.

2) Regional offices. In the six USDOL regional offices, some staff were formerly dedicated to working on UI issues and providing periodic UI state program reviews. That effort is now much reduced. To have effective regional oversite of state UI programs, a significant increase in dedicated UI regional staff is needed. Travel funding also would have to be substantially increased so that the regional staff can monitor, assess, and provide technical assistance to the states.

3) State staffing. At the state and local level, more staff are especially needed to assist claimants access the UI program. Returning more in-person resources to the local offices would help unemployed workers who have difficulty using remote application and job search systems. The vision that the UI national office had in the mid-1990s that UI would essentially leave the local workforce offices and become "a telephone on the wall" has not worked well, particularly for those claimants who have more difficulty negotiating computer and telephone claims-taking, such as older workers, workers with disabilities, workers with limited English language skills, low-wage workers, workers with less education, and workers with limited computer skills (Wandner 2010).

There should be sufficient state UI staffing to maintain a working organizational structure. Staffing cannot be entirely caseload-driven since many UI functions must be performed regardless of the caseload. One option is for each local workforce center to have at least four full-time ES staff along with some UI staff. While some staff can provide services from remote call centers, others would have to be in the local workforce centers. Local office staffing could also be strengthened if UI and ES staff were cross-trained and able to fill in for each other depending on the number of UI claimants and unemployed workers needing reemployment services.

There have been no recent studies of UI and ES staffing. The NCUC (1980) and the ACUC (1996) examined this issue several decades ago, and both found that UI and ES staffing was greatly underfunded. For UI, both the NCUC and ACUC recommended that Congress appropriate large increases in funding from increased FUTA revenue, paid for by raising the federal taxable wage base. The NCUC recommended a large increase in ES funding, with staffing set at four staff for each 10,000 members of the civilian labor force. Given the January 2023 civilian labor force of 165.8 million, the NCUC recommendation would result in 66,000 ES staff nationwide, vastly more than current staffing. None of these recommendations have been implemented.

## Recommendation

Staffing must be increased at the national, regional, state, and local levels to address the needs of unemployed workers. In local offices, UI and ES staff need to be cross trained so that they can support and fill in for each other. Much of the weakness of the current UI program is due to inadequate staffing at the local, state, and federal levels.

## MERIT STAFFING

### Issue

Ever since the enactment of Wagner-Peyser Act of 1933 and the Social Security Act of 1935, the state ES and UI programs were required to be administered by merit-system employees of state government. That requirement was abandoned, however, during the Trump administration.

The Committee on Economic Security (CES) believed that it was essential that state UI office staffing (and by implication the ES program) utilize a merit-based personnel system. In fact, the CES recommended that states be required to accept the provisions of the Wagner-Peyser Act, which included merit staffing as a condition for ES grants-in-aid. The CES report stated: " . . . the Federal Government should aid the States by granting them sufficient money for proper administration, under conditions designed to insure competence and probity. Among these conditions we deem the selection of personnel on a merit basis vital to success" (National Conference on Social Welfare 1985, p. 19).

Merit staffing mostly continued for state UI and ES staffing until it was challenged in 1997, when the state of Michigan attempted to privatize the delivery of Wagner-Peyser Act ES services under an unauthorized reorganization of the state workforce agency. USDOL decertified the state's ES program and withheld a part of its Wagner-Peyser Act grant-in-aid. Michigan sued USDOL in federal district court, and in 1998, the court concluded that USDOL had properly exercised its authority under the Wagner-Peyser Act to require the delivery of ES services by merit-based government staff (Balducchi and Pasternak 2004).

In 2020, however, the Trump administration upended nearly nine decades of public administration by allowing private entities to deliver ES and UI services. In January 2020, states were permitted to use a variety of staffing models to provide Wagner-Peyser Act ES funded activities (USDOL 2020a). Thereafter, the CARES Act of 2020 also permitted states to temporarily be relieved of the requirement to use only merit-staffed employees to deliver UI services (USDOL 2020b). The latter provision was enacted to meet the staffing needs projected to result from the enormous job losses associated with the COVID-19 pandemic. In most states, state workforce agencies could have requested temporary emergency hiring authority under existing state civil service rules. The Continued Assistance for Unemployed Workers Act of 2020 nevertheless renewed the temporary waiver of the merit staffing requirement for UI functions (USDOL 2020c). While the 2020 legislation was designed to give states flexibility while dealing with the extreme demands on the UI and ES programs during the pandemic, the effect has been to undermine the principles of merit staffing, which promotes the impartial and unbiased professional delivery of UI and ES services by public officials.

One potential problem with merit staffing, however, is that it can make it difficult for state agencies to staff up during recessions. Within a merit-staffing framework, however, there are several options for increasing flexibility.

1) Cross-train UI and ES employees, so that an expanded ES staff can support UI claims-taking during the claims surge that typically occurs at the beginning of recessions.

2) Significantly increase the technology tools available to claims-takers, adjudicators, and administrative law judges to allow them to increase their productivity.

3)  Redesign the UI program's business methods to speed processing and decision-making. An example is the New Jersey adjudication process of requiring employees and employers to email their perspective on the reason for the worker's separation from his job. This reduces the need for telephone calls if the employer and former employee agree.

## Options

In the post–COVID-19 pandemic period, there may be pressure to continue privatization of ES and UI staffing. Privatization, however, has been contrary to the intent of the UI program since its inception. Eliminating merit staffing would raise the possibility of inappropriate state influence in the dispensing of job referrals and payment of benefits, which are generally agreed to be inherently government functions. It also would erode public trust in the impartial and unbiased delivery of services. Three reform options could ensure the maintenance of merit staffing:

1)  USDOL could rescind the regulation that currently permits governors to use non-merit-staffed employees of state government to deliver Wagner-Peyser Act ES services.

2)  The administration could propose amending the Wagner-Peyser Act to require merit-staffing and include the merit standard found in Section 303(a)(1) of the Social Security Act

3)  Congress could opt to not extend the current waiver of merit staffing for the staffing of UI program services.

## Recommendation

To build public confidence in the provision of services, increase equity in the provision of services, and avoid inappropriate political influence, Congress should amend the Wagner-Peyser Act to require merit staffing. ES staff should be increased and cross-trained so that they can supplement UI staff during recessionary periods. An alternative would be promulgating a rule requiring merit staffing that is currently under consideration.

# 13
# Fraud and Overpayments

## UI FRAUD

### Issue

Fraud and overpayments have been ongoing issues for the UI program as they have been for other social insurance programs.[1] UI initiated a quality control program in the mid-1980s that was designed to help states assess the timeliness and accuracy of the administration of their UI program benefit payment process. The quality control effort developed into the current Benefits Accuracy Measurement program and is required by federal regulation.

The current approach to measuring improper payments, however, ignores the inherent tension between the requirement to quickly pay benefits and to continue making weekly payments until an adequate investigation has been completed. Staff underfunding plus the processing of the vast number of claims that are received exacerbate this tension.

The Improper Payments Elimination and Recovery Act of 2012, various executive orders, and other actions require that federal benefits be paid accurately, including requiring state UI programs to not exceed a 10 percent improper payment rate, but leave each program to define what constitutes "improper payments."

Historically, Congress has been more willing to provide administrative funding for fraud and overpayment prevention than for other administrative needs, so there have been robust programs in place.

Nevertheless, early in the COVID-19 pandemic, UI fraud was much more extensive than in the past. The decision to create a Pandemic Unemployment Assistance (PUA) program as part of the CARES Act in March 2020 breached the safeguards in the regular UI program. PUA covered previously uncovered workers, particularly self-employed and contract workers. But the state UI agencies that administered the program had none of the quarterly wage information about these newly covered employees' prior employment and wages that it regularly receives from employers covered by the regular UI program. It was difficult for the state agencies to determine whether, when, or why the PUA workers became unemployed. In addition, filing online PUA claims meant that state systems were vulnerable to domestic and foreign criminals, even through automated bots.

Other CARES Act programs heightened the potential for UI fraud, including in the Federal Pandemic Unemployment Compensation (FPUC) program, which allowed eligible individuals collecting certain UI benefits to receive an additional $600 in federal benefits per week for weeks of unemployment (note the initial $600/week was later reduced to $300/week). The Pandemic Emergency Unemployment Compensation program that allowed individuals who had exhausted benefits under regular unemployment compensation or other programs to receive up to 13 weeks of additional benefits also were rich targets. Benefits paid through the pandemic programs and the regular UI program greatly exceeded amounts paid in past recessions. For example, for the five and a half years between July 2008 and December 2013, total benefits paid approached $602.8 billion, while for the pandemic period April 2020 to May 2021 the amount paid was $896 billion.

The lack of employee information needed by the state UI agencies, combined with the ability of organized criminal groups to acquire and use stolen information, resulted in PUA fraud levels that were vastly greater than in the regular UI program. Six months into the pandemic, it became clear that there were significant fraud problems, not only in the PUA program but also in the IRS administered Paycheck Protection Program, another component of the CARES Act that provided forgivable loans to small businesses. USDOL gave $100 million in grants to state UI agencies to counter the fraud problem. State responses to PUA fraud had adverse effects on both the operation of the UI program and the validity of the UI program data. State UI agencies began cutting off benefits to individuals if any irregularities were detected, halting benefits for individuals with legitimate as well as illegitimate claims. This response to fraud in the PUA program resulted in many claimants experiencing long delays in benefits receipt. At the same time, UI data, especially for the PUA program, became suspect with respect to the number and timing of claims, with states inflating the count of claims by including fraudulent claims. There also were delays in the processing and counting of claims when states were overwhelmed with claims, including those they thought were fraudulent (Casselman et al. 2020).

Starting with the implementation of the PUA program, the UI system became overwhelmed with what has been called "criminal enterprise fraud" (Tucker and Thompson 2021). Criminal enterprises hacked into private and public sector repositories of individuals' personally identifiable information. This allowed criminals to apply for UI benefits in the name of individuals who had no knowledge of the applications in their names. The personally identifiable information needed to fraudulently collect PUA, harvested from massive past data breaches, was widely available for sale. These data were sufficient to file a fraudulent claim. It generally included at least a name, address, email address, Social Security number, and birth date. Some of the sources of hacked data were the 2013 hack of 3 billion Yahoo accounts, the 2018 hack of 500 million Marriott accounts, and the 2017 hack of Equifax, which affected 147 million people.

States have now identified ways to limit or reduce attacks on their systems including by looking for

- numerous Automated Clearing House deposits linked to a single bank account
- the use of the same Internet Protocol address to file or certify for UI benefits across many claims
- user identification and/or passwords that are similar or follow a particular pattern
- email addresses that following certain patterns
- Social Security numbers used to file claims in multiple states (generally more than three)
- a claimant name that does not match the name on the bank account
- a huge volume of bot attacks that overwhelm state systems but allow a few fraudulent claims to get through

## Options

With the end of the PUA program, the fraud and overpayment problems for the UI program have significantly diminished. Preparation should be made, however, to prevent a recurrence of these problems in the event of enactment of a similar temporary or permanent program that cover uncovered workers, such as the Jobseeker's Allowance. Three options might help:

1) Adopting a Canadian-like Record of Employment could substantially decrease organized crime fraud. Criminal groups would not be able to apply for UI benefits without submitting such a record, even if they obtained stolen identification information. For wage and salary employees, the record of employment could supplement quarterly wage records and provide the employee's reason for separation. In the case of 1099 workers who might apply for a future PUA-like program, the record of employment would be a source of separation and earnings information, although the base period would have to be the latest calendar year of 1099 data rather than four recent calendar quarters.

2) The state UI programs could be given access to the latest wages of uncovered workers. With congressional authorization, a database that only the state UI staff could search might be created using data from SSA or IRS. Access to the required data for state agency utilization might be accomplished through direct access to a centralized IRS data set, or perhaps by a variant of an existing system such as the UI Interstate Connection Network—which permits state UI agencies to request applicants' interstate wages—to access SSA data. The key aspect of such options would be the states' ability to verify whether program applicants are making legitimate claims. Obtaining these data would significantly reduce the probability of fraudulent claims as organized or other potential fraudsters would have very limited access to the wage information that legitimate applicants would have.

3) Fraud, including organized criminal fraud, could be reduced by requiring face-to-face initial claims and periodic face-to-face eligibility reviews. During periods of high unemployment, these face-to-face contacts could probably be done for only a random sample of claimants, with samples being larger in periods of low unemployment. This approach recognizes

that monitoring cannot be entirely automated to eliminate or even substantially reduce fraud. This effort would have to be undertaken by UI staff in local workforce offices and would require increased administrative funding to pay for sufficient staff to carry it out.

## Recommendation

USDOL should retain but improve their current fraud program. USDOL also should anticipate needing to limit fraud in future PUA-like or the proposed Jobseeker's Allowance program by gathering earnings data for gig/contract workers from IRS, contingent on congressional authorization.

## Notes

1. James Van Erden provided substantial input to this chapter.

# Part 5

# Summary and Conclusions

# 14
# Recommendations and Next Steps

As discussed in Chapters 2 through 4, the weakness of the federal-state U.S. UI program was foretold by the administrative structure created by the Social Security Act of 1935. It remained weak in its early years and has been further weakened over the past four decades. Making the U.S. UI program uniform state-to-state like in many other Western industrial nations requires comprehensive federal legislative reform involving nearly all components of the program. This chapter reviews key reform recommendations for the component parts of the program. It then suggests a path forward for comprehensive reform.

## SUMMARY OF KEY RECOMMENDATIONS

Recommendations for key UI reforms are listed below by UI component. The reforms generally should be mandated by Congress, but in the absence of federal legislative reform, states should consider adopting many of these recommendations to improve their UI programs on their own. A more complete discussion of the options and recommendations presented below is found in Chapters 8 through 13.

**Benefits** (See Chapters 8 and 9)

### Access and recipiency

Raising the current low UI recipiency rate requires several changes. Employers should be required to provide more and better information to potential claimants about the program and how to apply for benefits. They also should provide a Canadian-type record of employment to each separating worker, with an electronic copy sent to the state UI agency. Initial and continued claims filing must be simplified, tested, and standardized. A wide variety of additional smaller options should be implemented to enhance access to the program.

### Benefit standards

Four benefit standards for the regular UI program should be enacted by Congress, including three that have been advocated in the past: a maximum potential benefit duration of at least 26 weeks, a 50 percent wage replacement rate during periods of low unemployment, and a maximum weekly benefit amount of 66.67 percent of each state's average weekly wage in covered employment. The fourth benefit standard is a minimum benefit amount of approximately 30 percent of the state's average weekly wage.

To enhance access to benefits, Congress should eliminate waiting weeks and pension offsets. Partial earnings disregards need to be approximately 50 percent of the average weekly benefit amount. Congress also should expand nonmonetary eligibility by increasing the eligibility of workers separated from work for many compelling personal needs.

Furthermore, Congress should increase coverage for gig/contract workers by ensuring that workers who meet the modest ABC test are in covered UI employment. Relatively new entrants and some reentrants to the labor market would become eligible by requiring states to have alternative base periods and extended base periods. While it would be difficult to extend coverage to the self-employed, a voluntary program ought to be implemented, with a required evaluation and a sunset provision. New entrants to the labor force cannot be covered by a social insurance program but could be covered by a separate social welfare program if Congress so decides.

Extended Benefits should become a phased program, adding incremental weeks of benefit duration as unemployment rates increase. There ought to be four or five phased increases in benefit durations, with increasing additional weeks of benefits, based on the BLS total unemployment rate.

Finally, UI benefits should not be taxed.

### Finance (See Chapter 10)

To put the UI system on a sound financial footing, capable of paying out adequate benefits, Congress should raise the UI taxable wage base to at least 50 percent of the Social Security wage base, phased in over a five-year period. Tax rates also must be made more sufficient by 1) ensuring that the lowest state maximum tax rate is greater than the current 5.4 percent; 2) ensuring that administrative funding is more adequate; 3) requiring states to have a minimum number of rates in each tax schedule (e.g., 10); and 4) preventing states from refusing to move to higher tax schedules as required by state law when state trust fund accounts decline.

In addition, Congress should consider requiring employees in all states to contribute to UI financing in an amount up to half of UI total funding.

Since the current experience-rating system does not work well, it should be revised after studying several alternatives to the current system. Congress should consider establishing a reinsurance program, but only after a rigorous study.

The forward funding of benefits might be accomplished by enacting substantial incentives for states to forward fund their federal Trust Fund accounts, as well as by instituting substantial penalties for the failure to forward fund.

The inadequate financing that pays for UI and ES administration, EB costs, and loans to states should be increased sharply by having the federal UI tax applied to the new higher federal taxable wage bases with the federal tax rate set at a level sufficient to fully fund the current higher costs of more adequate program administration.

**Short-Time Compensation** (See Chapter 11)

To keep workers who otherwise would become unemployed attached to the labor force, short-time compensation should become a required program in all states. Neither employers nor employees should be charged for using the program during designated periods of high unemployment.

**Self-Employment Assistance** (See Chapter 11)

To help unemployed workers start their own businesses, Congress should make Self-Employment Assistance available in all states, including entrepreneurial training provided by the Workforce Innovation and Opportunity Act training programs. These programs would have separate performance measures from the regular UI program.

**Reemployment Bonuses** (See Chapter 11)

Reemployment bonuses, which have been found to speed unemployed workers' return to work, should be made an optional program, rigorously evaluated, and if successful and cost-effective, considered for inclusion as a permanent required program.

**Wage Insurance** (See Chapter 11)

Wage insurance has been implemented only as a small trade-related program. Thus, its effectiveness is unproven for a wider range of dislocated workers. It should be rigorously evaluated as part of a demonstration program.

**Reemployment Services** (See Chapter 11)

The U.S. Employment Service should be reestablished in USDOL. To achieve the significant benefits of reemployment services (e.g., job matching and job search) provided by ES to UI recipients that have proved to be cost effective, Congress should greatly increase the ES's funding, bringing total funding to approximately $1.7 billion (and then indexed), allowing for the greatly increased provision of these services to unemployed workers.

**Information Technology** (See Chapter 12)

The neglected state UI IT systems need to be modernized and made more effective. USDOL should be actively involved in ensuring that the new systems work, are effective, and are consistent between states by providing technical assistance and modular IT components. A nonprofit organization such as federally funded research and development center could provide effective IT and related services.

**Data Systems** (See Chapter 12)

To improve and make the UI data systems more usable for program assessment, administration, and research and analysis, the definitions for the terms used in the UI program should be revisited, refined, and uniformly used by all states. In addition, some data elements need to be made consistent, such as race and ethnicity, and new data elements should be introduced, such as hours worked. The UI office in USDOL could work with a federally funded research and development center, the BLS and the private sector in establishing these definitions.

Congress should fund the establishment of state UI and workforce longitudinal data systems in all states, with support from one or more nonprofit research organizations, probably a federally funded research and development center that also could guide and conduct research and evaluations. These data systems would have to be coordinated with the systems of the U.S. Department of Education and other federal agencies that have similar data systems.

**Research and Evaluation** (See Chapter 12)

Research and evaluation funding ought to be greatly increased and administered by a newly created USDOL UI research organization.

States also ought to be encouraged to conduct their own research, but research for the states and the federal government could be conducted by a combination of state universities, nonprofit research agencies, and for-profit research firms.

**Administration** (See Chapter 12)

The state and federal staffing levels funded by the UI federal tax—the UI program and ES programs at the national, state, and local levels—must be significantly increased to provide better, faster, and more accurate claims-taking and tax administration. More staff also are necessary to provide UI recipients with in-person reemployment services and referrals to training.

Both the UI and the ES programs should be statutorily required to operate under merit staffing rules with provisions for UI and ES staff to be cross-trained to accommodate peak load issues over the business cycle.

**Fraud** (See Chapter 13)

Traditional fraud and overpayment systems should be maintained and improved. New approaches ought to be implemented, such as local office staff conducting claimant eligibility interviews, developing and using a record of employment system to verify claimant identity and eligibility, and statutorily creating a searchable IRS-1099 earnings database that would be made available to UI state agencies on request. This last approach could greatly reduce fraud for a future Pandemic Unemployment Assistance type of program or a Jobseeker's Allowance, if enacted.

## CHOICES FOR THE ADMINISTRATIVE STRUCTURE OF THE UI PROGRAM

The current federal-state UI administrative structure is working poorly and is the cause of many of the weaknesses in the current UI program. That is because, lacking more vigorously enforced federal standards, the UI program has become a race to the bottom for many states, which has resulted in inadequate benefits and insufficient financing. To attain equity for all workers and all employers, a national program would be the best solution, making the UI administrative structure like the Title II Social Security program for Old-Age, Survivors, and Disability Benefits. While this is not politically practicable, a national program makes sense from a public administration perspective and would be much more cost effective.

The second-best solution is a federal program based on a single federal law but administered by the states. Because it would use the same rules in all states, its outcomes would be more equitable. States would continue to operate the programs, but the same program would exist in all states.

Political reality, however, probably means that neither the Congress nor the states are going to want to change the federal-state administration of the UI program. Nonetheless, whatever the structure of the administration of the UI program, many changes are necessary to create a stronger program. The reforms discussed here would achieve such a stronger and more equitable UI system.

## NEXT STEPS FOR BROAD UI REFORM

The United States deserves a UI program that is consistent with Congress's intent in the Social Security Act—that is, a true social insurance program that provides adequate UI benefits to all experienced unemployed wage and salary workers who become unemployed through no fault of their own. To achieve that goal, members of Congress should develop and enact comprehensive federal legislation for UI benefit reform that takes into account the changes to the U.S. economy and workforce that have occurred since the program was first enacted in 1935. The legislation also should provide for sufficient funding for the UI program and ensure that UI benefits and taxes are indexed such that they are in balance initially and remain in balance for many years. Reemployment services should be improved and funded such that permanently separated UI recipients are helped to return to work quickly. In the absence of federal legislative reform, states should enact legislative reform and administrative improvements to their own state UI programs.

This book has examined many options that could be components of comprehensive UI reform. Congress, however, is not currently considering such reform. It needs to hold hearings and examine all the potential components of reform. The Wyden-Bennet proposal would be a starting point. This book suggests some of the same or similar reforms that are in that proposal. It also proposes many alternatives to their recommendations and suggests other reforms that would improve the program.

In the United States, it is usually only during times of high unemployment that politicians become interested in comprehensive UI reform. By that measure, Congress should have enacted comprehensive UI reform during or immediately after the 2007–2009 or pandemic recessions. But it did not. Given the weakened state of the current UI program, however, Congress should not wait for the next recession. Rather, it should prepare now and develop comprehensive reform legislation that is introduced, debated, and tweaked until the necessary reforms are achieved.

# Appendix A
# A National UI Program

## What It Might Look Like, How It Would Work, and the Pros and Cons of Various Options

### FEDERAL PROVISIONS AND STANDARDS FOR ALL OPTIONS FOR COMPREHENSIVE UI REFORM

Any policy of comprehensive UI reform, including a national program, should apply evidence-based policy conclusions from an extensive body of UI research (O'Leary and Wandner 2018). Reform should require improved access to the UI program, uniform qualifying requirements, adequate benefit amounts and durations, and tax provisions that fully fund UI benefits through the following:

- an application process that all unemployed workers can easily complete online or via telephone—with in-person assistance available as needed
- an adequate benefit amount and duration with interstate equity
- an extended benefits program that is responsive to recessionary increases in unemployment
- a tax system that collects enough revenue to fully fund adequate benefits and does so in a more progressive manner through a substantially increased taxable wage base
- adequate administrative financing
- enhanced and more consistently delivered reemployment services

### Access

Create parity among the states regarding the percentage of unemployed workers receiving benefits, averaging approximately 50 percent (i.e., roughly the average percent of experienced workers who become unemployed through no fault of their own), although varying over the business cycle. This would be achieved by providing

- substantial and easy-to-understand information about how to apply for UI benefits

- a simple UI application form with prompts to help complete the application online or by telephone
- access to individual UI program staff who could assist with completing the application, if needed
- increased coverage of independent contractors and self-employed workers, mostly through expanding the federal definition of the employer-employee relationship for the UI program. (Nearly all wage and salary employees are currently covered by the UI program.)

**Benefits**

- Qualifying for benefits: unemployed workers must have earned at least $1,500 (subsequently indexed to wage growth) in one quarter and have some earnings in at least two quarters during a one-year period (the "UI base period").
- Benefit replacement rate: 50 percent of prior wages up to a maximum weekly benefit amount.
- Maximum weekly benefit: two-thirds of state (or national) average weekly wage.
- Maximum potential duration of regular UI benefits: 26 weeks in all states and jurisdictions.
- Extended benefits would be triggered on and off by the Bureau of Labor Statistics's (BLS's) measure of total unemployment, and the weeks of benefit eligibility would increase as the unemployment rate increases.
- Increase eligibility of workers to reflect changes in the labor force, including providing benefits for part-time workers, workers seeking part-time employment, workers following spouses/partners to new locations, workers quitting jobs to provide child or elder care, and disregarding pensions for older workers remaining attached to the labor force.

**Taxes/Financing**

- Taxable wage base: Social Security wage base ($160,200 in 2023).
- Tax rate: approximately 1.4 percent of taxable wages paid by each employer (Pavosevich 2020), varying year by year as needed, set by

the Social Security Administration's (SSA's) actuarial assessment, or by a schedule of rates varying with Unemployment Trust Fund solvency.

- Eliminate or replace current experience rating: shown to be difficult to administer and ineffective (Miller and Pavosevich 2019).
- Increase employee "ownership" of the UI program: consider splitting the tax between employers and employees similar to the approach of the Social Security old age insurance program.
- When insolvent, the Unemployment Trust Fund could borrow from the U.S. Treasury.

## NATIONAL UI PROPOSAL ADMINISTERED BY THE SOCIAL SECURITY ADMINISTRATION: HOW IT WOULD WORK

A national UI program should be adopted because the state UI programs have been shown to be 1) ineffective in providing equitable and adequate income replacement, 2) inefficient, and 3) slow to adapt to changing labor markets and technology. These deficiencies are especially problematic in times of national emergencies and when the UI program has been called upon to administer increasingly complex federal unemployment assistance programs.

### Program Administration

- A national program could be administered by the SSA—paying benefits, collecting taxes, administering UI work search requirements (the UI work test), and providing adequate self-service and staff-assisted reemployment services.
- The SSA would be best able to administer a national UI program because of its large staff with experience administering large social insurance programs, including paying benefits and collecting taxes, whereas USDOL has no such experience.
- State and local UI and ES staff would become federal employees of the SSA.
- Ease access to the UI program by creating a simple online national UI application form with prompts to assist applicants and the availability of robust telephone assistance as needed.

## Regular Benefits

- Improved program access and a single set of eligibility requirements consisting of minimum earnings requirements when workers become unemployed through no fault of their own would result in approximately 50 percent of unemployed workers receiving UI benefits (the UI recipiency rate), although the recipiency rate would vary over the business cycle. In 2018, the recipiency rate varied between states from a high of 52 percent to a low of 11 percent.
- Replacing 50 percent of prior wages up to a maximum of two-thirds of the national average weekly wage, such that the maximum benefit would be the same in all states and for all individuals.
- Maximum potential duration of benefits would be set at 26 weeks for all eligible unemployed workers.

## Extended and Emergency Benefits

- Extended benefits funded by federal general revenue.
- Extended benefits would increase in duration as unemployment rates rise, triggered on and off by state and national BLS civilian unemployment rates (see O'Leary and Wandner 2018).
- Emergency unemployment compensation enacted by Congress in times of emergency.

## Taxes

- Taxable wage base would be equal to that of Social Security ($160,200 in 2023).
- Tax rate of approximately 1.4 percent (Pavosevich 2020, Appendix 3), potentially varying annually as determined by actuarial analysis or a preestablished schedule of rates varying with Unemployment Trust Fund solvency.
- Taxes paid by employers. Alternatively, the tax burden could be shared by workers and employers to ensure that employees have a direct interest in program management.

## Data Systems

- A national UI program would have a single set of definitions for UI benefit and tax systems, including a single definition of "employers," "employees," "employment," and "wages."

- This shift to a single set of definitions would make it easier for multi-state employers to file quarterly wage reports and make tax payments. It also would improve the use of quarterly wage data for policy, program, and statistical analyses.

## Reemployment Services

- A rigorous work test would be included to ensure that UI recipients are unemployed through no fault of their own and are available for and actively seeking work.
- Greatly expanded reemployment services would be made available to assist in the rapid return to work, approximately doubling the funding for the Employment Service to provide UI claimants with staff-assisted services to speed their return to work.
- National programs for work sharing/short-time compensation and self-employment assistance would be established.

## Implementation

- Phase in over five years. SSA would develop new application, benefit payment, tax, and administrative systems, making use of the best processes currently used by the states.
- UI functions would be transferred to SSA and UI moved to co-located local offices or to new, separate UI offices by the end of the transition period.
- Existing state UI staff would be given the opportunity to transfer from state employment to working for the SSA to implement and operate the new UI program.

## TRANSITION

Starting on January 1, after the enactment of a national UI program:
- State UI agencies would become agents of USDOL for two years until the SSA could take over the administration of the UI program.
- Assuming a reasonably low national unemployment rate, state UI staff would begin transferring to the SSA.
- States would pay UI benefit recipients 50 percent of prior wages, up to a maximum of two-thirds of the national average weekly wage.

The maximum potential duration would be 26 weeks in all states and jurisdictions.

- The state UI tax would become a flat tax of approximately 1.4 percent on employers, paid on the Social Security wage base, to ensure a maintenance of effort by the states during the transition.

## PROS AND CONS OF A NATIONAL UI PROGRAM

### Pros

- Access, qualifying requirements, benefit, and tax provisions would be the same in all states, creating interstate and interpersonal equity in program administration and outcomes.
- Benefits would be more adequate and equitable for all UI recipients.
- Taxes would be sufficient to pay benefits, and with a higher taxable wage base for UI taxes, taxes would be more progressive due to the expanded wage base.
- The UI tax would be modest, raising the total employer Social Security-UI tax rate from 6.2 percent to approximately 7.4 percent, if employers were to pay the entire tax, or raising the tax to approximately 6.9 percent for both employers and employees, if the tax were shared.
- Reduced administrative costs from simplifying and consolidating administration from 53 jurisdictions.
- More flexible and timely response to congressional enactment of recessionary add-on federal UI programs.
- Improved defense and security from UI benefit payment and tax fraud.
- More timely and reliable reporting of UI unemployment, employment, and wage data.
- A single set of data definitions and a single data system would be advantageous for employers, employees, and analysts who want to understand and use UI program, employment, and wage data, including for the U.S. national income accounts.
- A single national definition and wage record would make it easier for unemployed workers to apply for UI benefits and be certain that all their wages would be counted since there no longer would be interstate claims for benefits.

**Cons**

- The current 53 state UI agencies would be eliminated, states would lose direct control of the UI system, and state UI employees would have to compete for jobs and transfer to the SSA.
- Likely opposition from some state governments, some members of Congress, and some employer groups, especially in high-wage, low unemployment industries and sectors, and employee groups opposed to an employee tax.
- There would be a potentially disruptive transition period of approximately five years during which time the state UI programs would have to continue administering their programs and maintain their level of effort, while SSA staff would have to learn to operate the UI program.

## CONCLUSIONS

While the UI system has been in decline for four decades, the COVID-19 recession was a wake-up call about how inadequate the current system really is. Without a massive increase in staffing and resources, USDOL would be unprepared to take the lead as a strong federal partner in a reformed UI program. It also is clear that many states have UI programs that are so weak that they were not able to deal with the onslaught of UI applications and new federal programs during the COVID-19 recession.

As a result, it is time to turn to the federal government to operate a national UI program. The SSA has effectively and efficiently run the Social Security old age assistance program for many years—a much larger program than UI. It is thus recommended that Congress create an effective, efficient, and equitable UI system that would be administered by SSA with expertise they would acquire from current federal and state UI staff members (see Wandner and King 2021).

# Appendix B
# How Much Would a
# National UI Program Cost?

Robert Pavosevich, Former Lead Actuary,
*USDOL Office of Unemployment Insurance*

Creating a single UI program in the United States and eliminating each individual state program would simplify the assessment and collection of UI taxes. Under the current federal-state structure as laid out in the Social Security Act (1935), employers pay two taxes quarterly—one a state tax that is based on the individual experience of the employer and is used only to pay for benefits to claimants; the second is a flat rated tax assigned to each taxable employer and is 0.6 percent on the first $7,000 of an employee's wages (the Federal Unemployment Tax Act tax). Revenues from this tax pay for the administration of the UI and Wagner-Peyser Act Employment Service programs in states, loans to states, and the federal part of the federal-state extended benefits system. In a national program, there would be one tax, the level of which would be determined by the specific assumptions about how this program would operate. This appendix describes the cost estimate for one potential national program.

## ASSUMPTIONS

This cost estimate for a proposed national UI program is based on the following assumptions:

- The national program would use average cost financing, rather than be a forward-funded program.
- The yearly tax rate would be set at an average of the total benefit costs (benefits divided by total wages) over the past 20 years (or inclusive of two recessions, whichever is longer).
- Access to the UI program would be facilitated such that on average approximately 50 percent of unemployed workers would receive UI benefits across the United States.

- Benefits would be set nationally and would be high relative to average wages in low-wage states and low in relation to average wages in high-wage states.
- All eligible claimants would receive a minimum benefit standard of 50 percent of their calculated base year average weekly wages,
  - with a maximum weekly benefit that is two-thirds of the nation's average prior year wages,
  - and be eligible for a maximum potential duration of 26 weeks.
- The provision of enhanced reemployment services to UI claimants and other job seekers and the administering of a rigorous UI work test. Funding for the Employment Service initially would be about doubled to approximately $1.5 billion per year.
- Cost estimates are retrospective for the period through 2019 and do not include extraordinary COVID-19 UI costs.
- The tax would include the amount of administrative financing necessary to operate the program.
- Yearly National UI Tax = Avg. of past 20 yrs. ben. costs + Administrative costs.

## ESTIMATE

The average of yearly benefit costs (total benefits as a percent of total wages) over the past 20 years (2000–2019) is 0.78 percent of total wages. Benefit costs include regular plus extended benefits, but not federal emergency benefits. Yearly benefit costs range from a low of 0.37 percent in 2019 (a boom year) to a high of 1.8 percent in 2009 (a recession year).

If claimants were paid benefits based on a new minimum benefit standard, then it is estimated that benefits would increase by approximately 25–30 percent over their current level. This estimate is based on state laws in existence in 2019, where 1) only two jurisdictions paid less than a 50 percent replacement rate in calculating their weekly benefit amounts (WBA), 2) eight jurisdictions paid fewer than 26 weeks for their maximum potential duration, and 3) only two jurisdictions maintained a maximum weekly benefit that was two-thirds of the average weekly wage in the prior year.

The amount needed to fund administrative costs is difficult to project. Potentially there could be tremendous savings achieved through economies of scale in a national program by eliminating much of the duplicative effort across states in the current program. At the same time, there would need to be some increase in funding to establish new computing and administrative systems needed for a new national program and increased reemployment services, so the current administrative funding level of about 0.11 percent of total wages (approximately $7.0 billion in 2020, reflecting a decline in UI administrative costs under SSA and an increase in the provision of reemployment services), would seem to be a reasonable level to include for administrative operations.

In total, estimating for 2020, a yearly tax rate of 1.13 percent of total wages = (0.78% × 1.30) + 0.11 percent appears to be an adequate level to fund a regular national UI program.

Based on historical data about U.S. business cycles, using an average cost formula of 20 years would still allow for a sufficient buildup in the UI program reserves to pay benefits in an average recession. For instance, a total collection of approximately $80 billion is estimated for 2020, which is well above the amount of benefits needed in an expansionary, nonrecessionary year (Figure B.1).

Converting the cost estimate of a national program into a percent of taxable wages depends on the level chosen for the taxable wage base (the maximum amount of annual earnings taxed for the collection of the UI tax). Increasing the taxable wage base from its current minimum level of $7,000 and using

**Figure B.1  Estimate of National Program Tax Rate**

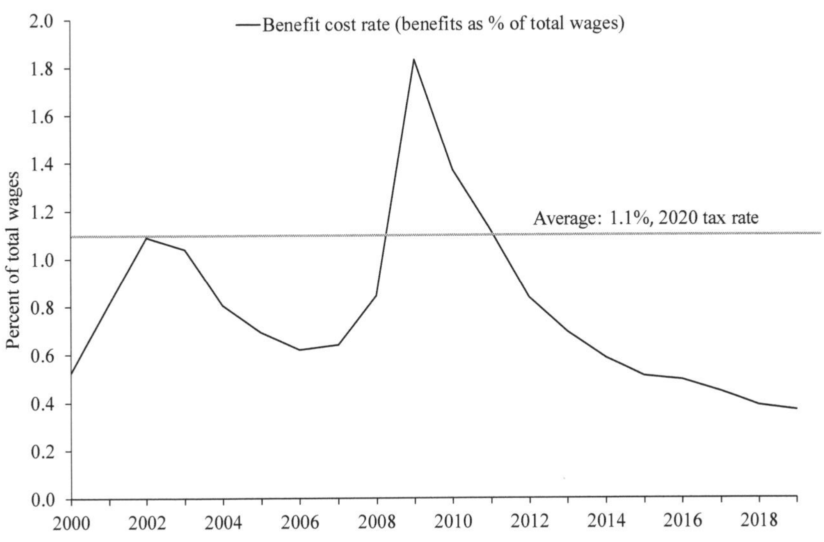

SOURCE: Estimate by Robert Pavosevich.

a yearly indexing formula will not impact the financing of the program since the necessary corresponding tax rate will be lower for any desired amount of tax revenue. However, a higher wage base will greatly reduce the regressivity of the tax towards low-wage employers since the proportion of their payrolls would then be taxed on a similar basis as high-wage employers. And for financing purposes, as long as the wage base is indexed each year, long-term deterioration in program finances would be prevented.

If the program were to adopt a wage base equal to the U.S. average wage in UI covered employment ($59,000 in 2019), then the UI tax rate needed to raise revenue sufficient to fund a UI program costing 1.1 percent of total wages would be 2.3 percent of taxable wages. If the same taxable wage base as the Social Security wage base ($160,200 in 2023) were used, then the UI tax rate for 2023 would be approximately 1.4 percent of taxable wages.

# References

Abraham, Katharine G., and Susan N. Houseman. 2014. "Short-Time Compensation as a Tool to Mitigate Job Loss? Evidence on the U.S. Experience during the Recent Recession." *Industrial Relations* 53(4): 543–567.

Advisory Council on Unemployment Compensation (ACUC). 1996. *Collected Findings and Recommendations: 1994—1996.* Reprinted from Annual Reports of the Advisory Council on Unemployment Compensation to the President and Congress. Washington, DC: Advisory Council on Unemployment Compensation.

Agbayani, Cassandra, Bruno Gasperini, James Moore, Neha Nanda, Luke Patterson, and Stephen Wandner. 2016. *Labor Market and DOL-Funded Employment Assistance for Older Workers: Literature Review Report.* Columbia, MD: IMPAQ International.

Almandsmith, Sherry, Lorena Oritz Adams, and Hans Bos. 2006. *Evaluation of the "Strengthening the Connections between Unemployment Insurance and the One-Stop Delivery Systems" Demonstration Project in Wisconsin.* Oakland, CA: Berkeley Policy Associates.

Alston, Lee J., and Joseph P. Ferrie. 1999. *Southern Paternalism and the American Welfare State: Economics, Politics, and Institutions in the South, 1865–1965.* Cambridge: Cambridge University Press.

Anderson, Patricia M., and Bruce D. Meyer. 2000. "The Effects of the Unemployment Insurance Payroll Tax on Wages, Employment, Claims and Denials." *Journal of Public Economics* 78(2000): 81–106.

Balducchi, David E., Randall W. Eberts, and Christopher J. O'Leary, eds. 2004. *Labor Exchange Policy in the United States.* Kalamazoo, MI: W.E. Upjohn Institute for Employment Research.

Balducchi, David E., and Christopher J. O'Leary. 2018. "The Employment Service–Unemployment Insurance Partnership: Origin, Evolution, and Revitalization." In *Unemployment Insurance Reform: Fixing a Broken System,* Stephen A. Wandner, ed. Kalamazoo, MI: W.E. Upjohn Institute for Employment Research, pp. 65–101.

Balducchi, David E., and Alison J. Pasternak. 2004. "Federal-State Relations in Labor Exchange Policy." In *Labor Exchange Policy in the United States,* David E. Balducchi, Randall W. Eberts, and Christopher J. O'Leary, eds. Kalamazoo, MI: W.E. Upjohn Institute for Employment Research, pp. 33–71.

Balducchi, David E., Stephen A. Wandner, Annalies Goger, Zachary Miller, Sandeep Shetty, Cassandra Agbayani, and Jasmine Eucogco. 2015. *Employer Views about the Short-Time Compensation Program: A Survey and Analysis in Four States.* Final Report. Columbia, MD: Impaq International.

Ball, Robert. 1985. "The 1939 Amendments to the Social Security Act and What Followed." In *50th Anniversary Edition: The Report of the Committee on Economic Security*. Washington, DC: National Conference on Social Welfare.

Bassi, Laurie J., and Daniel P. McMurrer. 1997. "Coverage and Recipiency: Trends and Effects." In *Unemployment Insurance in the United States: Analysis of Policy Issues*, Christopher J. O'Leary and Stephen A. Wandner, eds. Kalamazoo, MI: W.E. Upjohn Institute for Employment Research, pp. 51–89.

Becker, Joseph M. 1960. "Twenty-Five Years of Unemployment Insurance: An Experiment in Competitive Collectivism." *Political Science Quarterly* 75(4): 481–499.

Benus, Jacob M., Terry R. Johnson, Michelle Wood, Neelima Grover, and Theodore Shen. 1995. "Self-Employment Programs: A New Reemployment Strategy." Unemployment Insurance Occasional Paper No. 95-4. Washington, DC: U.S. Department of Labor, Employment and Training Administration.

Benus, Jacob M., Michelle L. Wood, Chris J. Napierala, and Terry R. Johnson. 1991. "Massachusetts Unemployment Insurance Self-Employment Demonstration: Interim Report to Congress." In *Self Employment Programs for Unemployed Workers*, Stephen A. Wandner, ed. Unemployment Insurance Occasional Paper 92-2. Washington, DC: U.S. Department of Labor, Employment and Training Administration, Unemployment Insurance Service, pp. 167–236.

Birnbaum, Michael. 2020. "How Europe Manages to Keep a Lid on Coronavirus Unemployment While It Spikes in the U.S." *Washington Post*, April 11.

Bivens, Josh, Melissa Boteach, Rachel Deutsch, Francisco Díez, Rebecca Dixon, Brian Galle, Alix Gould-Werth, Nicole Marquez, Lily Roberts, Heidi Shierholz, and William Spriggs. 2021. *Reforming Unemployment Insurance: Stabilizing a System in Crisis and Laying the Foundation for Equity*. A joint report of the Center for American Progress, Center for Popular Democracy, Economic Policy Institute, Groundwork Collaborative, National Employment Law Project, National Women's Law Center, and Washington Center for Equitable Growth. Washington, DC: Economic Policy Institute.

Blaustein, Saul J., Wilbur J. Cohen, and William Haber. 1993. *Unemployment Insurance in the United States: The First Half Century*. Kalamazoo, MI: W.E. Upjohn Institute for Employment Research.

Bogage, Jacob. 2021. "Another Big Job for Overwhelmed IRS." *Washington Post*, February 14.

Bureau of Labor Statistics (BLS). 2018. "Contingent and Alternative Employment Arrangements—May 2017." News release, June 7. Washington, DC: https://www.bls.gov/news.release/pdf/conemp.pdf (accessed January 19, 2023).

———. 2022. "Displaced Workers Summary." Economic News Release. Washington, DC: Bureau of Labor Statistics. https://www.bls.gov/news.release/disp.nr0.htm (accessed March 13, 2023).

Cahuc, Pierre. 2014. "Short Time Work Compensation Schemes and Employment: Temporary Government Schemes Can Have a Positive Economic Effect." Bonn, Germany: Institute of Labor Economics (IZA). https://wol.iza.org/articles/short-time-work-compensations-and-employment/long (accessed January 19, 2023).

———. 2019. "Short-Time Work Compensation Schemes and Employment: Temporary Government Schemes Can Have a Positive Economic Effect." *IZA World of Labor* 11(2): 1–11. https://wol.iza.org/uploads/articles/485/pdfs/short-time-work-compensations-and-employment.one-pager.pdf (accessed January 19, 2023).

Canada Employment Insurance Commission. 2021. *2019/2020 Employment Insurance Monitoring and Assessment Report.* https://www.canada.ca/content/dam/esdc-edsc/documents/programs/ei/ei-list/reports/monitoring2020/2019-2020_EI_MAR-EN.pdf (accessed January 19, 2023).

Card, David, Raj Chetty, and Andrea Weber. 2007. "Cash-on-Hand and Competing Models of Intertemporal Behavior: New Evidence from the Labor Market." *Quarterly Journal of Economics* 122(4): 1511–1560.

Carrns, Ann. 2021. "Are Stimulus Checks Taxable? Jobless Benefits?" *New York Times*, February 13, B:6.

Casselman, Ben, Patricia Cohen, Conor Dougherty, and Nelson D. Schwartz. 2021. "Fraud Entangles Lifeline to Pandemic Jobless." *New York Times*, September 12.

Century Foundation. 2020. *The Century Foundation's Top Policy Priorities for 2021.* New York: Century Foundation. https://tcf.org/content/report/century-foundations-top-policy-priorities-2021/ (accessed January 19).

Chocolaad, Yvette, and Stephen A. Wandner. 2017. "Research Capacity of State Workforce Agencies: Evidence from a National Scan, Including Two Case Studies and a Compendium of Recent Research." ETA Occasional Paper 2017-13. Washington, DC: U.S. Department of Labor, Employment and Training Administration.

Charkoudian, Lorig. 2021. Maryland House Bill 1002, "An Act Concerning Unemployment Insurance—Revisions and Required Study." Introduced February 5.

Cohen, Wilbur. 1985. "The Social Security Act of 1935: Reflections Fifty Years Later." In 50th Anniversary Edition: The Report of the Committee on

Economic Security. Washington, DC: National Conference on Social Welfare, pp. 3–14.

Committee on Economic Security. 1935. *Report to the President of the Committee on Economic Security.* Washington, DC: Committee on Economic Security.

Corson, Walter, Paul T. Decker, Shari Miller Dunstan, and Anne R. Gordon. 1989. "The New Jersey Unemployment Insurance Reemployment Demonstration Project: Final Evaluation Report." Unemployment Insurance Occasional Paper No. 89-3. Washington, DC: U.S. Department of Labor.

DeWitt, Larry. 2010 "The Decision to Exclude Agricultural and Domestic Workers from the 1935 Social Security Act." *Social Security Bulletin* 70(4). https://www.ssa.gov/policy/docs/ssb/v70n4/v70n4p49.html (accessed February 1, 2023).

Dube, Arindrajit. 2021. "A Plan to Reform the Unemployment Insurance System in the United States." Policy Proposal 2021-03. Washington, DC: The Hamilton Project, Brookings Institution.

Dunham, Kate, Annelies Goger, Jennifer Henderson-Frakes, and Nichole Tucker. 2005. Workforce Development in Rural Areas: Changes in Access, Service Delivery, and Partnerships. ETA Occasional Paper 2005-07. Washington, DC: U.S. Department of Labor, Employment and Training Administration.

East, Chloe N., and Elira Kuka. 2015. "Reexamining the Consumption Smoothing Benefits of Unemployment Insurance." *Journal of Public Economics* 132(C): 32–50.

Ehrenberg, Ronald G., and Ronald L. Oaxaca. 1976. "Unemployment Insurance, Duration of Unemployment, and Subsequent Wage Gain." *American Economic Review* 66(5): 754–766.

Employment and Social Development Canada. 2014. *How to Complete the Record of Employment (ROE) Form.* Ottawa: Government of Canada. https://www.canada.ca/en/employment-social-development/programs/ei/ei-list/reports/roe-guide.html (accessed February 9, 2023).

Ernst & Young. 2019. "State Unemployment Insurance Wage Bases for 2020." Tax News Update, U.S. Edition. https://taxnews.ey.com/news/2019-2186-state-unemployment-insurance-wage-bases-for-2020 (accessed March 13, 2023).

*Federal Register.* 2022. "Wagner Peyser Act Staffing." A Proposed Rule by the Employment and Training Administration on 04/20/2022. Washington, DC: U.S. Department of Labor, Employment and Training Administration. https://www.federalregister.gov/documents/2022/04/20/2022-07628/wagner-peyser-act-staffing (accessed February 18, 2023).

Feldstein, Martin. 1974. "Unemployment Compensation: Adverse Incentives and Distributional Anomalies." *National Tax Journal* 27(2): 231–244.

———. 1978. "The Effect of Unemployment Insurance on Temporary Layoff Unemployment." *American Economic Review* 68(5): 834–846.

Ganong, Peter, Fiona Greig, Max Liebeskind, Pascal Noel, Daniel M. Sullivan, and Joseph Vavra. 2021. *Spending and Job Search Impacts of Expanded Unemployment Benefits: Evidence from Administrative Micro Data*. New York: JPMorgan Chase and Co. Institute. https://www.jpmorganchase.com/content/dam/jpmc/jpmorgan-chase-and-co/institute/pdf/Spending-and-Job-Search-Impacts-from-Expanded-Unemployment-Benefits.pdf (accessed April 24, 2023).

Garcia, Jason, and Gray Rohrer. 2020. "Thousands of Jobless Floridians Face Meager Unemployment Benefits, Due to Cuts under Gov. Rick Scott." *Orlando Sentinel*, March 20. https://www.orlandosentinel.com/coronavirus/os-ne-health-coronavirus-florida-unemployment-insurance-20200320-btwwgumusrha3hzwxvk7bsdlre-story.html (accessed February 2, 2023).

Ghosh, Palash. 2021. "Sen. Ron Wyden Will Introduce a $500 Million Bill Seeking to Update State Unemployment Systems That Delayed Payments to Millions Last Year." *Forbes Business*, February 10. https://www.forbes.com/sites/palashghosh/2021/02/10/sen-ron-wyden-will-introduce-a-500-million-bill-seeking-to-update-state-unemployment-systems-that-delayed-payments-to-millions-last-year/?sh=58f6ab9f7f3b (accessed April 24, 2023).

Godfrey & Kahn. 2020. "Employer Alert: Wisconsin Mandates UI Notice for Employees at Separation." Milwaukee: Godfrey & Kahn.

Goldin, Claudia Dale, and Lawrence F. Katz. 2008. *The Race between Education and Technology*. Harvard University Press.

Gordon, Colin, and Thomas G. Paterson. 1999. *Major Problems in American History, 1920–1945*. Boston, MA: Houghton-Mifflin.

Gould-Werth, Alix, and H. Luke Shaefer. 2012. "Participation in Unemployment Insurance: Difference in Application Rates and Receipt among Applicants by Education and Race and Ethnicity. *Monthly Labor Review* 135(October): 28–41.

Groshen, Erica L., and Simon M. Potter. 2003. "Has Structural Change Contributed to a Jobless Recovery?" *Current Issues in Economics and Finance* 9(8): 1–7.

Gruber, Jonathan. 1997. "The Consumption Smoothing Benefits of Unemployment Insurance." *American Economic Review* 87(1): 192–206.

Gwyn, Nick. 2022. "State Cuts Continue to Unravel Basic Support for Unemployed Workers." Washington, DC: Center on Budget and Policy Priorities. https://www.cbpp.org/research/state-budget-and-tax/state-cuts-continue

-to-unravel-basic-support-for-unemployed-workers (accessed February 2, 2023).

Haber, William, and Merrill G. Murray. 1966. *Unemployment Insurance in the American Economy: An Historical Review and Analysis*. Homewood, IL: Richard D. Irwin.

Hamermesh, Daniel S. 1980. *Unemployment Insurance and the Older American*. Kalamazoo, MI: W.E. Upjohn Institute for Employment Research.

Harry S. Truman Presidential Library & Museum. 1950. "Special Message to the Congress on the Unemployment Insurance System." Independence, MO: Harry S. Truman Presidential Library & Museum. https://www .trumanlibrary.gov/library/public-papers/84/special-message-congress -unemployment-insurance-system (accessed April 24, 2023).

Hedin, Thomas J., Geoffrey Schnorr, and Till von Wachter. 2020. "An Analysis of Unemployment Insurance Claims in California during the COVID-19 Pandemic." California Policy Lab Policy Brief. Berkeley: California Policy Lab. https://www.capolicylab.org/wp-content/uploads/2020/05/May-21st- Analysis-of-California-UI-Claims-During-the-COVID-19-Pandemic.pdf (accessed February 2, 2023).

Houseman, Susan, Frank Bennici, Katharine Abraham, Chris O'Leary, and Richard Sigman. 2017. *Demonstration and Evaluation of the Short-Time Compensation Program in Iowa and Oregon: Final Report*. Washington, DC: U.S. Department of Labor, Chief Evaluation Office.

Jacobson, Louis S. 2009. "Strengthening One-Stop Career Centers: Helping More Unemployed Workers Find Jobs and Build Skills." Washington, DC: Brookings Institution, The Hamilton Project. https://www.hamiltonproject .org/wp-content/uploads/2023/01/Strengthening_One-Stop_Career _Centers_Helping_More_Unemployed_Workers_Find_Jobs_and_Build _Skills.pdf (accessed May 22, 2023).

Jacobson, Louis S., Robert J. LaLonde, and Daniel G Sullivan. 1993. "Earnings Losses of Displaced Workers." *American Economic Review* 83(4): 685–709.

Jacobson, Louis, Ian Petta, Amy Shimshak, and Reginia Yudd. 2004. "Evaluation of Labor Exchange Services in a One-Stop Delivery System Environment." ETA Occasional Paper No. 2004-09. Washington, DC: U.S. Department of Labor, Employment and Training Agency.

Johnson, Esther J. 1996. "New UIS Organization Chart/Functions." Note to UI Managers, February 1. Washington, DC. Unemployment Insurance Service, U.S. Department of Labor.

Katz, Lawrence F., and Alan B. Krueger. 2017. "The Rise and Nature of Alternative Work Arrangements in the United States, 1995–2015." NBER Working Paper No. 22667. Cambridge, MA: National Bureau of Economic

Research. https://scholar.harvard.edu/files/lkatz/files/katz_krueger_cws_resubmit_clean.pdf (accessed February 2, 2023).

King, Christopher T., and Peter R. Mueser. 2005. *Welfare and Work: Experiences in Six Cities.* Kalamazoo, MI: W.E. Upjohn Institute for Employment Research.

Kofman, Ava. 2020. "How North Carolina Transformed Itself into the Worst State to Be Unemployed." *ProPublica*, June 30. https://www.propublica.org/article/how-north-carolina-transformed-itself-into-the-worst-state-to-be-unemployed (accessed February 6, 2023).

Krueger, Alan B. 1999. "Labor Policy and Labor Research since the 1960s: Two Ships Sailing in Orthogonal Directions?" Working Paper No. 428. Princeton, NJ: Princeton University, Industrial Relations Section.

Krueger, Alan B., and Seth D. Harris. 2015. "A Proposal for Modernizing Twenty-First-Century Work: The 'Independent Worker.'" Hamilton Project Discussion Paper 2015-10. Washington, DC: The Hamilton Project, Brookings Institution.

Krueger, Alan B., and Andreas Mueller. 2010. "Job Search and Unemployment Insurance: New Evidence from Time Use Data." *Journal of Public Economics* 94 (3–4): 298–307.

Lachowska, Marta, Isaac Sorkin, and Stephen A. Woodbury. 2022. "Firms and Unemployment Insurance Take-up." Working Paper No. 22-14. Stanford, CA: Stanford Institute for Economic Policy Research.

Lachowska, Marta, Wayne Vroman, and Stephen A. Woodbury. 2020. "Experience Rating and the Dynamics of Financing Unemployment Insurance." *National Tax Journal* 73(3): 673–698.

Lane, Julia. 2020. *Democratizing Our Data: A Manifesto.* Cambridge, MA: MIT Press.

Lee, David S., Pauline Leung, Christopher J. O'Leary, Zhuan Pei, and Simon Quash. 2021. "Are Sufficient Statistics Necessary? Nonparametric Measurement of Deadweight Loss from Unemployment Insurance." *Journal of Labor Economics* 39(S2): S455–S506.

Lester, Richard A. 1962. *The Economics of Unemployment Compensation.* Princeton NJ: Princeton University, Industrial Relations Section.

Levine, Phillip B. 1997. "Financing Benefit Payments." In *Unemployment Insurance in the United States*, Christopher J. O'Leary and Stephen A. Wandner, eds. Kalamazoo, MI: W.E. Upjohn Institute for Employment Research, pp. 321–364.

Lieberman, Robert C. 1995. "Race, Institutions, and the Administration of Social Policy." *Social Science History* 19(4): 514–542.

Ljungqvist, Lars, and Thomas J. Sargent. 1998. "The European Unemployment Dilemma." *Journal of Political Economy* 106(3): 514–550.

MacLaury, Judson. N.d. "A Brief History: The U.S. Department of Labor." Washington, DC: U.S. Department of Labor.

Metz, Cade. 2022. "Uber Will Pay New Jersey $100 Million in Back Taxes." *New York Times*, September 13, B:4.

Meyer, Bruce D. 1995. "Lessons from the U.S. Unemployment Insurance Experiments." *Journal of Economic Literature* 33(1): 91–131.

Michaelides, Marios, Eileen Poe-Yamagata, Jacob Benus, and Dharmendraa Tirumasatta. 2012. "Impact of the Reemployment and Eligibility Assessment (REA) Initiative in Nevada." Employment and Training Administration Occasional Paper No. 2012-08. Washington, DC: U.S. Department of Labor, Employment and Training Administration.

Miller, Michael, and Robert Pavosevich. 2019. "Alternative Methods of Experience Rating Unemployment Insurance Employer Taxes." *Public Budgeting and Finance* 39(4): 28–47.

Mortensen, Dale T. 1977. "Unemployment Insurance and Job Search Decisions." *Industrial and Labor Relations Review* 30(4): 505–517.

Mower, Lawrence. 2020. "Ron DeSantis Was Warned about Florida's Broken Unemployment Website Last Year, Audit Shows." *Tampa Bay Times*, March 31. https://www.tampabay.com/news/health/2020/03/31/ron-desantis-was -warned-about-floridas-broken-unemployment-website-last-year-audit -shows/ (accessed February 7, 2023).

Mulligan, Casey B. 2012. *The Redistribution Recession: How Labor Market Distortions Contracted the Economy*. Oxford, UK: Oxford University Press.

Nadasen, Premilla. 2007. "From Widow to `Welfare Queen': Welfare and the Politics of Race." *Black Women, Gender + Families* 1(2): 52–77.

National Academy of Social Insurance. 2020. "New Task Force on Unemployment Insurance at the National Academy of Social Insurance." News release, December 22. Washington, DC: National Academy of Social Insurance. https://www.nasi.org/press/releases/2020/12/new-task-force -unemployment-insurance-national-academy (accessed February 7, 2023).

National Commission on Unemployment Compensation (NCUC). 1980. *Unemployment Compensation: Final Report*. Washington, DC: U.S. Department of Labor, Employment and Training Administration, National Commission on Unemployment Compensation.

National Conference on Social Welfare. 1985. *50th Anniversary Edition: The Report of the Committee on Economic Security of 1935*. Washington, DC: National Conference on Social Welfare.

Nelson, Daniel. 1969. *Unemployment Insurance: The American Experience, 1915–1935*. Madison: University of Wisconsin Press.

O'Leary, Christopher J. 1998. "The Adequacy of Unemployment Insurance Benefits." In *Research in Employment Policy: Reform of the Unemployment*

*Insurance System*, Vol. 1, Laurie J. Bassi and Stephen A. Woodbury, eds. Stamford, CT: JAI Press, pp. 63–110.

O'Leary, Christopher J., Paul T. Decker, and Stephen A. Wandner. 2005. "Cost-Effectiveness of Targeted Reemployment Bonuses." *Journal of Human Resources* XL(1): 270–279.

O'Leary, Christopher J., Robert G. Spiegelman, and Kenneth J. Kline. 1995. "Do Bonus Offers Shorten Unemployment Insurance Spells? Results from the Washington Experiment." *Journal of Policy Analysis and Management* 14(2): 245–269.

O'Leary, Christopher J., William E. Spriggs, and Stephen A. Wandner. 2021. "Equity in Unemployment Insurance Benefit Access." Upjohn Policy Paper No. 2021-026. Kalamazoo, MI: W.E. Upjohn Institute for Employment Research.

———. 2022. "Equity in Unemployment Insurance Benefit Access." *American Economic Association Papers and Proceedings* 112(May): 91–96.

O'Leary, Christopher J., David Stevens, Stephen A. Wandner, and Michael Wiseman, eds. 2019. *Strengths of the Social Safety Net in the Great Recession: Supplemental Nutrition Assistance and Unemployment Insurance.* Kalamazoo, MI: W.E. Upjohn Institute for Employment Research.

O'Leary, Christopher J., and Stephen A. Wandner, eds. 1997. *Unemployment Insurance in the United States: Analysis of Policy Issues.* Kalamazoo, MI: W.E. Upjohn Institute for Employment Research.

O'Leary, Christopher J., and Stephen A. Wandner. 2020. "An Illustrated Case for Unemployment Insurance Reform." Upjohn Institute Working Paper No. 19-317. Kalamazoo, MI: W.E. Upjohn Institute for Employment Research.

———. 2018. "Unemployment Insurance Reform: Evidence-Based Policy Recommendations." In *Unemployment Insurance Reform: Fixing a Broken System*, Stephen A. Wandner, ed. Kalamazoo MI: W.E. Upjohn Institute for Employment Research, pp. 131–210.

Oliver, John. 2021. "Unemployment: Last Week Tonight with John Oliver (HBO)." March 7. https://www.youtube.com/watch?v=jm9YKT0dItk (accessed April 24, 2023).

Organisation of Economic Co-operation and Development. 2009. "Generosity of Unemployment Benefits. Net Replacement Rates at Different Points during an Unemployment Spell, 2007. In percentage." Paris: OECD. https://www.oecd.org/employment/emp/43654254.pdf (accessed March 11, 2023).

——— N.d. Public Unemployment Spending." Paris: OECD. https://data.oecd.org/socialexp/public-unemployment-spending.htm (accessed March 13, 2023).

Pavosevich, Robert. 2020. "How Much Would a National Unemployment Insurance Program Cost?" Washington, DC: U.S. Department of Labor,

Office of Unemployment Insurance. Contained in an appendix to "Building a National Unemployment Insurance System," by Stephen A. Wandner and Christopher King. Austin, TX: University of Texas, Ray Marshall Center.

Rangel, Charles B. 2008. "Downturn in Economy Clearly Justifies Extending Unemployment Benefits Now." House Committee on Ways and Means Issue Brief, April 8. Washington, DC: U.S. House Committee on Ways and Means.

Roberts, Dorothy E. 1996. "Welfare and the Problem of Black Citizenship." *Yale Law Journal* 105: 1563–1602.

Robins, Philip K., and Robert G. Spiegelman, eds. 2001. *Reemployment Bonuses in the Unemployment Insurance System: Evidence from Three Field Experiments.* Kalamazoo, MI: W.E. Upjohn Institute for Employment Research.

Robinson, Jeff. 2021. "Examining Unemployment Insurance Finance in Washington State." Paper presented at the conference "Financing Unemployment Insurance: Research Workshop and Policy Forum," hosted by the W.E. Upjohn Institute for Employment Research, held in Kalamazoo, MI, April 23.

Schapitl, Ashley. 2021. "Wyden, Bennet, Brown Introduce Bill to Provide Down Payment on Unemployment Insurance Reform." Press release, September 27. Washington, DC: U.S. Senate Committee on Finance. https://www.finance.senate.gov/chairmans-news/wyden-bennet-brown-introduce-bill-to-provide-down-payment-on-unemployment-insurance-reform (accessed February 18, 2023).

Schmieder, Johannes F., Till von Wachter, and Stefan Bender. 2012. "The Effects of Extended Unemployment Insurance over the Business Cycle: Evidence from Regression Discontinuity Estimates over 20 Years." *Quarterly Journal of Economics* 127(2): 701–752.

———. 2016. "The Effect of Unemployment Benefits and Nonemployment Durations on Wages." *American Economic Review* 106(3): 739–777.

Simone, Sean. 2021. *The Failure of Big Data to Address Problems in the Workforce during the COVID-19 Era.* Atlanta: Federal Reserve Bank of Atlanta, Center for Workforce and Economic Opportunity. https://www.atlantafed.org/-/media/documents/cweo/workforce-currents/2021/04/16/the-failure-of-big-data-to-address-problems-in-the-workforce-during-the-Covid-19-era.pdf (accessed February 14, 2023).

Simon-Mishel, Julia, Maurice Emsellem, Michele Evermore, Ellen LeClere, Andrew Stettner, Martha Coven. 2020. *Centering Workers—How to Modernize Unemployment Insurance Technology.* Washington, DC: Century Foundation. https://production-tcf.imgix.net/app/uploads/2020/08/02153601/UI-mod-report_FINAL2.pdf (accessed February 14, 2023).

Simonetta, Susan. 2018. "UI Reform Proposals in the Fiscal Year 2017 Obama Budget Request." In *Unemployment Insurance Reform: Fixing a Broken System,* Stephen A. Wandner, ed. Kalamazoo, MI: W.E. Upjohn Institute for Employment Research, pp. 23–64.

Singletary, Michelle. 2021. "Refunds Coming to Millions Who Paid Taxes on Their Unemployment Benefits." *Washington Post*, April 4, G:2.

Snidar, Carrie. 2018. Email response to data request by Stephen Wandner from USDOL, ETA, from Carrie Snidar, Freedom of Information Act Disclosure Officer for ETA, December 20.

State of Florida Auditor General. 2019. *Reemployment Assistance Claims and Benefits Information System (CONNECT).* Information Technology Operational Audit. Tallahassee, FL: Department of Economic Opportunity. https://flauditor.gov/pages/pdf_files/2019-183.pdf (accessed February 14, 2023).

Stevens, David. 2012. *Documents and Presentations Enabled by or Related to the Administrative Data Research and Evaluation (ADARE) Project, 1998–2012.* Baltimore, MD: University of Baltimore, Jacob France Institute. http://www.jacob-france-institute.org/wp-content/uploads/ADARE-publications-presentations-compendium-11-8-12.pdf (accessed February 14, 2023).

Strategic Services on Unemployment and Workers' Compensation (UWC). N.d. *Organizations: The Association of Unemployment Tax Organizations.* Worthington, OH: UWC. https://www.uwcstrategy.org/employer-services/organizations/ (accessed February 14, 2023).

Tucker, Dorothy, and Carol Thompson. 2021. "Unemployment Scammer Spills Secrets: Illinois Easy Target because 'They Don't Check Anything.'" CBS Chicago, February 8. https://www.cbsnews.com/chicago/news/targeting-illinois-taxpayers-an-unemployment-scammer-spills-his-secrets/ (accessed February 14, 2023).

U.S. Chamber of Commerce Foundation. 2021. *Developing and Using Public-Private Data Standards for Employment and Earnings Records.* Washington, DC: U.S. Chamber of Commerce Foundation. https://www.uschamberfoundation.org/sites/default/files/media-uploads/T3%20Report_Employment%20and%20Earnings%20Records_Feb2021_FINAL%20%281%29.pdf (accessed February 1, 2023).

U.S. Department of Labor (USDOL). 1962. *Unemployment Insurance Legislative Policy: Recommendations for State Legislation, 1962.* Washington, DC: U.S. Department of Labor, Bureau of Employment Security.

———. 2014. "Wagner-Peyser Act Employment Services: State-by-State PY 2014 Performance." Washington DC: U.S. Department of Labor, Employment and Training Administration. https://www.doleta.gov/performance/results/Wagner-Peyser_act.cfm (accessed June 8, 2016).

———. 2015 Staffing Plan for the Office of Unemployment Insurance (May 19). Washington DC: USDOL.

———. 2017. "FY 2018 Department of Labor Budget in Brief." Washington, DC: USDOL. https//www.dol.gov/sites/default/files/FY2018BIB.pdf (accessed June 8, 2016).

———. 2018. "FY 2019 Department of Labor Budget in Brief." Washington, DC: USDOL. https//www.dol.gov/sites/dolgov/files/legacy-files/budget/2019/FY2019BIB.pdf (accessed June 8, 2016).

———. 2020a. "20 CFR § 652.215—Can Wagner-Peyser Act–Funded Activities Be Provided through a Variety of Staffing Models?" Ithaca, NY: Cornell Law School, Legal Information Institute. 20 CFR Parts 651, 652, 653, and 658 (Docket No. ETA-2019-0004), RIN 1205-AB87.

———. 2020b. "Coronavirus Aid, Relief, and Economic Security (CARES) Act of 2020—Summary of Key Unemployment Insurance (UI) Provisions and Guidance Regarding Temporary Emergency State Staffing Flexibility." Unemployment Insurance Program Letter No. 14-20, April 2. Washington, DC: U.S. Department of Labor, Employment and Training Administration. https://wdr.doleta.gov/directives/attach/UIPL/UIPL_14-20.pdf (accessed February 18, 2023)

———. 2020c. "Continued Assistance for Unemployed Workers Act of 2020 (Continued Assistance Act)—Summary of Key Unemployment Insurance (UI) Provisions." Unemployment Insurance Program Letter No. 9-21, December 30. Washington, DC: U.S. Department of Labor, Employment and Training Administration. https://www.dol.gov/agencies/eta/advisories/unemployment-insurance-program-letter-no-09-21 (accessed February 20, 2023).

———. 2020d. Semiannual Report to Congress. Office of Inspector General for the U.S. Department of Labor. Vol. 84, April 1–September 30, 2020. Washington, DC: U.S. Department of Labor, Office of Inspector General. https://www.oig.dol.gov/public/semiannuals/84.pdf (accessed February 15, 2023).

———. 2021. Unemployment Insurance Program Outlook: President's Budget 2021. Washington, DC: Office of Unemployment Insurance, Employment and Training Administration (March) https://oui.doleta.gov/unemploy/pdf/prez_budget_21.pdf (accessed June 23, 2023).

———. 2022a. Comparison of State Unemployment Insurance Laws 2020. Washington, DC: U.S. Department of Labor, Employment and Training Administration, Office of Unemployment Insurance. https://oui.doleta.gov/unemploy/comparison/2020-2029/comparison2020.asp (accessed March 21, 2023).

———. 2022b. *FY 2022: Congressional Budget Justification, Employment and Training Administration, State Unemployment Insurance and Employment Service Operations*. https://www.dol.gov/sites/dolgov/files/general/budget/2022/CBJ-2022-V1-07.pdf (accessed March 27, 2023).

U.S. Senate Committee on Finance. 2021. "Wyden, Bennet, Brown Introduce Bill to Provide Down Payment on Unemployment Insurance Reform." September 27, 2021. Washington, DC: U.S. Senate Committee on Finance.

Venator, Joanna. 2021. "Dual-Earner Migration Decisions, Earnings, and Unemployment Insurance." Working paper. Washington, DC: Washington Center for Equitable Growth. https://equitablegrowth.org/working-papers/dual-earner-migration-decisions-earnings-and-unemployment-insurance/ (accessed February 14, 2023).

Vroman, Wayne. 1995. *Alternative Base Periods in Unemployment Insurance: Final Report*. Washington, DC: Urban Institute.

———. 2012. "The Challenge Facing the UI Financing System." Unemployment and Recovery Project Working Paper No. 3. Washington, DC: Urban Institute.

———. 2016. *The Big States and Unemployment Insurance Financing*. Washington, DC: Urban Institute.

———. 2018. *Unemployment Insurance Benefits: Performance since the Great Recession*. Research Report, Center on Labor, Human Services, and Population. Washington, DC: Urban Institute. https://www.urban.org/sites/default/files/publication/96806/unemployment_insurance_benefits_performance_since_the_great_recession_2.pdf (accessed February 14, 2023).

Vroman, Wayne, Elaine Maag, Christopher J. O'Leary, and Stephen A. Woodbury. 2017. *A Comparative Analysis of Unemployment Insurance Financing Methods*. Final Report. Washington, DC: Urban Institute. https://www.dol.gov/sites/dolgov/files/OASP/legacy/files/A-Comparative-Analysis-of-Unemployment-Insurance-Financing-Methods-Final-Report.pdf (accessed February 14, 2023).

Wachter, Till von. 2019. "Unemployment Insurance Reform." *Annals of the American Academy of Political and Social Science* 686(1): 121–146. https://journals.sagepub.com/doi/full/10.1177/0002716219885339 (accessed February 14, 2023).

Wandner, Stephen A. 1997. "Early Reemployment for Dislocated Workers in the United States." *International Social Security Review* 50(4): 95–112.

———. 2010. *Solving the Reemployment Puzzle: From Research to Policy*. Kalamazoo, MI: W.E. Upjohn Institute for Employment Research.

———. 2013. "The Public Workforce System's Response to Declining Funding after the Great Recession." Unemployment and Recovery Project Working Paper No. 5. Washington, DC: Urban Institute. https://www.urban

.org/sites/default/files/publication/23821/412866-The-Public-Workforce
-System-s-Response-to-Declining-Funding-After-the-Great-Recession.pdf
(accessed March 22, 2023).

———. 2015. "The Future of the Public Workforce System in a Time of Dwindling Resources." In *Transforming U.S. Workforce Development Policies for the 21st Century*. Carl Van Horn, Tammy Edwards, and Todd Greene, eds. Washington, DC: Kalamazoo, MI: W.E. Upjohn Institute for Employment Research, pp. 129–166.

———. 2016. "Wage Insurance as a Policy Option in the United States." Upjohn Institute Working Paper No. 16-250. Kalamazoo, MI: W.E. Upjohn Institute for Employment Research. http://research.upjohn.org/up_working papers/250/ (accessed February 16, 2023).

Wandner, Stephen A., ed. 2018. *Unemployment Insurance Reform: Fixing a Broken System*. Kalamazoo MI: W.E. Upjohn Institute for Employment Research. https://research.upjohn.org/cgi/viewcontent.cgi?article=1268&context =up_press (accessed February 16, 2023).

Wandner, Stephen A. 2019. "Four Decades of Declining Federal Leadership in the Federal-State Unemployment Insurance Program." Upjohn Institute Working Paper No. 19-314. Kalamazoo, MI: W.E. Upjohn Institute for Employment Research. https://research.upjohn.org/up_workingpapers/314/ (accessed February 16, 2023).

———. 2020. "Options for Unemployment Insurance Structural and Administrative Reform: Proposals and Analysis." Upjohn Institute Policy Paper No. 2020-020. Kalamazoo, MI: W.E. Upjohn Institute for Employment Research. https://research.upjohn.org/cgi/viewcontent.cgi?article=1019&context=up _policypapers (accessed February 16, 2023).

Wandner, Stephen A., David E. Balducchi, and Christopher J. O'Leary. 2015. *Selected Public Workforce Development Programs in the United States: Lessons Learned for Older Workers*. AARP Research Report, Future of Work @ 50+. Washington, DC: AARP Public Policy Institute. http://www .aarp.org/content/dam/aarp/ppi/2015/aarp-selected-public-workforce -development-programs.pdf (accessed February 16, 2023).

Wandner, Stephen A., and Christopher King. 2021. "Building a National Unemployment Insurance System." Better Employment and Training Strategies Task Force Policy Brief. Austin: University of Texas at Austin, Ray Marshall Center. https://raymarshallcenter.org/files/2021/02/Natl-UI -Brief_Revd_WandnerKing_022421_FINAL.pdf (accessed February 14, 2023).

Wandner, Stephen A., and Christopher J. O'Leary. 2021. "Trends in Unemployment Insurance." Unpublished manuscript. W.E. Upjohn Institute for Employment Research, Kalamazoo, MI.

Wentworth, George, and Claire McKenna. 2015. "Ain't No Sunshine: Fewer than One in Eight Unemployed Workers in Florida Is Receiving Unemployment Insurance." Policy and Data Brief No. 1. New York: National Employment Law Project.

West, Rachel, Indivar Dutta-Gupta, Kali Grant, Melissa Boteach, Claire McKenna, and Judy Conti. 2016. "Strengthening Unemployment Protections in America: Modernizing Unemployment Insurance and Establishing a Jobseeker's Allowance." Washington, DC: Center for American Progress. https://cdn.americanprogress.org/wp-content/uploads/2016/05/31134245/UI_JSAreport.pdf (accessed September 29, 2017).

White House. 2021. "Fact Sheet: President Biden Announces Additional Steps to Help Americans Return to Work." May 10. Washington, DC: White House.

Whitman, Kevin, and Dave Shoffner. 2011. "The Evolution of Social Security's Taxable Maximum." Policy Brief No. 2011-02. Baltimore, MD: Social Security Administration, Division of Research, Statistics, and Policy Analysis.

Whittaker, Julie M. 2015. "Taxation of Unemployment Benefits." Congressional Research Service Report No. RS21356, November 16. Washington, DC: Congressional Research Service.

———. 2021. "Financing Self-Employment UI Programs." Paper present at the conference "Financing Unemployment Insurance: Research Workshop and Policy Form," hosted by the W.E. Upjohn Institute for Employment Research, held in Kalamazoo, MI, (April).

Williams, Callum. 2020. "Protectors v. Preservers: Labour Markets in the Rich World Will Diverge Again in 2021." The World in 2021. Economist, November 17, 125–126.

Woodbury, Stephen A. 2014. "Unemployment Insurance." Upjohn Institute Working Paper No. 14208. Kalamazoo, MI: W.E. Upjohn Institute for Employment Research.

Workforce Information Advisory Council (WIAC). 2020. "Enhanced Unemployment Insurance Wage Records Subcommittee: Expedited Recommendations, 2020." Washington, DC: U.S. Department of Labor, Workforce Information Advisory Council.

Wyden, Ron, and Michael Bennet. 2021. "Detailed Summary of Unemployment Insurance Reform Discussion Draft." Proposed by Senator Ron Wyden and Senator Michael Bennet, April 14. Washington, DC: U.S. Senate. https://www.bennet.senate.gov/public/_cache/files/2/6/2605ba7c-6493-4ffe-8808-ceea5dd8c43a/534E9D3A400B42ED29E3ECB1AE2A268D.ui-reform-discussion-draft-summary.pdf (accessed March 22, 2023).

Wyden, Ron, Michael Bennet, and Sherrod Brown. 2021. "Unemployment Insurance Improvement Act: Section-by-Section Summary." Washington,

DC: U.S. Senate, Finance Committee. https://www.finance.senate.gov/imo/ media/doc/Unemployment%20Insurance%20Improvement%20Act%20 -%20Section-by-Section.pdf (accessed March 23, 2023).

# Author

Stephen A. Wandner is a senior fellow at the National Academy of Social Insurance, a nonresident fellow at the Urban Institute, and president of Wandner Associates Inc. He worked for the U.S. Department of Labor for many years. At the Unemployment Insurance Service of the U.S. Department of Labor, he was an actuary, director of benefit financing, and deputy director of the Office of Legislation, Research and Actuarial Services. For the Employment and Training Administration he was the director of research and demonstrations. Throughout his government career, Dr. Wandner conducted and directed policy and economic analysis, research, and evaluations, as well as designed and implemented public workforce programs. He directed a series of 11 random assignment reemployment experiments, two of which were the basis for new federal employment programs. He has published over 30 articles. He co-edited and wrote chapters for seven books dealing with unemployment insurance, targeting employment services, reemployment services, job training, workforce experiments, and the relationship between the Supplemental Nutrition Assistance program and Unemployment Insurance. The Princeton Industrial Relations Section awarded him the Richard A. Lester Prize for the Outstanding Book in Labor Economics and Industrial Relations in 2010 for his book, *Solving the Reemployment Puzzle: From Research to Policy*. For the past 12 years, he has been an economic consultant. He recently was the principal investigator for the National Academy of Social Insurance's Unemployment Insurance Reform Task Force.

# Index

Note: The italic letters *f, n,* or *t* following a page number indicate a figure, note, or table, respectively, on that page. Double letters mean more than one such consecutive item on a single page.

Federal government, *cont.*
pandemic unemployment assistance,
12, 47, 94–95, 187–188
(*see also* Coronovirus Aid, Relief,
and Economic Security Act)
separate accounts for, UI taxes, 178–
179
Social Security responsibilities of,
21–22, 166
UI responsibilities of, 3, 6–7, 105
Federal Pandemic Unemployment
Compensation (FPUC), 187–188,
220
Federal Unemployment Account, federal
UI taxes into, 178
Federal Unemployment Tax Account
(FUTA), 102, 168
programs funded by, 142, 167, 215–
216
Federal Unemployment Tax Act, 28*f,*
106, 178, 243
Financial issues and UI reform
employee contributions, 165, 176–
177
experience rating, 165, 172–175
forward funding, 165, 175–176,
181*n*2
incentives and, 99, 100–102, 101*t*
(*see also* UI Modernization
program)
program administration and, 178–179,
237
reinsurance, 165, 179–181, 181*n*3
state tax rates, 165, 168–172, 181*n*1
taxable wage base, 165, 166–168,
228–229, 236–237, 238
Finland, STC/work sharing in, 69, 76*n*5
Florida, 53*f,* 55, 197, 206
duration of UI benefits in, 41, 131
recipiency rates for UI benefits in, 43,
43*f,* 63–64, 115
statutory components of UI in, 57,
58*f*–59*f*
unionization and UI benefits in, 33,
42*f*
For-profit businesses, 147–149, 199

FPUC. *See* Federal Pandemic
Unemployment Compensation
France, STC/work sharing in, 69, 76*n*5
Fraud and UI reform, 219–223, 223*n*1,
231–232
FUTA. *See* Federal Unemployment Tax
Account

GDP (gross domestic product), data
collection for, 203
Georgetown University. Center for Law
and Social Policy, UI reform, 79,
85
Georgia, 137, 206
regular UI benefits in, 43, 43*f,* 131
Germany
social insurance in, 17, 18
STC/work sharing in, 69, 76*n*5, 183
Gianforte, Gov. Greg, return-to-work in
Montana, 188
Gig workers. *See* Contractors
Great Depression, UI and, 17, 19, 79
Great Recession, UI reform and, 100,
131
Greece, STC/work sharing in, 69, 76*n*5

Hamilton Project, UI reform and, 79, 85
History of UI program in U.S., 17–31,
79–85
1935–1949 with varying
development, 22–24
Congressional commissions, councils,
legislation, 82–84
past presidential proposals for reform,
79–80
recent proposals for reform, 84–85
Social Security Act in, 17–22
USDOL in, 24–31, 81
Hungary, STC/work sharing in, 69, 76*n*5

ICON (UI Interstate Connection
Network), 154, 196–197, 222
Illinois, UI in, 131, 133, 206
Improper Payments Elimination and
Recovery Act (2021), 219
Industrial countries, UI in, 174, 176

# About the Institute

The W.E. Upjohn Institute for Employment Research is a nonprofit research organization devoted to finding and promoting solutions to employment-related problems at the national, state, and local levels. It is an activity of the W.E. Upjohn Unemployment Trustee Corporation, which was established in 1932 to administer a fund set aside by Dr. W.E. Upjohn, founder of The Upjohn Company, to seek ways to counteract the loss of employment income during economic downturns.

The Institute is funded largely by income from the W.E. Upjohn Unemployment Trust, supplemented by outside grants, contracts, and sales of publications. Activities of the Institute comprise the following elements: 1) a research program conducted by a resident staff of professional social scientists; 2) the Early Career Research Award program, which provides funding for emerging scholars to complete policy-relevant research on labor-market issues; 3) a publications program and online research repository, which provide vehicles for disseminating the research of staff and outside scholars; 4) a regional team that conducts analyses for local economic and workforce development; and 5) the Employment Management Services Division, which administers publicly funded employment and training services as Michigan Works! Southwest in the Institute's local four-county area.

The broad objectives of the Institute's activities are to 1) promote scholarship and evidence-based practices on issues of employment and unemployment policy, and 2) make knowledge and scholarship relevant and useful to policymakers in their pursuit of solutions related to employment and unemployment.

Current areas of concentration for these programs include the causes, consequences, and measures to alleviate unemployment; social insurance and income maintenance programs; compensation and benefits; workforce skills; nonstandard work arrangements; and place-based policy initiatives for strengthening regional economic development and local labor markets.